The Issues of Illegal Immigration and its Solutions in the Minority-Border Regions in Yunnan Province, China

Gang Luo

The Issues of Illegal Immigration and its Solutions in the Minority-Border Regions in Yunnan Province, China

A Look at Hekou Yao Autonomous County

SSAP

Springer

Gang Luo
Yunnan University
Kunming, China

Translated by
Yiquan Chen
Yunnan University
Kunming, China

Supported by a Grant from the Yunnan University Double First-Class Initiative

ISBN 978-981-19-1251-1   ISBN 978-981-19-1249-8 (eBook)
https://doi.org/10.1007/978-981-19-1249-8

Jointly published with Social Sciences Academic Press
The print edition is not for sale in China (Mainland). Customers from China (Mainland) please order the print book from: Social Sciences Academic Press.

This Springer imprint is published by the registered company Springer Nature Singapore Pte Ltd.
The registered company address is: 152 Beach Road, #21-01/04 Gateway East, Singapore 189721, Singapore

Contents

Chapter 1
Introduction

1 Topic Selection and Its Significance

(1) Topic Selection

On April 29, 2011, China's National Bureau of Statistics (NBS) released the "Major Figures on Residents of Hong Kong, Macao and Taiwan and Foreigners from the sixth National Population Census in 2010." With November 1, 2010 midnight as the cutoff, the census covered, for the first time, residents of Hong Kong, Macao and Taiwan and foreigners living within the territory of China.[1] Among the 1,020,145 residents who fell into this category and were counted, 234,829 were from the Hong Kong Special Administrative Region (SAR), 21,201 were from Macao SAR, 170,283 were from Taiwan, and 593,832 were foreign nationals. The ten areas with the highest concentration of these individuals were, in descending order: Guangdong Province with 316,138 persons; Shanghai with 208,602; Beijing with 107,445; Jiangsu Province with 64,177; Fujian Province with 62,564; Yunnan Province with 47,396; Zhejiang Province with 36,380; Shandong Province with 33,098; Liaoning Province with 23,834 persons; and Guangxi Zhuang Autonomous Region with 23,445. Aside from these, 97,066 persons lived in other provinces (autonomous regions or cities). The ten largest groups of expatriates living in China were, in descending order: 120,750 from the Republic of Korea, 71,493 from the US, 66,159 from Japan, 39,776 from

[1] "Residents of Hong Kong, Macao and Taiwan and foreigners" refer to the residents of Hong Kong, Macao and Taiwan and foreigners who had resided or would reside within the territory of China for over three months from the reference time of the census, while those shortly staying for business, travel or other purposes were not included. See the NBS website: http://www.stats.gov.cn/tjgb/rkpcgb/qgrkpcgb/t20110429_402722560.htm. Accessed July 11, 2011.

G. Luo, *The Issues of Illegal Immigration and its Solutions in the Minority-Border Regions in Yunnan Province, China*, https://doi.org/10.1007/978-981-19-1249-8_1

Myanmar, 36,205 from Vietnam, 19,990 from Canada, 15,087 from France, 15,051 from India, 14,446 from Germany and 13,286 from Australia. There were another 181,589 foreign residents from other countries living in China.[2]

When looking into the data, we can determine that the first-ever inclusion of residents of Hong Kong, Macao and Taiwan and foreigners living within the territory of China in the census was of special significance. Leading experts of immigration studies Tomas Hammar and Grete Brochmann share similar views about the definition of immigration. They both hold that an "immigrant is a person who migrates to a country and then actually resides there longer than a period of time, i.e., for more than three months."[3] Their definition has the following characteristics: first, "immigrant" is used in the narrow sense to refer only to people who migrate between countries, while people who migrate within their home countries are not included; second, both immigration and emigration are cross-border population movements by those who migrate to and reside in another country for more than a certain period (three months) at a time; third, people who stay in another country for less than three months are excluded. Moreover, scholars, students, artists and those who stay in another country as visitors for more than three months are not considered immigrants.[4] This definition applies to the corresponding group covered in the sixth National Population Census of the NBS. It is worth noting that in legal terms, foreigners include people of other nationalities and stateless persons. In China, the term "foreigner" refers to anybody who is not a Chinese national. Within certain contexts and for certain purposes, residents of Hong Kong, Macao and Taiwan are regarded as foreigners due to historical reasons.

Residents of Hong Kong, Macao and Taiwan and foreigners residing within the territory of China were included in the census for the first time by the NBS but were not classified as "immigrants." The main reasons for this are as follows: first, at the time, there was no official definition of "immigrant" in China, nor was there consensus among Chinese experts and scholars on this issue. Furthermore, even at present, China does not have uniform immigration legislation. Second, Chinese people typically associate "immigration" with outbound migration[5] among Chinese people. After all, China, with its vast territory and large population, does not suffer from a shortage of people, among all things. Therefore, the Chinese people may find it hard to understand the concept of "immigration" in China.[6] This deep-rooted mindset may make it difficult for the general public to understand the word "immigrants" in the population census. However, in terms of academic research, these 1,020,145 residents can be regarded as immigrants residing in the country. According to the

---

[2] The NBS website: http://www.stats.gov.cn/tjgb/rkpcgb/qgrkpcgb/t20110429_402722560.htm. Accessed July 11, 2011.

[3] Hammar (1985), Brochmann (1999).

[4] The analysis of the definition of immigrant, see Xu (2005), p. 6. Personally, I believe people residing in a country as guests include those staying there for business and travel.

[5] Outbound migration is the same as emigration. Trans.

[6] The sixth National Population Census in 2010 showed that the overall population was 1,370,536,875. See the NBS website: http://www.stats.gov.cn/tjgb/rkpcgb/qgrkpcgb/t20110429_402722560.htm. Accessed July 11, 2011.

official data, the nearly 1.02 million persons who "were residing in the territory of China and were counted in the census" did not include those immigrants "who were residing in the territory of China but not counted in the census,", i.e., illegal immigrants. I am interested in finding answers to the following questions: How many illegal immigrants are living within the territory of China? What are their motives for "immigrating" to China? What impacts do they have on local social and economic life? Finally, how should illegal immigrants in China be managed?

When analyzing the data, I came upon a perplexing question. Regarding the motivating factors of international migration, in the nineteenth century, American sociologist E.G. Ravenstein put forward the famous "push–pull theory," which holds that migration is the result of both push and pull factors.[7] In the "push–pull model," "push factors" refer to repulsive forces that are detrimental to people's subsistence and development in their places of origin, which can be wars, riots, catastrophes or deterioration of ecological environment or other factors with widespread effects on a region, or accidents or unfortunate incidents on a particular group of people, while the "pull factors" refer to the attraction of receiving places, which may be novel or exceptional opportunities for a specific group of people.[8] According to this theory, a rapidly developing China should have "pull factors" for some immigrants. Due to China's uneven economic development on its vast land, the eastern region with faster economic growth should have greater "pull factors" for immigrants, so there should be a greater number of immigrants in developed areas along the southeast coast, while southwestern China's Yunnan Province, relatively lagging behind in social and economic development, should have smaller "pull factors." If that is the case, why did Yunnan Province rank sixth in terms of the population of immigrants, higher than the better-off provinces of Zhejiang and Shandong? Aside from geographical factors, what are the other factors resulting in Myanmar and Vietnam ranking fourth and fifth among the top 10 countries of origin of foreign residents living within China?

I have long been concerned with border stability and security issues, especially nontraditional security issues, in the Yunnan border areas with a high concentration of ethnic minorities. Since the issue of *sanfei* (literally "three illegals," namely, illegal entry, illegal residence and illegal employment) has long concerned government departments, my previous studies focused more on the analysis of countermeasures to *sanfei* or illegal cross-border population movements and was not heavily theoretical. In fact, *sanfei*, or illegal cross-border population movements, can be included in the context of illegal international migration, and those people can be regarded as illegal immigrants in the Yunnan border areas; thus, relevant Chinese and foreign theories can be applied for analysis and further study. In terms of illegal immigrants in the Yunnan border areas, I am mostly interested in the following questions: Why do they choose Yunnan, a place that is relatively underdeveloped economically and socially,

[7] Some scholars hold that the "push–pull theory" is not a real theory, but the description and conclusion of the European immigration in the nineteenth century. See Qiu (2005).

[8] Li (2009).

as their destination? What are their motives? What effects do they have on the local society? And how should we manage illegal immigration?

(2) **Significance of the Topic**

The emerging population crisis in China is mostly reflected in low birth rates, population aging, and their adverse effects (or other crises derivative of the population crisis). China's increasing labor shortages, rapid economic development and stable political and social orders will certainly become greater "pull factors" for immigrants, in turn resulting in a greater number of immigrants in China. Meanwhile, the ensuing increase in illegal immigrants is bound to threaten the stability and security of China and its border areas in particular, thereby affecting China's social and economic order and the relations between China and countries of emigration, particularly China's neighboring countries.

National security has always been the top priority of all countries and the focus of academic research in China and other countries. However, in addition to traditional national security, illegal immigration also threatens the nontraditional security of a country. In recent years, the international community has attached greater importance to the study of nontraditional security. Additionally, referred to as "international public security," "nonmilitary security" and "new security," it is a concept increasingly applied in research and the practical actions of international relations. In contrast to traditional security issues, nontraditional security issues (with the exceptions of military, political and diplomatic conflicts) greatly threaten the survival and development of sovereign states and all humanity, including issues concerning economic security, financial security, ecological and environmental security, informational security, resource security, terrorism, religious infiltration, proliferation of arms and weapons, spread of diseases, cross-border crimes, smuggling and drug trafficking, illegal immigration, piracy and money laundering. China is still in the early stage in the study of "nontraditional" security issues. As nontraditional security is an important part of national security strategies, the study of these issues will be conducive to implementing sustainable development strategies in China, expanding its security space, and raising China's position in international security cooperation. Therefore, drafting national security strategies has become an essential theoretical subject of academic research. We must familiarize ourselves with the research performed by foreign scholars and draw up the schedule of our studies on that basis to understand the severity and complexity of nontraditional security threats faced by China and establish our own theories of nontraditional security with Chinese characteristics. At the same time, the study of illegal immigration is of theoretical value to exploring the theoretical basis and management approaches of national security in a globalized world and discussing the early warning mechanisms of China's national security and crisis management.

The negative effects of illegal immigration to China may not be obvious at present. However, we must pay due attention to this type of "hidden crisis." For the study of illegal immigration governance, an integral part of nontraditional security issues, we are in need of supranational management that focuses on international cooperation and national management based on national policies and laws, as well as subnational management at the regional and local government levels. By taking illegal immigration governance in the Yunnan border areas as an entry point, I seek to integrate the national, supranational and subnational management of illegal immigration and to explore effective approaches for managing illegal immigration in China.

China has large border areas with a high concentration of ethnic minorities. The stability and security of these areas play a decisive role in the entire country's stability and security. Stability in border areas is a reflection of national security. The ancient Chinese said, "The hinterland and border areas are like the heart and limbs. Cold trapped under the skin will cause intestinal diseases, as one's intestines and limbs are connected. Once the lips are gone, the teeth feel cold; when the limbs are wounded, the heart feels pain. Without limbs, the body is disabled; without borders, the country is in peril."[9] Other border areas with a high concentration of ethnic minorities aside from Yunnan are also facing various degrees of illegal immigration. Therefore, the study of illegal immigration governance in Yunnan will be of exemplary and practical value to these areas.

2 Literature Review

Only those directly related to this study are referred to as "related literature and studies." Considering that the related literature and studies are in large quantity and of similar content, I needed to select representative studies based on preliminary reading.[10]

(1) Causes of Immigration and Illegal Immigration

There are two causal factors in immigration and illegal immigration. First, the causes of immigration, i.e., motives and reasons citizens of any country have for migrating to another country (including the reasons for the persistence of international migration); and second, the reasons for illegal immigration. Why does illegal immigration even exist since people can migrate to another country by legal means and become legal immigrants?

As mentioned above, in terms of motives of immigration, the "push–pull" theory proposed by the American sociologist E.G. Ravenstein of the nineteenth century is one of the four overseas theories of the motives of immigration, namely[11]:

---

[9] (Western Han Dynasty) Heng Kuan, *The Discourses on Salt and Iron: About the Failure of the Qin Dynasty*.

[10] The object of this study is illegal immigration governance in the Yunnan border areas with a high concentration of ethnic minorities, with the focus on the management of illegal immigrants. There are three aspects of this study: first, the reasons for immigration and illegal immigration; second, the impact of illegal immigration on local society; third, illegal immigration governance. These are also the main aspects of the literature review.

[11] Ruan (2003), pp. 17–24. According to Ruan Zhengyu, there are four theories of immigration motives proposed by foreign scholars, namely, the neo-classical economic equilibrium theory, the historical-structuralist theory, the dual-labor market theory and the migration systems theory. I

The neo-classical economic equilibrium theory. The "push–pull" theory and the neoclassical economic equilibrium theory, both introduced by E.G. Ravenstein, are similar in that they conclude that immigration is the result of imbalanced economic development, especially wage gaps among countries. According to G.J. Borjas, both the neoclassical economic equilibrium theory and the "push–pull" theory, emphasize "the principle of utility maximization for individuals" in the process of migration. He holds that "individuals search for the country of residence that maximizes their well-being…the search is constrained by the individual's financial resources, by the migration regulations imposed by competing host countries and by the emigration regulations of the source country. In the migration market, various pieces of information are exchanged and various options are compared…The information gathered in this marketplace leads many individuals to conclude that it is profitable to remain in their birthplace. Conversely, other individuals conclude that they are better off in some other country."[12] It is concluded that income gaps among different regions will suffice to trigger migration. In the long run, the wages and working conditions of developed and developing countries can converge to equal levels, realizing overall economic equilibrium.

Since the neoclassical economic equilibrium theory is overly simplistic and has limited scope, it is not very useful for explaining the real situation of international migration. It predicts that people will migrate from densely populated areas to sparsely populated areas. This can be used to explain the migration of some areas but not migration in the opposite direction. For example, densely populated Germany has attracted many immigrants, and China, which has a large domestic population, has now begun to attract immigrants as well. The greatest drawback of this theory is that it disregards the influence on the migration of political factors, which are considered abnormal intervening factors. Joaquin Arango comments sardonically on the theory's underestimation of the influence on immigration by noneconomic factors, saying that it views all immigrants as workers while ignoring their other identities.[13]

The historical-structuralist theory. Deeply influenced by Karl Marx's ideas of capital and the capitalist mode of production, historical-structuralist theory has its roots in Marxist theories of political economy. Representative supporters of this theory, Alejandro Portes and Saskia Sassen, emphasize the disequilibrium in world politics and economy. They argue that imbalanced political and economic development is a massive pull factor for international immigration, and immigrants are merely a source of cheap labor. Colonialism, war and imbalanced political and economic development among regions have created many immigrant workers. They conclude that to reduce production costs and obtain cheap labor and raw materials, capitalism expands from core countries to peripheral ones, brings about fundamental changes in social, economic and political structures, erodes traditional ways of life, and produces

believe the fourth one is a type of world systems theory. The migration systems theory is a theory of the continuation of international migration.

[12] Borjas (1989).

[13] [Spain] Arango (2001).

a rootless proletarian class who are ready to go abroad. Lured to work in core countries' economic sectors as cheap labor at any time, they create enormous profits, which end up in the pockets of others. Therefore, international immigrant workers are an important part of the global labor supply system that keeps it running.[14]

Historical-structuralist theory is also partial and cannot be used to explain the complicated situation of migration among countries. The greatest shortcoming of neoclassical economic equilibrium theory is that it fails to examine the influence of political aspects on immigration, while historical structuralist theory overestimates the role of capital by regarding it as a decisive factor and underestimates the motives and behaviors of immigration.

Dual-labor market theory, also referred to as segmented labor market theory, was proposed by Michael Piore in 1979. It argues that the economy of developed countries is divided into two parts, capital-intensive primary sectors and labor-intensive secondary sectors, which result in the segmentation of the labor market. Natives of developed countries prefer to work in high-end sectors with higher wages, superior security and better working environments, while low-end sectors with lower wages, inferior security and poorer working environments need external labor forces. This practical and endogenous need bolsters immigration across national borders.

Dual-labor market theory adopts a unique perspective and makes a commendable contribution to academic research, as it is the first theory that analyzes the motives of immigration from the internal factors of receiving countries. However, the drawback is equally apparent for its one-sided observation. The reasons for international immigration are quite complex, and we should at least take into consideration the interaction between push and pull factors. Additionally, in regard to the pull factors or incentives of receiving countries, there is by no means only one factor of the market demand of developed countries.

The world systems theory. This theory is based on the "modern world system" put forward by Immanuel Wallerstain in 1974. It concludes that international immigration is the result of internal demands of developed countries, as well as forced involvement in the capitalist world market of underdeveloped countries. The expansion of capitalism stimulates the international flows of products, capital, information and the labor force. Unequal international relations make the labor force of underdeveloped countries the target of depredation by developed countries.[15] It is thus clear that immigration is the direct consequence of economic globalization, and the international flows of products, capital, information and labor force facilitate the population movements of the world.

World systems theory attributes immigration to economic globalization and takes into consideration the boost of products, capital, information and labor flows on immigration. It adopts a broader perspective and basically breaks through the limitation of the one-sided approach of the first three theories. However, none of these theories can fully elaborate on the complex and variable motives of international immigration. If there is any theory that takes immigrants' personal reasons into consideration

---

[14] Sassen (1998).

[15] Sassen (1998). Cited from Qiang (2010), p. 7.

regarding their immigration choices, then it shall surpass others in explaining the motives of immigration.

There are additional theories to account for the continuation or development of international immigration. The most representative ones are as follows. First, network theory holds that migrant networks are, in fact, sets of interpersonal ties that connect migrants, home-bound migrants, and their families and fellows through ties of kinship, friendship and shared community origin. They can provide various assistance, such as information, economic support, job opportunities and accommodation, to lower the costs and risks of migration to a large extent, thus promoting migratory movements.[16] This theory's central idea is that the large number of migrants residing in receiving countries will gradually establish extensive migrant networks, which will perpetuate and expand migration. Network theory is recommended by some foreign scholars, just as Joaquin Arango believes that, among all approaches of migration research, network theory is the most typical theory of our times.[17] Second, the cumulative causation theory. It holds that immigration is a self-perpetuating process. Migratory movements alter reality in a certain way and create new immigrants through a series of economic and social processes. Its basic posit is that the more immigrants someone knows, the more likely they are to immigrate, and those who immigrated once before are more likely to immigrate again.[18] Its core viewpoint is that migration is self-perpetuating because when it has become a habit, even when the circumstances contributing to immigration in the first place change, migratory behavior will continue,[19] as "second nature" or "unconscious migration." Third, migration systems theory. The so-called migration systems are a sort of space that comprises a group of relatively stable connections between receiving countries and sending regions. Moreover, this kind of connection is established through migratory movements based on various bonds.[20] The "various bonds" are actually macro- and microlevel structures that exist in migration systems.[21] The macrolevel structure refers to political and economic conditions of the global market, relations among countries, and the laws and regulations of receiving countries and sending countries on the control of migrants and their settlement. The microlevel structure mainly refers to chain migration, which makes the migration process safer and more reliable and helps new migrants learn more about the countries that they move into, find new jobs, and become accustomed to the environment as soon as possible. Families and communities play critical roles in chain migration. Once it is established, it will be self-perpetuating.

These are relevant theories regarding the motives of international immigration (including reasons for its continuation and development) proposed by foreign scholars. Despite some drawbacks, they adopt different perspectives and approaches

---

[16] Li (2009).

[17] [Spain] Arango (2001).

[18] Li (2009).

[19] Qiang (2010).

[20] [Spain] Arango (2001).

[21] The explanation about macro- and micro- level structure, cited from Qiang (2010), p. 8.

of academic research and offer inspiring answers to the questions of motives of international immigration (including reasons for its continuation and development), which are conducive to the writing of this book.

Why does illegal immigration even exist since people can migrate to another country by legal means and become legal immigrants?

The term "illegal immigration" was not strictly defined until the 1970s and 1980s. As it is not easy to give it a precise definition, relevant studies have been included in the scope of immigration research for many years.[22] Dr. Wang Xianfeng believes that illegal immigration theories are mostly based on the theoretical analysis of international immigration, which makes sense to a certain degree but is critically erroneous. There are bound to be major flaws in applying the theories of international immigration to define and study illegal immigration due to historical reasons and difficulties in theoretical research. For historical reasons, during the Cold War, legal immigration had much greater effects on the international community than illegal immigration, and the latter was considered only as a derivative of the former. Therefore, before the end of the Cold War, scholars and researchers mainly focused on the study of legal international immigration. Later, illegal international immigration began to increasingly influence the international community as a nontraditional security factor. At the same time, the understanding of this question was still based on the concepts, models or hypotheses of the mid-twentieth century due to the absence of pure theories regarding illegal immigration. This absence is manifested in two aspects: first, lacking a widely recognized research framework; and second, lacking accurate and representative data on illegal immigration. A substantive number of illegal immigrants were not recorded and thus were excluded from national statistical systems.[23]

Chinese scholars are not discouraged by the lack of overseas theories when analyzing the reasons for illegal international immigration, including the reasons for illegal immigration.

They published dissertations, including PhD dissertations and papers on journals, regarding the theories of illegal international immigration, most of which touched on the reasons for illegal immigration.

The most representative doctoral dissertations are as follows: 1. "The Research on Modern China's Illegal Immigration" by Wang Xianfeng (2004). It classifies the reasons for illegal immigration into two types, i.e., the "international causes of illegal immigration" and the "causes of illegal immigration in China." The former refers to political factors, economic factors, and historical, cultural and social factors.[24] In terms of political factors, illegal immigration emerged with the founding of countries. However, in the context of law, particularly from the perspective of international jurisprudence, modern illegal immigration developed with the birth of nation-states in modern history. After modern nation-states were established in most parts of the world and their sovereignty and citizenship identification grew stronger, each state built a set of complex and rigorous legal systems and management mechanisms

[22] Wen (2010a, b).

[23] Wang (2004).

[24] Wang (2004).

governing sovereignty and citizenship to put a strict limit on free movements across borders. Illegal immigration occurs when risk-takers manage to break movement limitations imposed by modern nation-states. In terms of economic factors, Wang Xianfeng argues that the imbalanced distribution of global wealth and job opportunities is an essential driver of illegal immigration worldwide. Unlike a green economy in a globalized world sought by legal immigrants, illegal immigrants pursue the illegal side of the international economic structure in economic globalization, i.e., the black or underground economy. In terms of historical, cultural, and social factors, there are three aspects for each of these factors. For historical factors: the previous immigration networks and their influences, colonial domination and ensuing connections, and the history of national development and continuous policy options; for cultural factors: the tendency of having the same ethnic characteristics and religious beliefs, the tendency of developing similar cultures by different nations due to historical reasons such as colonialism, and cultural identity of nations; and for social factors: changes in population structure and size, occupational discrimination generated in the process of social development (jobs which are deemed "cheap," including those of serving others, provide job opportunities for illegal immigrants), and racial discrimination. Regarding the "causes of China's illegal emigration,"[25] based on the facts of illegal emigration in China's coastal Fujian Province in the 1990s, the article holds that the main reasons for China's illegal emigrating flows are as follows: economic gaps and disparity between demand and supply in the international labor market; historical reasons, chain migration and the acceptance of smuggling, and the connivance and misleading of some local officials; and inconsistent and ineffective laws regarding the punishment of illegal immigration, such as smuggling among nations. In addition, there are also effects of political and humanitarian factors: better organized illegal immigration (including smuggling) involving more countries under the collusion of international smuggling syndicates and gangs; and poor access to legal immigration channels. 2. "The Study on the Problems of Legal Control of Illegal Immigration" by Xu Junhua.[26] This article attributes illegal immigration to four aspects, i.e., economic, political, legal and individual reasons. One distinctive feature of this article is its reference to legal reasons for illegal immigration.[27] In addition, in his article "Cross-border Immigration and National Security: A Study of Nontraditional Security", Ruan Zhengyu analyzes the actual motives of cross-border immigration from economic, political, natural, demographic, and environmental perspectives.[28] Finally, "The Research on European Union's Governance on Illegal Immigration" by Wen Feng analyzes the main reasons for illegal immigration within a regional organization, the European Union.[29]

[25] Wang (2004).

[26] Originally a PhD dissertation of Wuhan University in 2005, the article was published by Huazhong University of Science & Technology Press in October 2007, with the name of The Problems of Legal Control of Illegal Immigration.

[27] Xu (2005).

[28] Ruan (2003).

[29] Wen (2010a, b).

There are many journal articles about the reasons for illegal immigration, most of which conduct analyses from historical, policy, economic and social perspectives. The articles addressing the illegal immigration in the Yunnan border areas with a high concentration of ethnic minorities are as follows: "The Research on the Current Situation, Problems and Countermeasures of Cross-border Movement of People in the Yunnan Border Areas" by Professor Lu Gang and Professor Li Shou[30]; "Cross-border Movement of People in China-Myanmar Border Areas" by Professor Lu Gang[31]; "Elaboration and Analysis of the Situation of the Foreign Floating Population inside Yunnan's Border and Problems of Frontier Society"[32] and "Dynamics of Overseas Immigrants in Yunnan and the Analysis of Social Problems in Border Areas"[33] by Professor He Yue.

In addition to "The Study on the Problems of Legal Control of Illegal Immigration" by Xu Junhua, chapter six, titled "Illegal Emigration from Southern Zhejiang: Emigration Networks" in the book *Illegal Emigrants from Southern Zhejiang as Seen from the Global Perspective* written by Xia Fengzhen also analyzes the migration networks' catalytic role in illegal emigration in southern Zhejiang Province.[34] In Zhou Jianxin's book *On Peaceful Cross-border Dwelling Models: A Study of Peaceful Cross-border Dwelling Model of South China and Mainland Southeast Asia*, section III of chapter six, "Problems in Development of Cross-border Dwelling in South China", taking Guangxi border areas as example, analyzes the reasons for irregular movements of people.[35] Finally, in the book *Impact Factors of Immigration on the Current Sino-Russia Relations: An Analysis from the Perspective of Nontraditional Security* written by Qiang Xiaoyun, section V of chapter three, "Migration from China to Russia", analyzes the reasons for illegal migration from China to Russia.[36]

In summary, there are abundant and mature theories regarding the reasons for international migration (including the reasons for the perpetuation and development of international migration) proposed by foreign scholars, but there are few research papers regarding the theories of illegal migration. Meanwhile, Chinese literature on migration motives and reasons for illegal migration, with the exception of introducing relevant theories of foreign scholars, has mainly analyzed the political, economic, historical, cultural and social factors of the reasons for illegal migration or investigated the reasons from policy, legal, individual, natural, demographic and environmental perspectives. The research objects vary from illegal migration worldwide, illegal migration in the EU (a regional organization), specific countries such as the US and Russia, to that in southern Zhejiang, Fujian, and the border areas in Guangxi and Yunnan Provinces. There is less literature on the causes of illegal immigration in the Yunnan border areas with a high concentration of ethnic minorities.

[30] Lu and Li (2007).

[31] Lu (2006).

[32] He (2008).

[33] He (2009).

[34] Xia (2008).

[35] Zhou (2008).

[36] Qiang (2010).

When addressing this issue, some papers do not perform an in-depth study from the perspective of illegal immigration. At the same time, relevant theories proposed by both Chinese and foreign scholars are not applied in the analysis of the reasons for illegal immigration in specific areas of a country.

(2) **The Impacts of Illegal Immigration**

Like legal immigrants, illegal immigrants may also have positive impacts on receiving countries, such as replenishing the local workforce, taking up "inferior jobs," and promoting cultural exchanges. With that said, there are more negative impacts of illegal immigration. For example, illegal immigrants may affect and damage the immigration management systems of receiving countries; disturb social, political and economic orders; destroy the stability and security of local societies; disrupt normal exchanges between sending and receiving countries; and undermine friendly relations among countries.

As previously mentioned, foreign scholars have studied illegal immigration in the context of immigration and analyzed the impact of illegal immigration on receiving countries in the context of the impact of immigration on receiving countries. However, it was not until the 1990s that they began to pay more attention to the impact of illegal immigration from the following aspects[37]:

1. The impact of illegal immigration on border security control. This involves the impact of illegal immigration on the relevant management systems of border security, including the border security of both sending and receiving countries of illegal immigrants. A prominent research institute in this regard is the Center for Migration and Development (CMD) of Princeton University. Their research fields include the study of visa system security, immigration and domestic stability and asylum system reform for illegal immigrants and refugees.
2. The political, economic and social impact of illegal immigration on receiving countries. Alan Kessler, from the Center for Comparative Immigration Studies of the University of Texas, makes a thorough analysis and explanation regarding the interaction between illegal immigration and economic security in his article "Immigration, Economic Insecurity and the 'Ambivalent' American Public."
3. The impact of illegal migration on international security and international relations. In his paper "Refugees and International Security" presented to the fourth International Security Forum held in Geneva, Jeff Crisp performs preliminary research and exploration on refugees and international security issues.
4. The impact of illegal immigration on national security. When taking stock of the research results of foreign scholars, Chinese scholar Tian Yuan refers to it as "the threat of illegal immigration on national security," which I believe far outweighs the threat of immigration. Therefore, the viewpoints of foreign scholars introduced in his book are of significant reference value to our research on the impact of illegal immigration on national security.[38]

[37] The first three aspects of the study can be found in Wang (2004), p. 4.

[38] The viewpoints held by foreign scholars regarding the impact of illegal immigrants on national security can be found in Tian (2010), pp. 19–24.

Karen Jacobsen and Steven Wilkinson examine the security threats brought by immigrants from sub-Saharan Africa from economic, political and military spheres. They hold that immigrants will first increase the need of the receiving country for food, water, farming land and other scarce resources, thereby threatening the economic and environmental security of the receiving countries. The influx of immigrants will increase the complaint and hatred in these countries, leading to political and social turmoil and threatening the political security of the receiving countries. In the end, immigrants may also become the excuse of military actions of other countries, thus increasing the possibility of external military attacks and threats to military and strategic security.

Gary Freeman holds that the mass immigration after World War II posed certain threats to Australia's national security based on his study of immigration issues in Australia. The increase in immigrants whose political and cultural identities are distinct from local citizens will alter the receiving countries' cultural and social structures, affecting their political and social security, while internal social instability would trigger external insecurity.

Myron Weiner insists that a country's security primarily lies in its military security and opposes extending the scope of security to "individuals" at the microlevel or "international security" and "world security" at the macrolevel. At the same time, Myron Weiner broadens his study to nontraditional fields, such as social and economic fields. In his book *Security, Stability and International Migration*, he illustrates the threats posed by immigrants to receiving countries from political, social and economic perspectives. He points out that although immigrants may threaten national security, persecuting and rejecting them is equally problematic as denying their security hazards.

David T. Graham performs systematic research on population movements and national security from a new security perspective by switching from traditional fields (nation-centered and military-dominated) to nontraditional fields (more focused on "human" or "humanity"). He then establishes an analytical framework underpinned by a new security perspective and concludes that immigrants were a kind of security threat.

It was not until quite late that foreign scholars began their research on illegal immigration, and part of their research was still undertaken within the context of immigration studies. However, they carried out their research in various fields and changed their focus from traditional security to nontraditional security. The impacts of illegal immigration on national security, international security and international relations were also taken into consideration, in addition to the impacts on border security and the political, economic and social impacts on receiving countries. The previous research of some specific countries was later expanded to the entire world. The attitude toward immigrants, especially illegal immigrants, also changed, from opposing and expelling them in the past, to considering humanitarian principles on dealing with illegal immigration. Of course, this was done to defend the national interests of receiving countries, not in the interest of illegal immigrants. Unfortunately, academic studies of the impacts of illegal immigration targeted at specific areas of a country are not found in the literature of foreign scholars.

Chinese scholars' studies on the impacts of illegal immigration are mainly influenced by the aforementioned theories proposed by foreign scholars, and in some papers, the impacts of illegal immigration are still analyzed within the context of the impacts of immigration. In recent years, there have been more research papers specifically on the impact of illegal immigration.

Among these, the most representative PhD dissertations are as follows: 1. "Cross-border Immigration and National Security: A Study on Nontraditional Security" by Ruan Zhengyu. The topic "cross-border immigration and national security" can be characterized as "migration security."[39] In fact, the article analyzes the impact of cross-border migration (international migration) on national security from the perspective of nontraditional security. Chapter three, "The Interaction between Cross-border Migration and National Security," discusses at length the impact of cross-border migration (international migration) on economic, political, social, cultural, ecological and environmental security.[40] The article is refreshing in that it discusses the impact of overseas Chinese on modern China's economic security, talent security and political security.[41] 2. "The Study on the Problems of Legal Control of Illegal Immigration" by Xu Junhua. It describes the impacts of illegal migration as the "perils of illegal migration" and makes analysis from an innovative angle. It classifies the perils of illegal migration into the perils to destination countries and countries of origin, the influence on international relations and regular interstate exchanges, and the infringement of personal rights and property rights of illegal migrants themselves.[42] 3. In her article "Research on International Immigration and Immigration Policies," Li Fangtian analyzes the impacts of international immigration and immigration policies on national security, foreign policies and international security.[43] 4. The impact of illegal immigration on the EU is discussed in "The Research on European Union's Governance on Illegal Immigration" written by Wen Feng.[44]

For journal papers, from the perspective of nontraditional security, "The Impact of Migratory Movements on National Security" (Tian 2001) makes a comprehensive analysis on the impact of South Asian migration on the politics, economy, society and culture of receiving and sending countries and proposes the key argument that "cross-border immigration will not necessarily cause security problems, [because] certain preconditions are needed for those immigrants to be a source of security threats."[45] "International Immigration and Contemporary International Security: Impulses, Interactions and Challenges" (Zhou and Bai 2006) focuses on the negative security impacts of immigration, expands the research scope from national security to international security, analyzes the negative impacts of international migration on

[39] Ruan (2003).
[40] Ibid., 52–74.
[41] Ibid., 90–105.
[42] Xu (2005).
[43] Li (2009).
[44] Wen (2010a, b).
[45] Tian (2001).

sending countries' talent security, receiving countries' political ecology, identification and global ecological environment, and concludes that international immigration has become a nontraditional factor menacing international security.[46] Regarding the impacts of illegal immigration on specific countries, "On the Illegal Immigration in Malaysia" (Wen, 2010a, b) analyzes the negative impacts of illegal immigration on Malaysia's politics, economy, foreign relations and social security.[47] "The Problems of Illegal Immigration in Russia" (Xu, 2007) analyzes the negative impacts of illegal immigration on Russian society.[48] "The Research on the Current Situation, Problems and Countermeasures of Cross-border Movement of People in the Yunnan Border Areas" (Lu & Li, 2007) makes a detailed analysis of the positive roles and impacts of cross-border immigration and immigrants[49] in the border areas of Yunnan and their social issues and negative impacts.[50] "The Dynamics of Overseas Immigrants in Yunnan and the Analysis of Social Problems in Border Areas" (He, 2008) analyzes the security issues caused by *sanfei*[51] at the trading ports of border areas.[52]

In terms of books, *Immigrants and National Security: Research on the Derivation of Threats and Their Conditions* (Tian, 2010) analyzes the positive impacts of immigrants on the security of receiving countries, along with their threats to the economic, social and political security of receiving countries. Through empirical research on the relations between South Asian, French and German immigrants and national security, it is concluded that there are both positive and negative impacts of immigration; the consequences of immigration on various security areas are interconnected but difficult to offset; and specific conditions are required for immigrants to be a threatening factor of receiving countries' national security.[53] In the book *Nontraditional Security* (Lu, 2003), Chap. 16, "The Problems of Illegal Immigration in Nontraditional Security" studies the phenomenon of illegal immigration as a nontraditional security factor and addresses the political, economic, and social impacts of illegal immigration on receiving countries. The study of China's illegal immigration problems is currently based on the perspective of regarding China as a migrant-sending country.[54] *Impact Factors of Immigration on the Current Sino-Russia Relations: An Analysis from the Perspective of Nontraditional Security*, written by Qiang Xiaoyun, also studies immigration problems from the perspective of nontraditional security and addresses the impact of immigration on social orders, cultural security and economic security. In addition, it features an analysis of the impact of immigration on national

46 Zhou and Bai (2006).

47 Wen (2010a, b).

48 Xu (2007).

49 Regarding cross-border migration, floating population and illegal immigrants, see the analysis further below. –Author's note.

50 Lu and Li (2007).

51 Regarding the relations between *sanfei* and illegal immigrants, see the analysis further below. –Author's note.

52 He (2008).

53 Tian (2010), pp. 291–296.

54 Lu (2003).

image and the exploration of its impact on the relationship between countries and on international society.[55]

In summary, although both Chinese and foreign studies regarding the impact of illegal international immigration did not begin until quite late and some of them were still undertaken in the context of immigration, the perspectives have been expanded from traditional security to nontraditional security, as well as the impact on border security, the political, economic and social impact on receiving countries, and the impact on national security and international security and relations in terms of the impact of illegal immigration. The issue these studies have in common is that they focus on the impacts of illegal immigration on receiving countries and less so on sending countries. Most of the studies regard China as an immigrant-sending country (including illegal immigrants) and do not focus on the impact of illegal immigrants on China after they enter the country, along with the impact brought by illegal immigrants in China's border areas with a high concentration of ethnic minorities.

(3) **The Governance of Illegal Immigration**

The purpose of studying the causes and impacts of illegal immigration is to resolve this particular issue of governing illegal immigration. The governance of illegal immigration can be undertaken from different aspects. Taking the relevant policies and legal systems as a reference, this book performs its analysis based on the theories or strategies of governance.

As mentioned above, it was quite late when the strict definition of "illegal immigration" was finally provided, and most of the relevant overseas studies were included in the study of immigration. Similarly, it was not until the late 1990s that the concept of immigration governance was introduced. The previous studies on immigration governance focused on the study of policies, which in turn led to the confusion of the studies of immigration or illegal immigration governance and relevant policies.

In the few overseas studies specifically on immigration governance in China, China was regarded as an immigrant-sending country. For example, the report "Recent Trends in Chinese Migration to Europe: Fujianese Migration in Perspective," published by the International Organization of Migration (IMO) in March 2002, provides a detailed study of migrants from Fujian Province, particularly their illegal immigration to other countries. In 2002, the Bureau of International Information Program of the US Department of State also released the "Human Trafficking from China" and "Trafficking in Persons Report," which perform thorough analyses of the contemporary issues of human trafficking and illegal immigration.[56]

Other relevant studies mainly focus on immigration in the EU and the US, while studies in the political dimension focus on the study of immigration policies and strategies and countermeasure analysis of immigration governance. For example, *Transnational Chinese: Fujianese Migrants in Europe*, published by Stanford University Press, applies meticulous fieldwork research of Fujian migrants, provides a large amount of important and accurate source materials, and analyzes and reflects on

[55] Qiang (2010).

[56] Ruan (2003).

the immigration policies of EU members by considering the characteristics of new migrants from China. In 2006, *Europe and Its Immigrants in the 21st Century: A New Deal or a Continuing Dialog of the Deaf?*, edited by Delnetrios G. Papadelnetriou, was published. It proposes a series of measures regarding the future of immigration in Europe, economic costs and benefits of immigration, citizenship, and social and economic integration.[57]

The research on illegal immigration governance by Chinese scholars can be divided into four types, according to the subjects of research: international organizations, such as the EU; specific foreign countries; China as an immigrant-sending country; and China as an immigrant-receiving country.

Two PhD dissertations on the immigration governance of the US, namely, "Immigrants and Their Economic Impacts on the United States Since 1965" (Ouyang, 2010)[58] and "Research on Muslim Immigrants in the United States: South Asian and Arabic Immigrants" (Ma, 2010),[59] discuss various problems of immigration in the US but not much of its governance. Regarding immigration governance in the EU, chapter four, titled "International Regulations: The Incentive Mechanisms in the EU's Immigration Politics" in Chen Zhiqiang's dissertation "Research on the EU's Immigration Politics," analyzes the motives of the immigration policies of the EU and its member states, the issues of immigration, the tug of war between the EU and its member states, among all EU member states and their political parties, final results and future trends.[60] When referring to multilevel governance, it admits that regulations, the rule of law, and dialogs of supranational actions have become the core of politics, which are exactly the power source of human rights protection for immigrants. Treaties between states, the *Geneva Agreement*, the *International Convention on Civil and Political Rights*, and the UNHCR constitute the regulations of cross-border human rights protection. The rights and freedoms to which individuals are entitled are guaranteed to prevent the unlimited role of sovereign states on immigration matters. At the same time, it also points out that when sovereign states remain dominant, it would be a utopian dream and naive to overestimate the role of international regulations.[61] "The Research on European Union's Governance on Illegal Immigration" (Wen, 2010a, b), an essential publication in terms of illegal immigration governance, proposes the models of national governance, supranational governance, subnational governance, and multilevel governance of illegal immigration in the EU.[62]

---

[57] Delnetrios G Papadelnetriou, "Europe and Its Immigrants in the 21st Century: A New Deal or a Continuing Dialog of the Deaf?", MPI and the Luso-Americin Foundation, March 2006.

[58] Ouyang (2010).

[59] Ma (2010).

[60] Chen (2007).

[61] Chen (2007).

[62] Wen (2010a, b).

"The Study on the Problems of Legal Control of Illegal Immigration" (Xu, 2005) is a representative study of illegal immigration governance from the perspective of legal control.[63] "The Research on Modern China's Illegal Immigration" (Wang, 2004) is more closely targeted, which proposes measures to manage illegal immigrants in China and measures of international cooperation and further elaborates measures to manage illegal Chinese emigrants (sending) and illegal foreign immigrants (receiving).[64]

For journal articles, "Elaboration and Analysis of the Situation of the Foreign Floating Population inside Yunnan's Border and Problems of Frontier Society" (He, 2008) argues that the management of overseas immigrants in Yunnan Province was uneven and inadequate and sometimes ineffective. It analyzes the problems and weaknesses of the management of overseas immigrants, yet it does not elaborate on improvement measures.[65] In another article, "The Dynamics of Overseas Immigrants in Yunnan and the Analysis of Social Problems in Border Areas," Professor He Yue analyzes the main problems in managing the foreign floating population in Yunnan but fails to suggest any solution.[66] In "The Research on the Current Situation, Problems and Countermeasures of Cross-border Movement of People in the Yunnan border areas," Professor Lu Gang and Professor Li Shou make their observations and recommendations for cross-border immigration governance in the Yunnan border areas. However, they do not provide concrete analysis due to space limitations.[67]

For books, Research on the Legal System *of International Immigration* of the *EU* (Hao, 2011) draws on the EU's legal system of international immigration, analyzes the way forward for China's legal regulations of international immigration, envisages the concept of enhancing border management, and ensuring legislative harmonization and institutional coordination.[68] The *Immigration Law* (Liu, 2010) analyzes specific legal issues concerning the governance of illegal immigration, such as "the problems of the *Passport Law of the PRC* and their solutions" and "the solutions to the problems in the *Exit-Entry Administration Law of the PRC"*.[69]

In summary, Chinese and foreign research on illegal international immigration can be divided into two categories: research on illegal immigration governance in the context of immigration governance and that specifically on illegal immigration governance. Immigration governance in other countries mainly focuses on the study of relevant policies, which has led to confusion between the study of immigration or illegal immigration governance and the study of relevant policies. Moreover, there is not much literature directly relevant to immigration governance in China. Chinese scholars have shifted their attention from immigration governance in hot spot areas or countries such as European countries and the US to that in China, and

---

[63] Xu (2005).

[64] Wang (2004).

[65] He (2008).

[66] He (2009).

[67] Lu and Li (2007).

[68] Hao (2011).

[69] Liu et al. (2010).

the means of governance they have proposed range from macrolevel policy adjustment and microlevel countermeasures to specific legal controls. However, there are few research papers that provide empirical analyses by combining relevant theories and practices.

There are common problems in Chinese and foreign studies on the following topics: “motives and causes of illegal immigration”, “impacts of illegal immigration”, or “illegal immigration governance”: 1. The importance of the research on illegal immigration was not highlighted due to historical reasons. Furthermore, most studies have included illegal immigration in the scope of immigration, which ignored the essential differences of these two concepts. 2. The studies focused on immigrant-receiving regions or countries such as European countries and the US, but less so on traditional immigrant-sending regions and countries, especially on “reverse flows” from developed countries to developing countries and “parallel flows” among developed countries or developing countries. 3. They overlooked the immigration inflows of emerging economies, such as China, “ignoring” the impacts of illegal immigration on these countries. A small number of Chinese scholars have begun to pay attention to the problems faced by China as an immigrant-receiving country, but unfortunately, they have not performed any systematic research from the perspective of international immigration based on relevant theories.

3 Research Design and Main Approaches

(1) Research Design

The prerequisite of research is the objective existence of genuine problems. “The most foolish scholars study nonexist problems. The first step for scientific discovery is to find real problems.”[70] Therefore, this book first defines relevant concepts and clarifies the differences and connections of illegal immigrants, refugees, and *sanfei*. It also defines the scope of the research to specify the “Yunnan border areas with a high concentration of ethnic minorities.” On this basis, the book then analyzes the current situation of illegal immigration in the Yunnan border areas with a high concentration of ethnic minorities to prove the existence of the question, which is the precondition of its governance.

The governance of illegal immigration must address both its symptoms and root causes. We must understand and analyze the reasons for the problem to then make calibrated responses. More importantly, we need to decide whether illegal immigration is even in need of a solution. When the impact of a specific problem is minor and the benefits outweigh the costs, then all that is needed is some improvement measures. This book analyzes the negative consequences of illegal immigration in the Yunnan border areas with a high concentration of ethnic minorities from multiple aspects to highlight the necessity and urgency of governance.

[70] Ji (2008).

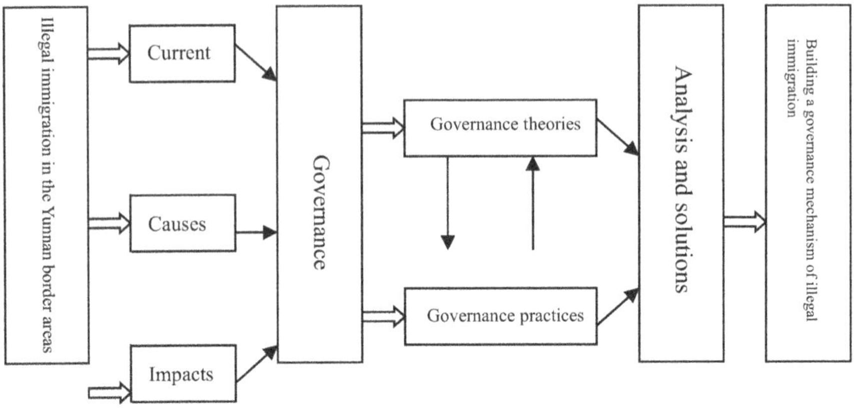

Fig. 1 Research design

The book focuses on the governance of illegal immigration in the Yunnan border areas with a high concentration of ethnic minorities, including the current situation, causes and impact. There are two parts: governance theories and governance practices, which are closely related to one another. Governance practices are the practices undertaken under the guidance of theories, without which practices are "blind"; moreover, they represent the sole criterion for testing theories and will surely react to them by challenging and correcting them for continuous improvement and development. This is why, from the perspective of development, governance theories and practices are both under constant changes and development and face the challenges of emerging issues. This book analyzes the problems faced by the governance theories and practices of illegal immigration in the Yunnan border areas with a high concentration of ethnic minorities and then seeks corresponding solutions.

Governance, also referred to as a governance mechanism, is a mechanism in which multiple factors each play their own individual roles. It consists of the subject, object, basis, methods, performance evaluation and risk forecast of governance. By taking illegal immigration governance in Yunnan border areas with a high concentration of ethnic minorities as a starting point, this book seeks to establish a governance mechanism for illegal immigration in border areas with Chinese characteristics. The research design is as follows: Fig. 1.

(2) **Main Research Methods**

1. Literature Review Methods

Literature collection and research are the crucial basis and prerequisite of sociologic studies. This can inspire our research and help us avoid getting sidetracked by collecting and analyzing the research results of Chinese and foreign scholars on specific questions and understanding their research methods and viewpoints. After collecting Chinese and foreign literature related to the "illegal immigration in the Yunnan border areas with a high concentration of ethnic minorities and its governance" based on the three aspects of "immigration motives and causes of illegal immigration," "impacts of illegal immigration" and "illegal immigration governance," I selected the research papers that would be helpful for writing this book.

2. Investigation Methods

Investigation is vital for acquiring first-hand materials, increasing perceptual knowledge, and understanding facts. Although the assertion of "no investigation, no right to speak" does not necessarily apply to all questions, the research object of this book is a question under constant changes. Therefore, it is not easy to guarantee the timeliness of relevant literature. Meanwhile, since there have been few studies regarding "illegal immigration and its governance in the Yunnan border areas with a high concentration of ethnic minorities," it is necessary to perform an investigation in this regard. The investigation methods applied in this book are as follows:

(1) Field investigation. I visited Hekou Yao Autonomous County of Honghe Prefecture to ascertain the actual situation from the competent authorities and front-line officers involved in illegal immigration governance, illegal immigrants and their families, as well as to collect their comments and suggestions regarding illegal immigration governance by questionnaires, field observations, symposiums, and interviews.
(2) Individual interview. I conducted face-to-face interviews with local sociology experts and scholars, along with supervisors and officials in the substantive departments of Yunnan Province. Their insightful and unique observations brought my analyses closer to the facts of the question.

3. Comparative Study

Comparative study involves either vertical or horizontal comparison. This book horizontally compares the theories and practices of illegal immigration governance in China, other countries (France, the US, Italy, Russia, etc.) and international organizations.

4. Integrated Theoretical and Empirical Research

Based on previous studies, this book takes stock of the issues of illegal immigration governance in the Yunnan border areas with a high concentration of ethnic minorities from the perspectives of "immigration motives and causes of illegal immigration," "impacts of illegal immigration" and "illegal immigration governance," aiming to build a policy-guided governance mechanism guaranteed by the rule of law. This requires empirical analysis to assess whether the theoretical hypotheses of governance mechanisms are valid. Finally, this book verifies the relevant governance theories based on the materials collected in the investigation process.

References

Arango, J. (2001). Explaining migration: A critical view. *International Social Science Journal (Chinese Edition)*, (3).

Borjas, G. J. (1989). Economic theory and international migration. *International Migration Review*, Special Sliver Anniversary Issue: 23.
Brochmann, G. (1999). *Mechanisms of immigration contro*. Berg Press, 7p.
Chen, Z. (2007). *The Research on the EU's Migration Politics*. Northeast Normal University.
Hao, L. (2011). *EU Legal Regime of International Migration Research*. People's Publishing House.
Hammar, T. (1985). *European immigration policy: A comparative study*. Cambridge University Press, 11p.
He, Y. (2008). Elaboration and analysis of the situation of the foreign floating population inside Yunnan's border and problems of frontier society. *Journal of Yunnan Normal University (Social Sciences Edition)* (2)
He, Y. (2009). Dynamics of overseas immigrants in Yunnan and the analysis of social problems in border areas. *Journal of Yunnan Normal University (Social Sciences Edition)* (1).
Ji, X. (2008). *The cowshed: Memories of the Chinese cultural revolution*. Huayi Publishing House
Li, F. (2009). *The Research on International Immigration and Immigration Policies*. PhD diss., Nankai University
Liu, G., et al. (2010). *Chinese Immigration Law*. Economic Press China.
Lu, G., & Li, S. (2007). The research on the current situation, problems and countermeasures of cross-border movement of people in the Yunnan Border areas. *Journal of Humanities*, (Lu, G.eds.) Yunnan University Press.
Lu, Z. (2003). *Nontraditional security*. Current Affairs Press
Lu, G. (2006). Cross-border movement of people in China-Myanmar border areas. *Journal of Yunnan Nationalities University (Social Sciences Edition)*, (6).
Ma, L. (2010). *The Research on American Muslim Immigrants: South Asian and Arabic Immigrants*. PhD diss., Minzu University of China.
Ouyang, Z. (2010). *Immigrants and Their economic impacts on the United States since 1965*. Northeast Normal University.
Qiang, X. (2010). *Impact factors of immigration on the current Sino-Russia relations: An analysis from the perspective of nontraditional security*. Current Affairs Press.
Qiu, L. (2005). The research on international immigration: History and current situation of international immigration and China's countermeasures. *Overseas Chinese Histories Studies*, (1).
Ruan, Z. (2003). *Cross-border immigration and national security: A study on nontraditional security*. PhD diss., Jinan University.
Sassen, S. (1998). *The mobility of labor and capital* Cambridge University Press.
Tian, H. (2001). The impact of migratory movements on national security. *Journal of Contemporary Asia-Pacific Studies* (4).
Tian, Y. (2010). *Immigrants and national security: The research on the derivation of threats and their conditions*. World Affairs Press.
Wang, X. (2004). *The Research on Modern China's Illegal Immigration*. Jinan University.
Wen, F. (2010a). *The research on European Union's governance on illegal immigration*. PhD diss., Jinan University.
Wen, F. (2010b). On the illegal immigration in Malaysia. *Southeast Asian Studies*, (3)
Xia, F. (2008). *illegal immigrants from Southern Zhejiang as seen from the global perspective*. Nankai University Press.
Xu, J. (2005).*The study on the problems of legal control of illegal immigration*. PhD diss., Wuhan University.
Xu, H. (2007). The problems of illegal immigration in Russia. *International Information*, (6).
Zhou, J. (2008). *On peaceful cross-border dwelling models: A study of the peaceful cross-border dwelling model of South China and Mainland Southeast Asia*. Ethnic Publishing House.
Zhou, Y., & Bai, Q. (2006). International immigration and contemporary international security: Impulses, interactions and challenges. *Around Southeast Asia*, (6).

Chapter 2
Overview of Illegal Immigration in Yunnan Border Areas with a High Concentration of Ethnic Minorities

This chapter analyzes fundamental or prerequisite questions, including the definition and clarification of relevant concepts and the current situation of illegal immigration in the Yunnan border areas with a high concentration of ethnic minorities. There is more than one way to define or clarify a concept, and the ways to understand it vary from different angles. In addition, there are many interpretations of the same concept at different times. Therefore, before discussing any question, we must give a unified definition of a concept and elaborate the reason or basis of this definition to facilitate the discussion in the same context. Meanwhile, the chapter analyzes the current situation and problems of illegal immigration in the Yunnan border areas with a high concentration of ethnic minorities to lay the foundation for further examination of its governance.

1 Definitions and Clarifications of Core Concepts

The core concepts of this book are the Yunnan border areas with a high concentration of ethnic minorities, illegal immigration therein, and governance thereof.

1.1 Frontier and Border

When referring to Yunnan Province, many people think about a "frontier area" or "ethnic minorities" or a frontier area with a high concentration of ethnic minorities. These two ideas define the public's general impression of the province.

"Frontier" and "ethnic minority" are two distinct concepts. According to Professor Zhou Ping, "frontier" refers to the periphery within a country's territory or boundaries. It is a particular area within a country. However, not every country regards a peripheral area within its territory as a frontier area. Furthermore, countries with

G. Luo, *The Issues of Illegal Immigration and its Solutions in the Minority-Border Regions in Yunnan Province, China*, https://doi.org/10.1007/978-981-19-1249-8_2

frontier areas have different views regarding the scope of these areas. A "frontier area" literally refers to a designated remote land. After the establishment of the state, "land" is an area under the jurisdiction of the state. However, the connotation of a "frontier" extends far beyond its literal definition.[1] After the founding of the People's Republic of China, the concept of a frontier became closely related to that of ethnicity. In discussing the concept or topic of a frontier area or frontier issues, the term "frontier area with a high concentration of ethnic minorities" became widely used. Even when discussing "areas with a high concentration of ethnic minorities," what is meant is a "frontier area with a high concentration of ethnic minorities." The word frontier became used less frequently, and the concept has become subsumed under that of ethnicity.[2]

A frontier is a multidimensional concept, and its political, geological and legal interpretation are of primary importance.

Based on his analysis of frontier areas' political attributes from the perspective of their formation, Professor Zhou Ping argues that the prerequisite of a modern frontier area is the founding of nation-states. Since the Revolution of 1911, China has embarked on the journey of building a nation-state. Throughout this process, the concept of delimitation of frontiers according to national boundaries has been framed, and this new approach replaced the old perception of treating frontier areas as peripheral zones and lands of "rude tribes" under the rule of an empire. China became a true nation-state after the founding of the People's Republic of China, and a new concept of a "frontier" came into being: the areas close to the national boundary.[3] The approach of "binding" the concept of a frontier with that of a nation-state is clearly based on the governance of a modern country because the precondition of national jurisdiction is the existence of established national boundaries. Moreover, favorable policies for less developed frontier areas should be adopted based on administrative regions.

From a geographic point of view, frontier areas include both land frontiers and maritime frontiers. Land frontiers are the areas along the inner side of a country's land boundaries that meet two requisite conditions: first, borderlines with neighboring countries; and second, unique natural, historical and cultural characteristics. Based on this standard, China's land frontiers consist of the northeastern provinces of Heilongjiang, Jilin and Liaoning, as well as the Inner Mongolia Autonomous Region, Gansu Province, Xinjiang Uyghur Autonomous Region, Xizang Autonomous Region, Guangxi Zhuang Autonomous Region, and Yunnan Province. However, He Danpeng holds that, strictly speaking, we cannot consider the entire territories of the Inner Mongolia Autonomous Region, Guangxi Zhuang Autonomous Region, and the provinces of Heilongjiang, Jilin, Liaoning and Yunnan as land frontiers. Specifically, the hinterland areas of Guilin and Wuzhou in the northeastern part of Guangxi Zhuang Autonomous Region, the city of Harbin and its neighboring areas in southern Heilongjiang Province, the areas other than Yanbian

[1] Zhou (2008a, b).

[2] Ibid., 90.

[3] Zhou (2008a, b).

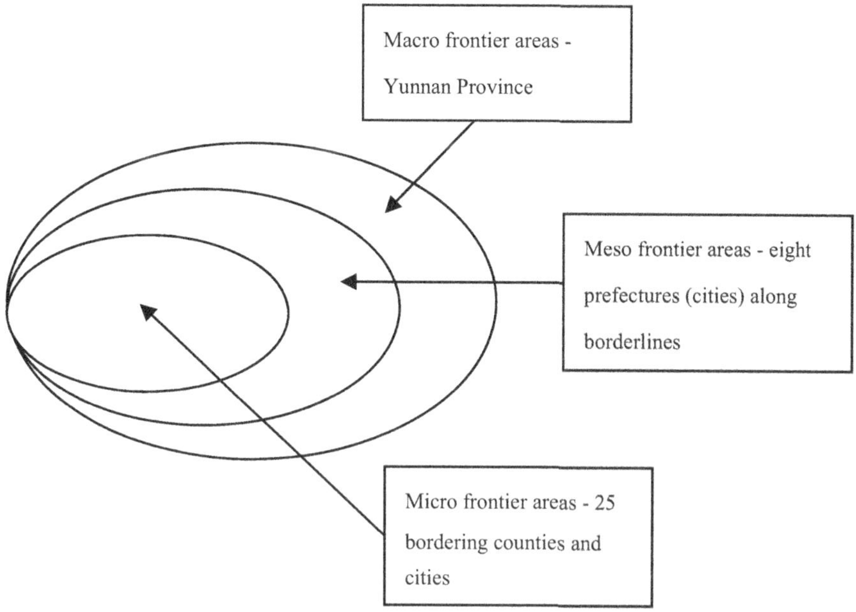

Fig. 1 Diagram of frontier delimitation in Yunnan

and Changbai Korean Autonomous Prefectures, the city of Ji'an in Jilin Province, the areas surrounding Dandong in Liaoning Province, and the areas aside from the prefectures and districts along the national borders in Yunnan Province cannot be considered frontier areas. To put it simply, in a narrow sense, all of the counties along the borderlines are modern China's frontier areas.[4]

However, I am afraid I must disagree with his approach. Taking Yunnan Province as an example, it is a typical land frontier area that meets the geographic standard of frontiers. Of course, we can make further divisions from macro, meso and micro perspectives for the convenience of academic study (see Fig. 1). From the perspective of national macromanagement, Yunnan is a typical land frontier area; in terms of provincial meso-management, Yunnan Province's eight prefectures (cities) along the borderlines can be regarded as frontier areas[5]; and the 25 bordering counties (such as Hekou County) are border areas, as well as typical frontier areas at the micro level. Therefore, it is relevant to study the problems of frontier areas by taking border areas as an example, despite their particular significance in terms of law.

[4] He (2009).

[5] There are 16 prefectures (cities) and 128 counties (cities or districts), among which eight prefectures (cities) and 25 counties are at the border areas. The eight prefectures (cities), i.e., Honghe Prefecture, Wenshan Prefecture, Xishuangbanna Prefecture, Dehong Prefecture, Nujiang Prefecture, Pu'er City, Baoshan City, and Lincang City, are referred to as the eight prefectures (cities) along the borderlines. Five of them are ethnic autonomous prefectures.

From a jurisprudence perspective, a frontier is not a legal concept. In other words, the Chinese and overseas legal communities have never defined frontiers in legal terms. The legal concepts relevant to frontiers are "border" or "border area" and its corresponding border management system. The basis of a state's border delineation is the state boundary, i.e., the lines defining the limits of a state's territory and those defining a state's territorial control (particularly territorial jurisdiction). A state's territory consists of territorial land, waters, airspace and subsoil, while the boundaries are divided into land boundaries, water boundaries and air boundaries. The terms "border" and "border area" refer to the area at both sides of the borderlines. Boundaries are the "lines" that divide territories, while border areas are the "areas" on either side of these lines. The division and size of the "areas" are determined by all states according to their own situations.

Neighboring countries often manage border areas with their domestic laws and bilateral treaties signed between each other for the convenience and interests of their residents' economic and social life. This management system established according to laws and regulations is the border management system, which includes maintenance of boundary marks, cooperation in public services, resource utilization and environmental protection, and proper settlement of events in border areas.[6] Neighboring countries may agree on the scope and delimitation of border areas by signing bilateral treaties to facilitate border management. For example, Article 13 of the *Interim Agreement on Handling Border Issues between the People's Republic of China and the Socialist Republic of Vietnam* stipulates the following: 2. The term "border residents" in this agreement means village (town) residents living within the boundaries of each country; 3. The term "border areas" in this agreement means counties (cities) within the boundaries of each country. Article 13 of the *Boundary Treaty between the People's Republic of China and the People's Democratic Republic of Laos* reads that the term "border residents" in this Treaty means county residents living within the boundaries of each country. In the *Agreement between the Government of the People's Republic of China and the Government of the Union of Myanmar on China-Myanmar Border Areas Management and Cooperation*, Article 1 reads as follows: In this Agreement, 1. the term "border areas" means the counties (cities) on the Chinese side and townships on the Myanmar side as specified in Annex I to this Agreement. 2. The term "border residents" means permanent residents of either country living in the border areas. In the above three bilateral treaties, there are two criteria for the determination of border areas: first, the areas within the boundaries of each country; and second, counties, cities or townships in accordance with the administrative division of both countries.

This shows that border areas in legal terms are different from frontier areas based on political and geological perspectives. Frontier areas are larger and include border areas. In addition, a border management system is a specific way of managing frontier areas. Taking Yunnan Province as an example, its frontier areas only refer to the 25 counties and cities that share borders with other countries.

---

[6] Regarding the border management system, see Shao Jin, *International Law* (Beijing: Peking University Press, Higher Education Press, 2000), 109–110.

To facilitate investigation, this book selects 25 border counties and cities in Yunnan Province, i.e., border areas in Yunnan Province as the research subjects. In addition, Yunnan is home to the largest number of ethnic groups. The sixth National Population Census showed that 45,966,000 residents (3.43% of China's total population) were counted in Yunnan Province, ranking 12th in the country and 3rd in Western China. Among the residents registered for the population census, 15,337,000 (33.37%) belonged to ethnic groups, and 30,629,000 (66.63%) were of Han ethnicity.[7] In addition, there are 16 cross-border ethnic groups with over 5,000 residents living in Yunnan Province and neighboring countries, totaling 10,410,000, accounting for 78.6% of the population of ethnic groups in Yunnan Province.[8] Most of these cross-border ethnic groups reside in 25 border counties throughout Yunnan Province. Therefore, the border areas in this book are those areas with a high concentration of ethnic minorities and are thus referred to as the Yunnan border areas with a high concentration of ethnic minorities.

Hekou Yao Autonomous County is a typical border area with a high concentration of ethnic minorities in Yunnan Province; thus, its problems of illegal immigration governance are somewhat representative in these areas. This is one of the critical reasons for choosing Hekou County as the primary investigation site in this book.

1.2 Migration and Illegal Migration

To understand the concept of an "illegal immigrant," one must first comprehend the respective meanings of "illegal" and "migration," as well as the relations among "illegal immigrant," "*sanfei*" and "refugee."

1. **Migration**

No agreement has been reached regarding the definition of migration among Chinese and overseas scholars or international organizations. One researcher even holds that "there is nothing objective about the definitions of migration, as they are the result of state policies introduced in response to political and economic goals and public attitudes."[9] I am afraid I cannot agree with this. State policies are a vital factor

[7] See: http://society.yunnan.cn/html/2011-05/09/content_1603043_2.htm. Accessed August 12, 2011.

[8] "Cross-border ethnic groups" refer to the same ethnic groups residing in China and neighboring countries who live in connected or adjacent areas and share basically the same languages and cultures. They initially resided in the same regions but later lived in two or more countries due to migration and boundary changes. The 16 cross-border ethnic groups in Yunnan Province are as follows: Yi, Hani, Zhuang, Miao, Yao, Buyi, Dai, Bulang, Lahu, Wa, Jingpo, De'Ang, Lisu, Achang, Nu and Dulong. See Fang Tie, "The Distribution, Origins and Characteristics of Cross-border Ethnic Groups in Yunnan Province," *Journal of Guangxi University for Nationalities (Philosophy and Social Science Edition)*, no. 5 (September 2007). It is worth noting that the population of cross-border ethnic groups with over 5,000 residents in Yunnan Province and neighboring countries does not originate from the latest data of the sixth National Population Census.

[9] [Australia] Castles (2001), p. 22.

in defining migration, while international organizations have been working toward a unified definition, and some international treaties have made some progress in specifying migration. Although not sharing the same views about the meaning of migration, Chinese and overseas scholars have begun to reach somewhat of a common understanding. After reviewing relevant definitions and considering China's reality, I found it necessary and possible to define migration.

1. Definitions in Dictionaries

Encyclopedia Americana states that human migration is the permanent change of residence by an individual or group over some distance.[10] It holds that there are two elements in human migration: "over some distance" and "permanent change of residence." "Over some distance" indicates that the people's movement should reach a certain spatial distance, but does not clarify whether this involves traveling over state boundaries, i.e., cross-border movement. The description is ambiguous in that it seemingly involves either moving within one country or across countries. Meanwhile, "permanent change" means permanent residence after moving, which does not match the reality that modern migrants reside for different lengths of time after their movements. The definition of migration in the *Dictionary of the Social Sciences* is a permanent change of residence from an original location to a destination due to geographic or spatial movement.[11] It still does not identify if this involves cross-border movement, and it emphasizes that the change is permanent. *Encyclopedia of China (Society)* reads, "human migration means people's movement across administrative boundaries to another residence. The people who migrate are called migrants."[12] It stresses the movement across administrative boundaries, which often refers to regional division within a country. The dividing lines between states are called "state boundaries" or "borderlines." Therefore, this definition can be applied for domestic migration but not international migration.

The *Practical Chinese Dictionary* gives a distinctive explanation to *yimin*: ① [verb] to move to another place or another country; ② [noun] people who move to another place or another country.[13] It divides *yimin* into two categories: the behavior of moving and the people who move, i.e., the behavior itself and the subject of the behavior. It also suggests that migrants include internal and international migrants but does not specify the duration of residence after moving to the new place. In addition, it should be noted that in English, "migration" refers to the movement and "migrant" refers to a person who moves from one place to another. However, in the Chinese language, *yimin* means both the behavior and the subject of behavior, the usage of which entails the assessment in specific contexts.

From the definitions in the dictionaries mentioned above, we may determine that the word *yimin* encompasses international migrants (or cross-border migrants) and internal migrants, including both the behavior of moving and the people who move.

---

[10] Encyclopedia Americana, Beijing (1994).

[11] Dictionary of the Social Sciences, Taipei (1973).

[12] Encyclopedia of China, Beijing (1991).

[13] Practical Chinese Dictionary, Beijing (2008).

Nevertheless, there is no explicit provision regarding the length of stay following the movement, the boundaries to cross for migration, or the nature of these boundaries.

2. Definitions Made by International Organizations

The definitions made by international organizations are clearly relevant to international migration and are as follows:

International Organization for Migration (IOM): International migration means the movement of persons away from their countries of birth or countries of origin and across an international border to a country where they are not residents for short-term or long-term residence. Movements due to holidays, short business visits, medical treatment, or religious pilgrimage were not included.[14] It features the reference of "international border" and "short-term or long-term residence" (therefore, international migrants consist of short-term migrants and long-term residents) and the exclusion of movements due to holidays, short-term business visits, medical treatment or religious pilgrimage.

The Special Commission of Inquiry on Human Rights of the United Nations Educational, Scientific and Cultural Organization (UNESCO): International migrants are the people who live in a country other than their countries of birth and have attained important social connections in the residing country. They also include the following three types of migrants: (1) residents who have left their countries of origin (and thus are not protected by the law of these countries) and are now living in the territory of another country; (2) residents who are not entitled to the identification of legal rights in receiving countries (such as the status of refugees, citizens and others); and (3) residents who are not guaranteed the protection of law based on diplomatic protocols, visas or other agreements.[15] This definition points out that international migrants include both legal and illegal migrants. In addition, the three types of migrants listed above are protected by neither the law of their countries of origin nor that of the receiving country and are not entitled to legal protection based on diplomatic protocols, visas or other agreements. Immigrants who are not protected by law should be considered illegal immigrants.

The United Nations: International migrants are individuals who have resided in a country other than their countries of origin for more than one year, except diplomats residing in other countries and military personnel of peacekeeping troops stationed in other countries.[16] This definition excludes diplomats and military personnel from

[14] This definition is cited from Luyi (2011), p. 10. In contrast, the IOM held that at the international level, no universally accepted definition for "migrant" exists. The term migrant has usually been understood to cover all cases where the decision to migrate was taken freely by the individual concerned for reasons of "personal convenience" and without intervention of an external compelling factor; it therefore applied to persons, and family members, moving to another country or region to better their material or social conditions and improve the prospects for themselves or their family. Xu (2005, pp. 5–6.) Wen Feng made a similar statement in his dissertation Wen (2010, pp. 43–44.) I believe that we should adopt the latest definition cited by Hao Luyi.

[15] The UNESCO website: http://portal.unesco.org/she/en/ev.phpl. Cited from Luyi (2011), p. 10.

[16] Li (2005).

international migrants and specifies the minimum residence of international migrants as one year.

3. Definitions Made by Scholars

Australian researchers and scholars on migration studies Stephen Castles defined migration as the process of crossing the boundary of a political or administrative unit for a certain minimum period.[17] Well-known experts on migration studies Tomas Hammar and Grete Brochmann hold that a migrant is a person who migrates to a country and then actually resides there longer than a short period, i.e., more than three months. Both inward and outward movements of people are cross-border movements. People who move to another country and reside there longer than a certain period (three months) are immigrants in the receiving countries and emigrants from the countries of origin (countries of birth).[18] The definitions made by these three experts are of critical reference value. They clarify that people's inward and outward movements are movements across the boundaries of states and political or administrative units for a certain period of time. Moreover, the latter two experts further specify that the duration is no less than three months.

Chinese scholars have made clear distinctions between internal migrants (such as *sanxia yimin*, i.e., migrants who relocated due to the construction of the three gorges dam on the Yangtze River) and international migrants. Several representative views on international migrants are as follows: (1) According to Wu Qianjin, international migrants do not include the people who move from rural areas to cities within one country, and these people are distinguished from refugees. International migration is the movement of people across state boundaries. It comes from the free will of individuals and groups, without coercion from the government.[19] This definition excludes the following three categories of people from international migrants: internal migrants, refugees, and nonvoluntary migrants. forced migrants (international migrants are those who migrate voluntarily, free of government compulsion). I have different views regarding the last two categories, which I will discuss further below. (2) Weng Li argues that international migration is a social phenomenon that occurs after the establishment of states. It is the movement of citizens who exit their own countries and enter another country or region for either short- or long-term residence, according to the law of their countries of citizenship and countries of destination, as well as the relevant international treaties and practices.[20] Weng's definition, made from the lens of law, involves two significant problems. First, it only considers the migrants who legally move to another country, with no indication of illegal migrants; second, it regards migration as the behavior itself (exit and entry), while neglecting the subject of migration, i.e., migrants. (3) Hao Luyi contends that

[17] [Australia] Castles (2001), p. 21.

[18] Tomas Hammar, *European Immigration Policy: A Comparative Study* (Cambridge: Cambridge University Press, 1985), 11; Great Brochman, *The Mechanism of Control* (Oxford: Berg Press, 1999), 7.

[19] Wu (2004).

[20] Li (2001).

international migration refers to voluntary or nonvoluntary movements across borders for a certain period of stay in another country or region other than their countries of citizenship or birth. Hao further points out that the term "*guoji yimin*" may refer to the behavior (international migration) or the subject of the behavior (international migrants). The duration of stay following the movement does not play a decisive role in the definition of migration. Moreover, the scope of migration expands with the change in duration. It includes permanent migration and temporary movement, such as overseas study or longer business visits. Hao also holds that the differences in the scope of migration result from specific regulations regarding the duration of migration among countries. Therefore, when studying migration problems in various countries, it is important to pay particular attention to national legislation.[21] Hao's definition of international migration requires further improvement, as it clarifies two types of international migration, voluntary and nonvoluntary migration, yet confines migration to the behavior of moving. Hao further explains that migration refers to both the behavior of moving and the subject of the behavior. In addition, Hao specifies the duration of residence and recognizes that the duration varies according to different laws. Each country may determine, where appropriate, the length of stay for their definition of migration. Of course, this does not affect their identification of a uniform length of stay according to relevant international conventions of which they are signatories. It is in fact the transfer of sovereign rights and the exercise of these rights. Hao Luyi's definition and further explanation of international migration are relatively objective, as they relate to the actual situation; however, further improvement is still needed.

4. Definition Used in This Book

The definition of migration used in this book draws upon the definitions in the dictionaries mentioned above, as well as the definitions made by international organizations and Chinese and overseas scholars, and then combines China's actual situation to integrate the country's particular circumstances. Moreover, the definition targets the research subject, i.e., the Yunnan border areas with a high concentration of ethnic minorities. As a specific and unique region, Yunnan Province faces illegal immigration problems of specific and unique meanings.

Yimin refers to both the migrants themselves and the act of migrating. Migrants are the people of one nationality who move across borders to another country or region. In this book, the term "migrants" refers only to international migrants who move across national borders (domestic migrants are excluded). Furthermore, the book does not touch on the Chinese who emigrate to other countries or regions and only focuses on the immigration of foreigners (people who are not Chinese citizens, including stateless persons) into the territory of China. Strictly speaking, the territory of China includes China's mainland, Hong Kong SAR, Macao SAR, and the Taiwan region. However, for historical reasons, the "territory within China" in this book refers to mainland China, and "foreigners" refer to expatriates, stateless persons, and

[21] Luyi (2011).

residents of Hong Kong, Macao and Taiwan. Residents of Hong Kong, Macao and Taiwan are regarded as "foreigners" for historical reasons.

In terms of subjective attitude, international migrants must have the purpose of moving to another country and staying there. As the purpose of staying in another country is a mental state, there are only two ways to ascertain it: first, direct interviews or investigation, or indirect inquiries through questionnaires; and second, observations about objective behaviors based on the principle of "subjective thinking is embodied in objective behaviors." The investigation in this book was done in these two ways. However, considering the definition of immigrants, it is simpler to adopt a more recognizable objective standard, i.e., "having resided within the territory of China for over three months, or being certain they will do so."

Based on the analysis above, I concluded that *yimin* refers to foreigners (including stateless persons and residents of Hong Kong, Macao and Taiwan) who have resided within the territory of China for over three months or been certain they would do so, excluding those shortly staying for business, travel or other purposes. In addition, my research subject does not include people staying in China for family visits, cross-border farming and grazing, religious pilgrimage, market fairs, or short-term business visits with no intention to reside there.

To understand this definition, it is important to pay attention to the following aspects:

1. The definition only focuses on the one-way migration of foreigners into the territory of China and does not consider Chinese migrants to other countries or regions. By combining these two categories, one can develop a more comprehensive definition of international migrants: foreigners (including stateless persons) who have resided in a country or region for a certain period of time (over three months) or been certain they would do so, excluding those staying for business, travel, religious pilgrimage, short-term business visits and other purposes without the intention to reside there.
2. The term "have resided for over three months or been certain they would do so" is the criterion indicating the purpose of residence, as well as the particular requirement for the length of stay. The reasons for setting the length of three months are as follows: First, China is a country with a large population; thus, we must maintain a high level of vigilance regarding immigrants. Setting the length of three months and integrating immigrants in the management process will help properly manage these people.[22] Second, although without a unified duration for the identification of immigration among international organizations, overseas scholars and certain countries, there are regulations regarding the minimum length of three months. This will facilitate communication and exchanges with the international community to set the length of three months.

[22] There is no unified regulation regarding the duration of immigrants' "residence" or "stay." For example, the UN considers immigrants who reside in another country for over one year as permanent residents, while other international organizations or countries set the time limit of five years, three years, six months, three months, etc. Three months is the shortest duration of immigration in the literature I have reviewed.

Third, as mentioned previously, in the sixth National Population Census, the NBS, for the first time, incorporated residents of Hong Kong, Macao and Taiwan and foreigners residing within the territory of China. They included residents of Hong Kong, Macao and Taiwan and foreigners who had resided within the territory of China from the reference time or been certain they would do so, excluding those temporarily staying for business, travel or other purposes. Although relevant departments did not classify these people as "immigrants," the length of three months adopted in this book as one of the criteria may comply with the legislative intent of these departments and scholars.

2. **Illegal Immigrants**

Immigrants can be categorized into different types according to various standards, such as internal migrants and international migrants (border crossing); legal immigrants and illegal immigrants (legality); individual immigrants, group immigrants and mass immigrants (size); short-term immigrants, mid-term immigrants and permanent immigrants (duration); and surviving immigrants and immigrants seeking further development (motivation).[23] These standards can be applied for the research from different perspectives, while this book focuses on how to distinguish legal immigrants from illegal ones.

Xu Junhua performs an in-depth investigation regarding the definition of illegal immigrants. After enumerating the definitions made by the IOM and the Organization for Economic Cooperation and Development (OECD), he divides the definitions formulated by Chinese scholars into three categories: first, the subject of behavior; second, the behavior itself; and third, a combined definition that refers to the behavior and subject of behavior. Finally, he concludes that we should adopt the combined definition of "illegal immigrants,", i.e., both the subject of behavior and the behavior itself. The focus should be the behavior, and thus the legal control of illegal immigrants is the control of their behavior. Meanwhile, based on the subject and the behavior, illegal immigrants can be classified into two types: immigrants who stay illegally and those who arrive illegally based on the subject and immigrants who enter illegally and those who enter legally but stay illegally based on the behavior.[24] I agree with the definition that combines the behavior and the subject while holding the view that the governance or legal control of illegal immigrants should also be "combined" without a skewed focus because the control of illegal immigration is also the control of illegal immigrants. Focusing on either side signifies failing to realize that the behavior and subject of illegal immigration are combined. Moreover, there is no need to divide illegal immigrants based on the subject and the behavior. Instead, we can divide them into migrants who (exit) enter illegally and their behavior and immigrants who enter legally but stay illegally and their behavior. Nonetheless, this definition does not take into consideration the time limit for illegal (exit) entry and legal entry but illegal stay, and in practice may be confused with *sanfei*.

[23] Xu (2005).

[24] Xu 2005, pp. 6–8.

Hao Luyi divides international migrants into four types: legal immigrants, illegal immigrants, forced immigrants and returned immigrants.[25] She holds that legal immigrants are those who move to the receiving country for short- or long-term residence from their countries of citizenship or birth according to relevant laws, international treaties or practice, and they include labor immigrants (immigrant workers), technical immigrants, investment immigrants, family immigrants, and other immigrants.[26] In contrast, illegal immigrants are those who enter the receiving country without valid legal documents or permission. She further divides illegal immigrants into two types: people who enter another country against its laws and regulations, often referred to as illegal immigrants[27]; and people who legally enter another country but overstay their permits, thus becoming overstayers, or people without legal identities (people in no possession of valid passports or similar documentation) who stay in another country by using altered documents or the documents of others, often referred to as illegal residents.[28] The characteristics of her definition of illegal immigrants are as follows: First, although she divides illegal immigrants according to the subject of immigration, there are two (indispensable) elements of "illegal entry" and "illegal overstay"; however, she does not set a time limit for illegal immigrants.

I believe there are three key points in the definition of illegal immigrants. First, illegal immigration is an irregular situation compared with legal immigration. Therefore, illegal immigrants form some immigrants, and their definition should be developed based on the definition of immigrants. Second, the subject and behavior of illegal immigration should be combined when defining illegal immigrants. Third, the definition of illegal immigrants should be developed based on the actual situation of specific countries while considering the specific contexts of the research, as well as the relations between illegal immigrants and relevant concepts.

Now that we have defined the concept of immigrants, let us next discuss the term "illegal." In terms of law, illegal and law-breaking are two distinct yet related concepts. Illegal means that the actions or facts are not protected by laws and regulations due to the lack of a legal basis. Law-breaking means the actions or facts are against laws and regulations; thus, there will be legal consequences. Illegal actions do not necessarily break the law (such as illicit cohabitation), and the perpetrators will not necessarily be brought to justice. However, lawbreakers will have to be held legally responsible for their actions. In fact, during my investigation, I discovered that

[25] Luyi (2011), pp. 14–23.

[26] Ibid., 14.

[27] Professor Liang Shuying holds that illegal border-crossing includes the following acts: 1. Using forged or altered documents to falsely pass border inspection; 2. Using documents of others or documents transferred by others to enter another country; 3. Entering without permission; 4. Landing in the country again and not leaving after being escorted to the departure vehicle based on the announcement of deportation; 5. Entering another country not according to the specified period and location (entry ports); 6. Avoiding inspection and entering another country; 7. Entering another country by hiding important facts or providing false information. See Liang Shuying, "The Measures to Address Illegal Immigration," *Pacific Journal*, no. 7 (2007).

[28] Luyi (2011), pp. 15–16.

relevant substantive departments and officials in charge of illegal immigration governance, or even scholars of illegal immigration, were unclear or indifferent toward the distinction between illegal and law-breaking. They claimed that illegal immigrants are those who break the law and should be held accountable according to laws and regulations. The term *Feifa yimin* used in this book can be taken to mean either "illegal immigrants" or "law-breaking immigrants," along with their behavior in a broad sense. However, in fact, these terms refer to "law-breaking immigrants" who should be held accountable for breaking the law and their behavior. For receiving countries, "laws" means their domestic laws, rules and regulations, as well as the rules in the bilateral agreements and treaties signed with sending countries and the multilateral treaties to which both receiving and sending countries had acceded.

Based on the above analysis, I conclude that illegal immigrants refer to foreigners (including stateless persons and residents of Hong Kong, Macao and Taiwan) who have illegally entered and resided within the territory of China or foreigners who have stayed in China (or were certain to reside) for over three months after their legal entry, excluding people staying for less than three months for family visits, cross-border farming and grazing, religious pilgrimage and short-term business visits with no intention to stay permanently.

It is important to note two issues to understand this definition:

1. This definition only refers to the one-way illegal immigration of foreigners to China and does not consider the illegal migration of Chinese citizens to other countries or regions. When the two aspects are combined, the definition of illegal international migrants will become complete: foreigners (including stateless persons) who have illegally entered and resided in one country or region, foreigners who have overstayed in one country or region for a certain period of time (over three months or were certain to reside for over three months) after their legal entry, excluding people staying for family visits, cross-border farming and grazing, religious pilgrimage and short-term business visits with no intention to stay permanently.
2. Theoretically speaking, illegal immigrants should bear corresponding legal responsibility for their illegal acts. However, some countries may adopt different measures to address this problem at different times, for example, to ignore it, make exceptions, or even provide a path to legalization for illegal immigrants. Therefore, "should bear corresponding legal responsibility" differs from "must bear corresponding legal responsibility."

3. Illegal Immigrants and Related Concepts

1. Illegal Immigrants and Sanfei

"*Sanfei*" refers to foreigners (including stateless persons and residents of Hong Kong, Macao and Taiwan, likewise below) of illegal entry, illegal residence and illegal employment. Technically speaking, the term "*sanfei*" is not a legal concept but what substantive departments call particular groups. The words "illegal entry, illegal residence and illegal employment" were included in the *Exit-Entry Administration Law of the People's Republic of China* adopted at the 27th session of the 11th National

People's Congress.[29] However, during the investigation for this book, I discovered that the substantive departments were more familiar with *sanfei*, but not much with illegal immigrants, and even less with the relationship between the two.

I believe it is easier to identify *sanfei* in that foreigners who perform one or more acts of illegal entry, illegal residence and illegal employment can be recognized as such. Illegal entry matters the most because it is one of the three conditions, and once people enter China illegally, their residence and employment in China are illegal. In practice, there are other cases, such as legal entry but illegal overstay; legal entry but illegal overstay and illegal employment; and legal entry, legal residence but illegal employment.[30]

The determination of illegal employment is based on the status of the worker. Employment is illegal either because of the worker's illegal entry or illegal overstay or because employment is forbidden on his or her visa type, albeit legal entry and legal residence. Article 43 of the *Exit-Entry Administration Law of the People's Republic of China* (hereafter the *Exit-Entry Administration Law*) specifies the scope of illegal employment of foreigners. It stipulates the actions of foreigners that shall be deemed illegal employment: working in China without obtaining work permits or work-type residence permits in accordance with relevant regulations; working in China beyond the scope prescribed in the work permits; or foreign students working in violation of the regulations on the administration of foreign students working to support their study in China or working beyond the prescribed scope of jobs or the prescribed time limit.[31]

For the same reasons, "illegal marriage"[32] as described in this book refers to the marriage between a citizen of China's mainland and a foreigner under the status of illegal entry or legal entry but illegal overstay. Marriage is illegal due to the latter's illegal status. In the case of Hekou County, the marriages between refugees in Hekou County and foreigners (including stateless persons and residents of Hong Kong, Macao and Taiwan) under the status of illegal entry or legal entry but illegal overstay are also illegal for the same reason.

The concepts of "*sanfei*" and "illegal immigrant" are closely related, and the latter is part of the former. Foreigners under the status of illegal entry, illegal residence and illegal employment are referred to as *sanfei*, while foreigners who have entered

---

[29] Article 45 of the *Exit-Entry Administration Law of the People's Republic of China*, source: http://news.xinhuanet.com/politics/2012-07/01/c_123353064_4.htm. Accessed July 1, 2012.

[30] There are cases of legal entry, legal residence but illegal employment in China. For example, foreigners (including stateless persons and residents of Hong Kong, Macao and Taiwan) holding student visas (travel authorization certificates for residents of Hong Kong, Macao and Taiwan) and tourist visas working illegally in China's mainland. "Illegal" means that the act of working is illegal, not the work itself (such as prostitution). –Author's note.

[31] Article 43 of the *Exit-Entry Administration Law of the People's Republic of China*, source: http://news.xinhuanet.com/politics/2012-07/01/c_123353064_4.htm. Accessed July 1, 2012.

[32] In this book, illegal marriage refers to the marriage between a foreigner (including stateless persons and residents of Hong Kong, Macao and Taiwan) under the status of illegal entry, or legal entry but illegal overstay and a citizen of China's mainland. Relevant substantive departments address this type of marriage as illegal marriage.

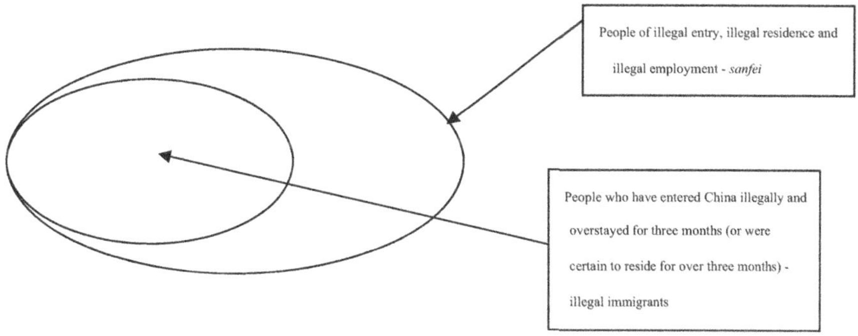

Fig. 2 The relationship between sanfei and illegal immigrants

China illegally or who have overstayed in China for over three months after their legal entry (or were certain to stay for over three months) are considered illegal immigrants. Therefore, it can be concluded that the difference between *Sanfei* and illegal immigrants lies in the different durations of illegal entry and illegal residence. Once *sanfei* have entered China illegally or overstayed for over three months (or were certain to reside for over three months), they became illegal immigrants. In other words, illegal immigrants are *sanfei* who have been in illegal status for a certain amount of time, i.e., the former forming a subset of the latter (see Fig. 2).

It is essential to understand the connections between these two concepts for the governance of illegal immigrants. China's current laws, rules, regulations and practices for addressing the problem of *sanfei* can be mostly applied to the governance of illegal immigrants. Of course, some differences exist between them. Particularly in international exchanges, the concept of illegal immigrants is more acceptable for the international community. The special features of illegal immigrants should be considered for their governance.

2. **Illegal Immigrants and Refugees**

The relations between refugees and illegal immigrants are quite complex. Hao Luyi holds that the term "forced immigrants" refers to refugees and asylum seekers and in a broad sense includes people who relocate to other countries due to environmental deterioration or loss of homes due to construction.[33] This shows that she draws a line between refugees and legal immigrants, illegal immigrants and returned immigrants based on people's subjective attitudes. However, it is not easy to make such a distinction in practice. It is better to follow the regulations of relevant international treaties to identify the status of refugees.

---

[33] Luyi (2011), p. 18.

On July 28, 1951, the *Convention Relating to the Status of Refugees* was adopted by the United Nations Conference of Plenipotentiaries on the Status of Refugees and Stateless Persons, convened in Geneva. For the first time, the definition and scope of refugees were clearly stated at a universal international convention. According to Article 1 of the Convention, the term "refugee" shall apply to any person who: has been considered as a refugee under relevant agreements, treaties and protocols established by the International Union or the Constitution of the International Refugee Organization; as a result of events occurring before January 1, 1951 and owing to well-founded fear of being persecuted for reasons of race, religion, nationality, membership of a particular social group or political opinion, is outside the country of his nationality and is unable or, owing to such fear, is unwilling to avail himself of the protection of that country; or who, not having a nationality and being outside the country of his former habitual residence as a result of such events, is unable or, owing to such fear, is unwilling to return to it.[34] Professor Liang Shuying concludes that there are three conditions for refugee status: first, residing outside of one's country of nationality or country of habitual residence; second, unable or unwilling to avail oneself of the protection of one's country of nationality or is unable or unwilling to return to one's country of habitual residence; and third, a well-founded fear of being persecuted. "Fear of being persecuted" refers to mentally or psychologically suffering from the dread or fear of abuse or persecution against oneself. It is not necessarily actual persecution but the situation in which one fears persecution, which is not out of imagination or fabrication.[35] Professor Wang Tieya states, "in the *Convention Relating to the Status of Refugees*, one of the basic requirements of being considered a refugee is the fear of being persecuted. Moreover, rather than being imaginary or fabricated, this fear shall be well founded by facts and legitimate reasons, the combination of subjective and objective factors. However, it is not necessary to reach a certain level or actual persecution to meet the requirements for being considered a refugee. When the fear of being persecuted is well founded, his seeking or attaining refugee status will not be prejudiced even when the persecution has not yet occurred."[36]

In 1982, China announced its accession into the *Convention Relating to the Status of Refugees and the Protocol Relating to the Status of Refugees* adopted by the UN in 1967. In addition, China adopted the definition of refugees stipulated in the 1951 *Convention Relating to the Status of Refugees*. Nevertheless, China has yet to establish relevant laws and regulations, which has resulted in shortcomings in identifying and managing refugees. This will be discussed further below.

Illegal immigrants and refugees, although largely different in definition and distinctive in theory, are not easy to distinguish in practice. Despite the difficulty in distinguishing between them based on immigrants' subjective attitudes, there is the possibility of mutual conversion under certain conditions. After entering a country

[34] Liang (2000), p. 310. The Convention Relating to the Status of Refugees adopted by the UN in 1967 removed the time limit mentioned above.

[35] Liang (2008).

[36] Wang (1995), pp. 89–90.

of destination, some illegal immigrants may make false asylum claims in exchange for refugee status and become refugees if they succeed. However, when their refugee applications are found untrue and thus rejected, they will remain illegal immigrants. Meanwhile, refugees usually enter another country illegally and retain their status of illegal entry and illegal residence before their refugee status is confirmed. Putting the time limit aside, they are defined as illegal immigrants.

Xu Junhua concludes that, aside from differences in concept, there are other distinctions between illegal immigrants and refugees: 1. Legal basis. Refugee status is recognized by the country where refugees reside or international organizations of refugee protection and rescue based on international treaties, i.e., the 1951 Convention Relating to the Status of Refugees and the 1967 Protocol Relating to the Status of Refugees. However, there are no unified international standards or relevant international treaties regarding the identification of illegal immigrants. They are recognized based on particular criteria, i.e., immigration laws or other domestic laws and regulations of various countries. 2. Legal status. Countries make efforts to combat and prevent illegal immigrations. Therefore, apart from basic human rights, illegal immigrants are not protected by the law of their residing country in terms of social benefits and employment guarantees. Meanwhile, refugees are protected and assisted by international law and are granted legal status by international treaties and legal documents. 3. Treatment. Refugees and their families are entitled to the rights and treatment granted by their residing country, which have acceded into the international treaties mentioned above, especially the "nonrefoulement principle."[37] Illegal immigrants who are not entitled to this right are usually repatriated to the country of residence or citizenship.[38]

Expert of international migration studies Joaquin Arango states that theoretical research on immigration must regard refugees as a fundamental research object.[39] The "theoretical research on immigration" includes the research on both legal and illegal immigrants. That is, Joaquin Arango suggests that the theoretical research on illegal immigrants must also regard refugees as one of its fundamental research objects. This conclusion was drawn by logical reasoning, which another scholar,

---

[37] The "nonrefoulement principle" means states shall not expel or return a refugee in any matter to the territories where his or her life or freedom would be threatened. This includes no refusal, no expulsion and no extradition at frontiers. Article 33(1) of the 1951 Convention reads: "No Contracting State shall expel or return ("refouler") a refugee in any manner whatsoever to the frontiers of territories where his [or her] life or freedom would be threatened on account of his [or her] race, religion, nationality, membership of a particular social group or political opinion." This is the most critical principle of refugee protection stipulated by the Convention. Liang Shuying, "Principles of Dealing with Illegal Entry Refugees," *Pacific Journal*, no. 6 (2008): 4.

[38] Xu (2005).

[39] [Spain] Joaquin Arango, "Explaining Migration: A Critical View," *International Social Science Journal (Chinese Edition)*, no. 3 (2001).

Tian Yuan, shares the same views. Tian Yuan includes illegal immigrants in the category of immigrants[40] and further argues that refugees shall not be excluded from immigrants and shall be considered on a case-by-case basis. In previous and current practice, only a small portion of refugees are recognized by the international community or receiving countries; thus, the vast majority cannot obtain refugee status and in turn cannot enjoy the status and rights of cross-border immigrants granted legal refugee status. Most refugees live in refugee camps, and many have gradually become foreign residents or illegal residents seeking self-sufficiency. The exclusion of these refugees from immigrants will affect the comprehensive review and study of immigrant issues.[41] At the same time, during my investigation in Hekou County, I came upon illegal immigrants and marriages between refugees and illegal immigrants in the refugee settlement area. Therefore, the refugee issues of Hekou County will also be discussed in this book.

1.3 Governance and Illegal Immigration Governance

The English word "governance" means control, guidance or manipulation, which overlaps with the meaning of government. The distinction between governance and government is that the former refers to the ways and means of governance, while the latter refers to the entities (organizations) in charge of governance. In addition, governing refers to the act of governance itself.[42] In Chinese, *zhili* means: 1. (verb) to rule or manage: to rule a country; 2. (verb) to revamp or dredge: to dredge the Huaihe River.[43]

The Commission on Global Governance states that "governance is the sum of many ways individuals and institutions, public and private, manage their common affairs. It is a continuing process through which conflicting or diverse interests may be accommodated and cooperative action taken. It includes formal institutions and regimes empowered to enforce compliance, as well as informal arrangements people and institutions either have agreed to or perceive to be in their interest."[44]

Chinese scholar Yu Keping claims that governance means the use of authority within a given scope to maintain order to satisfy the general public's needs. The purpose is to wield power to guide, control and regulate all kinds of activities of citizens in various institutional relations, in turn maximizing public interests.[45]

---

40 Tian (2010).

41 Tian (2010).

42 Qiao Weibin, (2002).

43 Beijing, (2008).

44 The Commission on Global Governance, (1995).

45 Yu (2000).

After taking stock of the definitions above, Wen Feng concludes that governance is the process of social management, undertaken by actors at all levels within a given scope, to establish a series of formal and informal rules to maintain normal social orders through democratic negotiation to maximize common interests. Governments do not have all legitimate rights to themselves; aside from the government, social organizations and individuals may also participate in economic and social regulatory activities.[46]

I believe that the explanation of governance is abstract and vague. From the practical needs of illegal immigration governance, we must transform the concept of governance into an easy-to-use program or route. American scholar James N. Rosenau proposes four questions regarding the elements of governance: Who? Why? How? and Results (effects)?[47] Considering the research object of this book, we can also divide the elements of governance into four parts: Who (subject)? Why (reasons)? How (methods)? and Effects (comprehensive assessment).

This book analyzes illegal immigration governance in Yunnan border areas with a high concentration of ethnic minorities in terms of the four aspects mentioned above. Furthermore, it discusses this problem by combining theories and practices at the state, international and local levels based on relevant laws and policies. Meanwhile, as *Feifa yimin* (illegal migration) includes the subject of behavior and the behavior itself, its governance shall also take both aspects into consideration. The governance of illegal migration is also the handling of illegal migrants. In other words, the object of illegal migration in this book includes the behavior of illegal migration (such as illegal entry and exit) and its related issues, as well as illegal migrants (the legal status of illegal migrants).

2 Categories and Characteristics of Illegal Immigration in Yunnan Border Areas with a High Concentration of Ethnic Minorities

2.1 Overview of the Yunnan Border Areas with a High Concentration of Ethnic Minorities

It should be noted that the Yunnan border areas with a high concentration of ethnic minorities refer to 25 counties and cities along the state border, covering an area of 92,000 km^2 (46.09% of the area of the eight border prefectures and cities). The eight border prefectures and cities and their 25 subordinate counties and cities are as follows:

---

46 Wen (2010).

47 [United States] James N. Rosenau, *Governance Without Government*, trans. Zhang Shengjun, Liu Xiaolin et al. (Nanchang: Jiangxi People's Publishing House, 2001), 35.

Wenshan Prefecture: Maguan, Funing, Malipo;
Honghe Prefecture: Jinping, Lüchun, Hekou;
Xishuangbanna Prefecture: Jinghong, Menghai, Mengla;
Pu'er City: Menglian, Lancang, Ximeng, Jiangcheng;
Lincang City: Zhenkang, Gengma, Cangyuan;
Baoshan City: Tengchong, Longling;
Dehong Prefecture: Luxi, Yingjiang, Longchuan, Ruili;
Nujiang Prefecture: Lushui, Fugong, Gongshan.

Among these 25 border counties and cities, with the exception of three counties (Funing, Hekou and Mengla) at lower altitudes, all other places are at an elevation of over 1,500 m (see the figure below). Among the 56 counties and cities under the jurisdiction of the eight border prefectures and cities, 46 (82.15%) are under the jurisdiction of autonomous prefectures and ethnic autonomous counties, while 22 (88%) of the 25 border counties and cities are under autonomous governance (the exceptions being Tengchong, Longling and Zhenkang).[48] It can be concluded that the 25 border counties and cities are typical border areas with a high concentration of ethnic minorities.

The 4,060 km borderlines in Yunnan Province (bordering Vietnam, Laos and Myanmar) can be divided into three parts per the terrain and neighboring countries: the 1,353 km China-Vietnam borderlines that connect one city, two prefectures and seven counties of China, and Vietnam's provinces of Lai Chau, Lao Cai and Ha Giang; the 710 km China-Laos borderlines that connect Mengla County (Xishuangbanna Prefecture) and Jiangcheng County (Pu'er City) and Lao's provinces of Louang Namtha, Oudomxai and Phongsali; and the 1,997 km China-Myanmar borderlines that connect China's 19 counties and cities in the prefectures of Nujiang, Baoshan, Dehong, Lincang, Pu'er and Xishuangbanna with Myanmar's Kachin State and Shan State.[49] (Fig. 3).

海拔分布	Altitude
西藏	Xizang
四川	Sichuan
贵州	Guizhou
广西	Guangxi
缅甸	Myanmar
老挝	Laos
越南	Vietnam
贡山县	Gongshan County
福贡县	Fugong County
泸水县	Lushui County

(continued)

[48] Lu (2011).

[49] Ibid., 12.

(continued)

海拔分布	Altitude
腾冲县	Tengchong County
盈江县	Yingjiang County
龙陵县	Longlin County
陇川县	Longchuan County
瑞丽市	Ruili City
潞西市	Luxi City
耿马县	Gengma County
镇康县	Zhenkang County
沧源县	Cangyuan County
西盟县	Ximeng County
孟连县	Menglian County
澜沧县	Lancang County
勐海县	Menghai County
景洪市	Jinghong County
江城县	Jiangcheng County
勐腊县	Mengla County
金平县	Jinping County
绿春县	Lüchun County
河口县	Hekou County
麻栗坡县	Malipo County
马关县	Maguan County
富宁县	Funing County

2.2 Categories and Characteristics of the Yunnan Border Areas with a High Concentration of Ethnic Minorities

1. Categories of Illegal Immigrants in the Yunnan Border Areas with a High Concentration of Ethnic Minorities

Illegal immigrants in the Yunnan border areas with a high concentration of ethnic minorities can be divided into different categories according to numerous criteria.

First, illegal immigrants as described in this book refer to foreigners (including stateless persons and residents of Hong Kong, Macao and Taiwan, likewise below) who have illegally entered and resided within the territory of China or foreigners who have overstayed in China for over three months (or were certain to reside for over three months) after their legal entry, excluding people staying for less than three months for family visits, cross-border farming and grazing, religious pilgrimage and

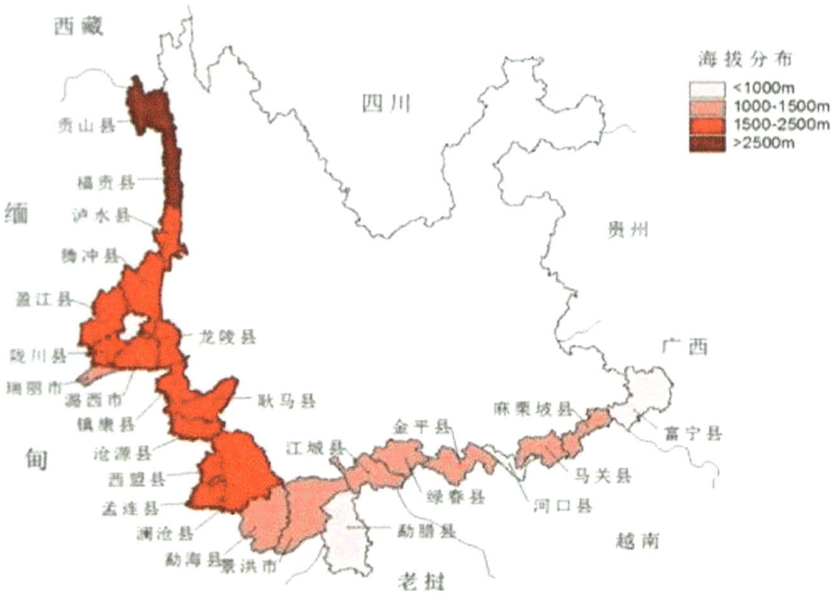

Fig. 3 Locations and Altitudes of the 25 Border Counties and Cities in Yunnan Province[50]

short-term business visits with no intention to reside there. Taking the above as the criteria, we can classify the illegal immigrants in these areas into two categories: foreigners who have illegally entered and resided within the territory of China for over three months (or were certain to reside for over three months) and foreigners who have overstayed in China for over three months (or were certain to reside for over three months) after their legal entry. The distinction between these two types of illegal immigrants is the way of their entry.

Second, based on their means and sources of substance, we can divide them into four types: illegal immigrants seeking business opportunities who make a living from small business (by running stalls or street-vending); illegal immigrant workers who make a living by working for others; illegal immigrants joining families and friends, then depending on financial aid from them; and illegal immigrants who seek life support by marrying Chinese citizens. However, of course, there are no absolute criteria, and one immigrant may belong to several types or change to another type.

Third, if we look into their means or sources of substance based on China's existing laws and regulations, we can further divide the illegal immigrants in these areas into other types: illegal immigrants of "legal subsistence" (illegal immigrants who mainly depend on the financial aid of families and friends) and illegal immigrants of "illegal subsistence" (illegal immigrants who seek life support by the illegal marriage with Chinese citizens. Illegal acts are different from law-breaking acts. According

[50] Source: http://image.baidu.com/i?ct=503316480&z=&tn=baiduimagedetail&word. Accessed October 31, 2011.

to China's current laws, authorities do not hold intermarried couples accountable, merely not recognizing or protecting the legal effect of their marriage); illegal immigrants of "law-breaking subsistence" (for example, illegal immigrants who run stalls against the rules. Administrative departments will hold them accountable for their law-breaking acts, but these acts do not constitute crimes), and illegal immigrants of "criminal subsistence" (for example, illegal immigrants who live on the proceeds of crime, such as drug and human trafficking). They will be punished for their criminal acts according to China's *Criminal Law*.)

Fourth, based on marriage status, we can divide them into intermarrying illegal immigrants and those who married people of other statuses (Chinese citizens or refugees). This is a particular distinction used during the investigation of illegal immigrants in Hekou County. More details can be found in later chapters.

2. Characteristics of Illegal Immigrants in Yunnan Border Areas with a High Concentration of Ethnic Minorities

Professor Lu Gang holds that the cross-border immigration and floating population in the areas along state boundaries in Yunnan Province possess distinctive local features in terms of five aspects[51]: 1. two-way flows; 2. a large floating population; 3. various complicated motivations; 4. numerous sources and complex structure; and 5. spindle-shaped geological distribution.[52]

There are two fundamental differences between the research subject of this book and the cross-border migration and floating population. First, cross-border migration and floating populations include both legal and illegal migration and floating populations, while the illegal migrants covered in this book only refer to illegal migration and floating populations. Second, cross-border migration and floating populations include both inward and outward migration and floating populations, while this book only studies inward migration and floating populations in China. Despite these fundamental differences, of the five features mentioned above, illegal immigrants in the Yunnan border areas with a high concentration of ethnic minorities exhibit the last four of them.

In addition, illegal immigrants in the Yunnan border areas with a high concentration of ethnic minorities exhibit other features as follows:

1. Characteristics of Illegal Immigrants' Marriage

As previously mentioned, illegal immigrants must make a living after entering the territory of China. According to their means or sources of substance, they can be

---

51 Lu Gang and Li Shou, (2007): 73.

52 More active cross-border immigration and a larger floating population in the middle-and-lower part of China-Myanmar borderlines, especially category-1 and category-2 ports of Ruili and Wanding (Dehong Prefecture), Jinghong and Daluo (Xishuangbanna Prefecture), and Nansan (Zhenkang County, Lincang City). In contrast, other areas, with the exceptions of Hekou Port (Honghe Prefecture) in the middle of the China-Vietnam border, Mohan Port (eastern part of Xishuangbanna Prefecture) along the China-Laos border, and Pianma Port (Lushui County, Nujiang Prefecture) at the upper part of the China-Myanmar border, see less immigration and floating population. See Lu and Li (2007), p. 73.

divided into illegal immigrants seeking business opportunities, illegal immigrant workers, illegal immigrants joining families and friends, and illegal immigrants seeking marriage. In addition, based on the definition of illegal immigrants described in this book, illegal immigrants are those who intend to stay on a long-term basis and have resided within the territory of China for over three months or were certain to reside there for over three months. In other words, illegal immigrants with the intention of long-term residence must find a sustained and stable livelihood. *Sanfei* typically resorts to temporary stalls and street vending, odd jobs and seasonal jobs, the assistance of families and friends, or even some criminal acts. On the other hand, for illegal immigrants, their small businesses and employment are unlawful because of their status; thus, any employment they take is unlawful.

For illegal immigrants in the Yunnan border areas with a high concentration of ethnic minorities, the chance to legalize their status is slim; thus, they may choose to immigrate to China by marrying Chinese citizens. In this manner, they are provided with housing, farming land and basic life support. In particular, their children can hopefully become Chinese citizens and thus have better access to education and employment. Therefore, the vast majority of illegal immigrants in the Yunnan border areas with a high concentration of ethnic minorities are those seeking marriage. This is the prominent feature of illegal immigrants in these areas.

2. Geographical Characteristics of Illegal Immigrants

Geographical means the way in which the physical features of a place are arranged. The geographical characteristics of illegal immigrants in the Yunnan border areas with a high concentration of ethnic minorities are as follows:

First, illegal immigrants in those areas mainly migrate from countries that share borders with Yunnan, i.e., Vietnam, Laos and Myanmar. In addition, some illegal immigrants originate from other countries with geographical proximity to Yunnan, such as Thailand. At the ports of Tengchong, Ruili, Wanding, Jinghong and others along the China-Myanmar border, there are people of other nationalities with dark skin, high-bridged noses, sunken eyes and curled hair, who locals refer to as "Heigala" (black foreigners). These are "Indians and Pakistanis of Myanmar citizenship," originally from the region sharing borders with India, Bangladesh (formerly East Pakistan) and the northwestern part of Myanmar.[53] During the investigation in the Yunnan border areas with a high concentration of ethnic minorities, no illegal immigrants from countries or regions located far from Yunnan, such as Europe, the United States, Africa, Japan or South Korea, were found. Apart from economic, cultural and other reasons, geographical proximity is an essential factor that must not be neglected.

Second, the countries of origin of the illegal immigrants in these areas are relevant to their geographical proximity to Yunnan. For example, in Hekou County, which is close to Vietnam, most of the illegal immigrants in the county originate from Vietnam. Similarly, most of the illegal immigrants in Cangyuan County, which shares a border with Myanmar, come from Myanmar.

---

[53] Lu and Li (2007).

3. Ethnic Characteristics of Illegal Immigrants

The ethnic characteristics of the illegal immigrants in the Yunnan border areas with a high concentration of ethnic minorities are as follows:

First, the countries that share borders with these areas (the main countries of origin of illegal immigrants in these areas) consist of multiple ethnic groups closely related to nearly 20 ethnic groups in the Yunnan border areas, including Han. According to previous studies, the main ethnic groups in neighboring countries, such as Thai (Thailand), Lao Loum (Laos), Kinh (or Viet), Nung, Thai and other ethnic groups (Vietnam), Shan (northern Myanmar), Ahom (northeastern India), and Thai (Cambodia and Bangladesh), share the same origin (i.e., Guyue people) as the ethnic groups that speak Zhuang-Dai languages, such as Dai, Zhuang and Buyi, along the borders in Yunnan. Some of these people still share the same languages and religious beliefs, as well as similar customs. In many cases, they are, in fact, the same ethnic groups living in different countries: Khmer (Cambodia's main ethnic group), Wa, Bulang and De'Ang (three ethnic groups which speak Mon-Khmer languages, one of the South Asian language groups, in Yunnan), Kawa and Palaung (Myanmar), Mon and Khmer (Thailand) people are also closely related ethnic groups of the same origin. Other such groups include the Miao, Yao, Hani, Lahu and Yi peoples, who all originated in China and later relocated to Vietnam, Laos, Myanmar, Thailand, and other neighboring countries, as well as Jingpo-Kachin in western Yunnan Province, northern Myanmar's Kachin State and northeastern India.[54]

Second, the ethnic self-identification of illegal immigrants in these areas and people of the same ethnic groups. Here, ethnic self-identification refers to that of ethnic groups in China's border areas. It is the identification or confirmation of members of ethnic groups for the identity of themselves and the groups to which they belong and a process of psychological acculturation of ethnic groups and their members. For illegal immigrants joining families and friends and those seeking marriage, their ethnic self-identification, such as "speaking the same languages and sharing similar lifestyles" and "belonging to the same ethnic group makes it easier to have life together," reveals typical characteristics of these regions.

4. Historical Characteristics of Illegal Immigrants

Illegal immigrants of any country are influenced by the features of a specific era, and illegal immigrants in the Yunnan border areas with a high concentration of ethnic minorities are no exception. Illegal immigration in these areas can be divided into two phases, beginning from the founding of the People's Republic of China in 1949.

First, one-way outflow occurred between the 1950s and the late 1970s. The impact and damage of China's nationwide ultraleft campaigns, such as the People's Commune, the Great Leap Forward, and the Cultural Revolution, on the Yunnan border areas, along with the infiltration and instigation of overseas hostile forces and religious groups, resulted in an outflow of over 10,000 residents in border counties of Nujiang Prefecture.[55] Taking the ethnic group of Jingpo in Dehong Prefecture as an

---

[54] Lu (2011), 28.

[55] Lu and Li (2007).

example, the first population census showed a population of 101,900. However, the second census revealed an obvious negative growth of 43.28% (57,800 residents).[56] It was when the Great Leap Forward was launched between these two censuses. Under the influence of ultraleftist guidelines, these areas underwent economic failure due to adventurous policies seeking instant success and people's communes being "large in size and collective in nature." Furthermore, ultraleftist policies regarding ethnic and religious issues identified the cultural traditions of ethnic groups as being of the "four olds" or "feudal superstitious activities" and thus banned them. Some Jingpo people recalled that the government prohibition of the manau dance was the direct cause of their "joining relatives" abroad. Unable to maintain their own cultural traditions, many Jingpo families relocated to Myanmar, thereby leading to a sharp decline in their population in China.[57] According to the definition mentioned above, these people in the border areas who migrated abroad are considered illegal migrants.

Second, there has been a two-way movement of illegal migrants since China's reform and opening-up. China's rapid economic and social development, political stability and improved livelihood in border areas have become strong pull factors for the residents of countries bordering Yunnan, especially among their residents living along the borderlines. It is difficult for these people to move to China by legal means under the current laws and regulations; thus, they often choose to immigrate by joining families and friends and seeking marriage, business and job opportunities. Most illegal immigrants live in the Yunnan border areas with a high concentration of ethnic minorities, but there are signs of them moving to the interior part of Yunnan and other provinces in China's mainland. At the same time, border residents in these areas also relocate to neighboring countries close to Yunnan. Many people in other places of Yunnan Province and interior China move abroad from these areas and become illegal immigrants residing in other countries. According to the government statistics of Myanmar's Special Region 4, there are currently 4,320 Chinese citizens from 27 provinces, districts and cities residing in Mongla, opposite China's Daluo port. Their typical duration of residence ranges from one year up to 10 years.[58]

---

[56] The Institute of Population of the Chinese Academy of Social Sciences, *The 1985 China Population Statistics Yearbook* (Beijing: China Social Sciences Press, 1986). Cited from Chen Xiaojing, "The Study on Ethnic Self-Identification in the Pattern of Pluralistic Unity of the Chinese Nation: Theoretical Exploration and Empirical Analysis of the Needs of Bai People in Han Communities" (MA diss., Yunnan University), 12.

[57] Chen Xiaojing, "The Study on Ethnic Self-Identification in the Pattern of Pluralistic Unity of the Chinese Nation: Theoretical Exploration and Empirical Analysis of the Needs of Bai People in Han Communities" (MA diss., Yunnan University), 12.

[58] Lu and Li (2007).

It is worth noting that the criteria for illegal immigrants who immigrate to neighboring countries next to Yunnan are not China's law and regulations but those of the destination countries. In fact, there are no specific criteria for illegal immigrants under China's current laws and regulations, and the people who come to China illegally are known as *sanfei* in practice. Therefore, we must further explore how to better deal with the two-way movement of illegal immigrants based on the characteristics of the new era.

3 Current Situation of Illegal Immigration in Hekou County

Now that the core concepts of the Yunnan border areas with a high concentration of ethnic minorities, illegal immigrants and governance have been defined, this section analyzes the current situation of illegal immigrants in these areas. Among the 25 border counties and cities in Yunnan, Hekou Yao Autonomous County of Honghe Hani and Yi Autonomous Prefecture were chosen as the main investigation sites. Hekou County, a place exhibiting major illegal immigration problems, has a higher proportion of illegal Vietnamese immigrants to China. During the on-site investigation, it was found that substantive departments were familiar with *sanfei*, illegal marriage and refugees, but not as much with illegal immigration, and even less so with *sanfei* who had resided in China for over three months, i.e., illegal immigrants. Therefore, the analysis of the current situation and relevant issues of illegal immigrants in Hekou County is based on the investigation of regular *sanfei*, the marriage of illegal immigrants (intermarrying illegal immigrants and those who married people of other status), and refugees. Of course, it should be noted that there are significant differences between refugees and illegal immigrants. However, as mentioned above, refugees are closely associated with *sanfei* and intermarried people, and their situations will be discussed briefly in the book.

3.1 Locations and Methods of Investigation

Connected by mountains and rivers with the provinces of Lao Cai and Lai Chau in Vietnam, the counties of Hekou, Jinping and Lüchun at Honghe Prefecture's border areas cover newly established boundaries of 425.953 km (including water boundaries of 145.726 km and land boundaries of 280.227 km), which account for approximately 10.5% of the land boundaries of Yunnan Province and 156 entry and exit routes and paths. It does not take much effort to pass national borders illegally due to the mountain terrain and lack of natural barriers in these areas.

According to the public security and frontier defense authority of Honghe Prefecture, as of July 2011, there were 727 *sanfei* of other nationalities (all Vietnam citizens,

52 males and 675 females) under their jurisdiction, including 31 illegal immigrant workers, 45 overstayers and 651 marriage immigrants.[59] The jurisdiction of the public security and frontier defense authority of Honghe Prefecture covers the entire prefecture, or at least the border counties of Hekou, Jinping and Lüchun. However, the data of these *sanfei* may not be accurate.[60]

Hekou Yao Autonomous County, a county in the southeastern part of Yunnan Province that faces the Vietnamese City of Lao Cai across the river, is located 469 km from Kunming, 296 km from Vietnam's capital city Hanoi, and 416 km from the largest port in northern Vietnam, the port of Haiphong. It converges with the Yunnan-Vietnam Railway, Kunming-Hekou Highway and Honghe Channel, all of which are connected to Vietnam, making it a convenient path from Yunnan Province and southwestern China to Southeast Asia and the South Pacific. There are two towns and four townships (including one ethnic township): Hekou Town, Nanxi Town, Laofanzhai Township, Qiaotou Miao and Zhuang Township, Yaoshan Township and Lianhuatan Township, and four farms: Hekou Farm, Basa Farm, Nanxi Farm and Mahuangbao Farm. Among the 104,609 residents in Hekou County home to 24 ethnic groups, including Yao, Miao, Dai and Hani, 40,195 (38.42%) are of Han ethnicity, while 64,414 (61.58%) belong to ethnic groups.[61] Southern Hekou County shares a boundary of 193 km in length (including 120 km of land boundaries and 73 km of water boundaries) with Vietnam's Lao Cai city, Muong Khuong County and Bat Xat County in Lao Cai Province, which belong to the first part of the China-Vietnam borders in the territory of Yunnan. In addition, there are four ports that connect Hekou County with Vietnam, namely, Hekou Port (a national port), Basa Port, Laoka Port, and Xindian Port, along with 114 border-crossing routes and paths (Fig. 4).

---

[59] Li Piyin, "Brief Discussion on the Impact of Sanfei on Local Public Security and Countermeasures," http://www.legaldaily.com.cn/police_and_frontier-defense/content/2011-07/26/content_2810179.htm?node=23297. Accessed August 30, 2011.

[60] The 2008 statistics of *sanfei* population in Maguan County alone was 650. Maguan County is located in Wenshan Zhuang and Miao Autonomous Prefecture, next to Hekou County to the southwest, and bordering Vietnam to the south. With 138 km boundary lines in its area, it has four towns and 11 villagers' committees, and shares the same mountains and rivers with 65 villages in the counties of Muong Khuong, Bac Ha, Xin Man, and Hoang Su Phi of Vietnam. As of October 2008, there were 650 *sanfei* (32 males and 618 females) in the following areas of Maguan County: Dulong (155), Jinchang (142), Xiaobazi (154), Jiahanjing (62), Renhe (34), Muchang (56), Gulinjing (15), Dalishu (6), Shanche (2), and Miechang (24). Among these, 282 of them overstayed for 1–3 years and gave birth to 127 children; 178 overstayed for 3–10 years and gave birth to 183 children, and 190 overstayed for over 10 years and gave birth to 219 children. See "Public Security in the Border Areas of Maguan County," http://www.yn.xinhuanet.com/live/2008-10/06/content_14564855.htm. Accessed October 11, 2011.

[61] Statistics Bureau of Hekou County, "Major Figures of the Sixth National Population Census," the People's Government of Hekou County's website: http://xxgk.hk.hh.gov.cn/readinfo.aspx?InfoId=7a88100bb55346758d12b90abe45a8ad. Accessed June 30, 2011.

Fig. 4 Map of Hekou Yao Autonomous County[62]

河口瑶族自治县	Hekou Yao Autonomous County
本县位于红河州东南部,面积1313平方公里,辖2镇、3乡、1民族乡,25个行政村。人口7万多人,有汉、瑶、苗、壮、彝、傣、布朗等民族。 本县地处云贵高原南部,最高点大尖山,海拔2354米,最低点为元江与南溪河汇合处,海拔76米。属热带山地季风雨林湿热型气候,立体气候明显,气温较高,年平均气温22.6°C本县有"热带水果"之乡的美誉,盛产香蕉、菠萝。县城已被批准为国家级口岸和开放城镇	The county is located in the southeastern part of Honghe Prefecture, covers an area of 1,313 km^2, and includes two towns, three townships, one ethnic township and 25 administrative villages. It has a population of over 70,000, consisting of Han, Yao, Miao, Zhuang, Yi, Dai, Bulang and other ethnic groups Situated at the southern part of the Yunnan-Guizhou Plateau, it has the highest elevation of 2,354 m at Dajian Mountain, and the lowest elevation of 76 m at the junction of the Yuan River and Nanxi River. With a typical hot and humid climate in tropical montane monsoon rainforests, it features distinctive weather changes, and an average high temperature of 22.6°C Renowned as the "home of tropical fruits," due to its production of bananas, pineapples and other fruits, it has been approved as a national-level port and open town
清水河	Qingshuihe

(continued)

[62] Source of the map of Hekou County: http://www.lvyou114.com/map/4/4537.html. Accessed May 10, 2012.

(continued)

河口瑶族自治县	Hekou Yao Autonomous County
个旧市	Gejiu City
地古白	Digubai
嘎马	Gama
莲花滩	Lianhuatan
干龙井	Ganlongjing
下母鸡坡	Xiamujipo
勐桥	Mengqiao
老新街	Laoxinjie
莲花滩	Lianhuatan
中岭岗	Zhonglinggang
石板寨	Shiban Village
八角	Bajiao
新龙	Xinlong
牛塘	Niutang
向阳寨	Xiangyang Village
达沟河	Dagouhe
水槽	Shuicao
梁子	Liangzi
瑶山	Yaoshan
金竹梁	Jinzhuliang
马古坡	Magupo
太阳寨	Taiyang Village
老范寨	Laofan Village
贵良	Guiliang
半坡	Banpo
茶坪	Chaping
五队	Wudui
芭蕉寨	Bajiao Village
水碓湾	Shuiduiwan
坝洒农场	Basa Farm
坝洒	Basa
南溪农场	Nanxi Farm
蚂蝗堡农场	Mahuangbao Farm
河口 (河口镇)	Hekou (Hekou Town)
班菲	Banfei
老街	Lao Cai
保胜	Bao Thang

(continued)

(continued)

河口瑶族自治县	Hekou Yao Autonomous County
越南	Vietnam
爱卓	Aizhuo
地西北	Dixibei
普玛	Puma
马鞍底	Ma'andi
马拐塘	Maguaitang
金平苗族瑶族傣族自治县	Jinping Miao, Yao and Dai Autonomous County
滴水层	Dishuiceng
屏边苗族自治县	Pingbian Miao Autonomous County
屏边 (玉屏镇)	Pingbian (Yuping Town)
白河	Baihe
腊哈	Laha
大尖山	Dajian Mountain
斑鸠河	Banjiuhe
古林箐	Gulinjing
团结	Tuanjie
竹林寨	Zhulin Village
薄竹箐	Baozhujing
大南溪	Dananxi
棍惹	Gunre
马若河	Mayanhe
龙堡	Longbao
南溪镇	Nanxi Town
篾厂	Miechang
老汪山	Laowangshan
桥头	Qiaotou
东瓜岭	Donggualing
中寨	Zhong Village
下湾子	Xiawanzi
老街子	Laojiezi
木厂镇	Muchang Town
孟康	Muong Khuong
斋河	Zhaihe
邮政编码:661,300	Zip Code: 661,300
元江	Yuan River
南溪河	Nanxi River

(continued)

(continued)

河口瑶族自治县	Hekou Yao Autonomous County
新桥河	Xinqiao River
马关县	Maguan County
清水	Qingshui

During the research phase for this book, I paid multiple visits to Hekou County to investigate the problem of illegal immigration through means such as local yearbooks and archives, interviews with government officials, symposiums with relevant departments, questionnaires, interviews with refugee and illegal immigrant families, and on-site investigation at border-crossing routes and trafficking ports and ultimately learned much about the local situation.

How many illegal immigrants are there in Hekou County? Based on my on-site investigation, I observed that the data produced by the regulatory departments varied due to different criteria and manners of calculation. They made no distinction between refugees and *sanfei* who had entered China, resided and worked here illegally for less than three months with no intention of long-term residence and illegal immigrants. Moreover, they confused illegal marriages with interracial marriages; some interracial couples legally registered their marriages according to China's laws and regulations. In addition, the numbers are constantly changing. Therefore, failing to update data in a timely manner is another cause of inaccurate statistical calculations and differences among departments.

After learning of the situation described above, I adopted the following investigation system:

First, "top-down and bottom-up" two-way inquiry from regulatory departments. I sent a letter that gave a detailed explanation of the inquiry enclosed with a questionnaire to Hekou County's regulatory departments in charge of illegal immigration (see Annex I)[63]; I held discussions with front-line officers from relevant departments and produced written documents based on the answers to the questionnaire; finally, I organized and held symposiums and discussions, while the relevant departments undertook studies on key issues.

Second, inquiry from illegal immigrants was conducted through observation, family visits and questionnaires (see Annex II). There are three categories of immigrants I interviewed: 1. sanfei who have entered China, resided and worked here illegally for less than three months with no intention of long-term residence; 2. foreigners who have entered China illegally, or have entered China legally but overstayed for over three months or were certain to stay for over three months and did not marry Chinese citizens or refugees; 3. foreigners who have entered China illegally, or have entered China legally but overstayed for over three months or were certain to stay for over three months and married Chinese citizens or refugees. The first category

[63] These departments include the Bureau of Civil Affairs (Office of Refugee Affairs), Public Security and Frontier Defense Checkpoint, Public Security Bureau (Exit & Entry Administration Department), Public Security and Frontier Defense Department and National Security Bureau of Hekou County. I extend my deep gratitude to the leaders and front-line officers of these departments.

is referred to as "regular sanfei", and the second and third categories are referred to as "irregular sanfei", i.e., illegal immigrants. The reason for taking "marrying Chinese citizens or refugees" as a criterion is for the convenience of statistical calculations and the fact that there are different measures to deal with those who do and those who do not. The second category is called "intermarrying illegal immigrants (it does not exclude the possibility of them marrying other illegal immigrants)," and the third category is called "illegal immigrants who married people of other status." This chapter introduces the number of these three categories of illegal immigrants and their distribution. Their immigration motivation, impact on local society and governance will be discussed in later chapters.

It is worth noting that Professor Lu Gang divides foreigners staying in China into three types from the perspective of cross-border immigration in the Yunnan border areas with a high concentration of ethnic minorities. First, business owners and workers who run stalls, operate shops, or work for others at ports and medium- and small-sized towns along the borders. Local governments often group them together for better management, leading to the creation of specific communities, such as the "China-Vietnam Street" in Hekou County. Second, Indochinese refugees include refugees from Vietnam, Laos and Myanmar. Third, sanfei refers to foreigners under the status of illegal entry, illegal employment and illegal residence. Although different from the division I make in this book, his approach is highly inspiring for my studies.[64]

3.2 *Current Situation of Illegal Immigrants*

(1) **Regular Sanfei**

Regular *sanfei* refers to people who have stayed in China for less than three months for family visits, cross-border farming and grazing, religious pilgrimage, market fairs, short-term business visits, and other purposes with no intention to stay permanently. They either entered China illegally or stayed overtime after their legal entry. Most of them came from Vietnam, some from Myanmar or Laos, but no residents of Hong Kong, Macao or Taiwan were found in Hekou County. They either stayed for a few hours or several days, weeks or months (but less than three months). They did not have the intention or purpose of long-term residence, and their actual length of stay was less than three months (one-time continuous visit).

The border crossings in Hekou County are very busy, with nearly 10,000 people crossing the borders every day at peak times. People passing these crossings need to bring their documents, go through the required processes, and pay a fee. Regular

---

[64] For classification and analysis, see Lu and Li (2007), pp. 67–70. As for the first category, the authors did not indicate if "business owners and workers" have legal status. They can be seen as legal from logical reasoning. As to the second category, "Indochinese refugees," this book includes refugees living in Hekou County as part of the research subject. Finally, the third category, "*sanfei*" refers to the regular *sanfei* described in this book. However, they do not introduce the concept of illegal immigrants, nor make further division based on their marriage status.

sanfei usually choose unauthorized crossing points on the border to gain illegal entry into the country, and those who have overstayed after their legal entry also choose to leave at these crossing points. The fundamental cause of illegal entry and exit is the difficulties in controlling these points of crossing. For the same reason, it is difficult to have access to the number of regular *sanfei* and their information. From January to August 2011, the Public Security and Frontier Defense Department of Hekou County found and handled a total of 516 regular *sanfei*. Most of them had crossed the borders illegally for odd jobs and small businesses (street vending), such as working on a banana plantation, peddling handicrafts or street food. The department believed that these 516 people represented a small portion of the regular *sanfei* in the area.

I selected two locations for on-site observation to investigate the actual situation of illegal entry and exit through these unauthorized crossing points.

One is Bazihe ferry in Nanxi Town. The Bazihe River, a natural border between China and Vietnam, was named after its shape, similar to the Chinese character "*ba*" (eight). It was lunchtime when we arrived. Two Vietnamese young men walked across the river at leisure and went for lunch at a restaurant on the Chinese side. A few minutes later, another two Vietnamese youths crossed the river freely and walked backed to Vietnam from the Chinese side. Approximately 30 min later, the two men, who had finished their lunch, returned to Vietnam across the river. I took a quick photo of them, and they paid no mind to me. In a time span of approximately 30 min, six people crossed the border illegally, with no one even stopping to question them. I spoke with a 35-year-old Chinese man originally from Sichuan. He laughed at my questions and said he always went over there (Vietnam), but nobody cared for because he rented some land to grow pineapples on the opposite side (Vietnam). He pointed at seven or eight motorcycles opposite and said they were used to carry passengers. If you are not a frequent passenger, you would be charged a small amount of money afterward, such as 10 or 20 yuan, goods would be charged according to the weight. There are people on the lookout on the China side who do not work for the government, and he does not know who they are. When goods are delivered from the other side, they are also charged tariffs for on the China side. The military forces station around the ferry sometimes came to patrol, but they do not do anything about the people crossing the border. This is an unauthorized crossing point not only for people but also for trafficked goods.

Another site is a ferry in Hekou County. I was standing on the side of a highway, next to a publicity board that reads "Illegal Border Crossing Is Strictly Prohibited." Opposite the publicity board is Vietnam's Lao Cai Province, connected with Hekou Port by a bridge. Four or five diesel-powered Vietnamese tin boats that can drive at a fast speed berthed at a ferry under the bridge to the left. Then, 15 or 16 passengers were transferred by three boats within 15 min. According to a local friend, it would cost approximately 30 yuan for a round trip, and no document was required. This was a typical entry and exit behavior.

Based on my on-site observation, I learned about the reasons for the inaccurate calculations of regular *sanfei* and the "difficulty in border control," which will be discussed later.

2. **Intermarrying Illegal Immigrants**

It was difficult to count the number of illegal immigrants in this category, and the estimates provided by the government varied. When marrying among themselves, illegal immigrants usually choose not to register their marriages officially and would only mark the occasion with a banquet, according to their own customs. In addition, their scattered and highly mobile residence makes it difficult to count them. With the help of a friend, I found some places populated by a larger proportion of these illegal immigrants.

At Mahuangbao Farm in Nanxi Town of Hekou County, close to the China-Vietnam border on the China side, there are a group of Vietnamese illegal immigrants, referred to by locals as "stateless persons," whose number ranges between 20–30 (7–8 households) and 300–350 (50–60 households).[65] These people began to move to China following the end of the China-Vietnam War in the 1980s and have lived close to the border on China's side. The place where they live had been subject to border dispute, but since the dispute was resolved, it has been China's territory. They did not enter China because of the war and thus were not regarded as refugees but only as "stateless persons,", i.e., illegal immigrants by the Chinese government. The local government tried to repatriate them multiple times but failed for three reasons. First, two-way repatriation requires verification of illegal immigrants' identity by the Vietnamese authorities and their agreement in receiving repatriated immigrants. However, these people had lived in China for a long time, and the Vietnamese authorities were not able to verify their identities. Furthermore, Vietnam's counter-repatriation measures stipulate that Vietnamese citizens who moved to China after 1975 shall not be recognized as Vietnamese, and the Vietnamese government organized interception against them.[66] Their Vietnamese citizenship had been revoked for most of them, and the Vietnamese government does not accept their repatriation. Second, one-way repatriation is restricted for its violation against relevant international treaties and the bilateral treaty of handling border issues between China and Vietnam.[67] Third, illegal immigrants who had been sent back by two-way or one-way repatriation often returned to their places of residence in China through unauthorized crossing points because their citizenship was revoked, they missed their families and friends living in China, or other reasons.

I chose a place called Laoaochang near Mahuangbao Farm in Nanxi Town, Hekou County, as the site of illegal immigration investigation. My original plan was to bring them together and distribute questionnaires (see Annex II), but my friend believed this was inappropriate, so I chose to make inquiries by family visit. Most of these illegal immigrants married Chinese citizens (border residents) or refugees; thus, there were

---

[65] According to incomplete statistics of relevant departments, there were 343 "stateless persons" at most. However, because of their high mobility and changes in marriage, this book only uses a relatively reliable number.

[66] Zhou (2008), p. 299.

[67] One-way repatriation refers to the repatriation by relevant departments to send illegal immigrants back to their country by unauthorized crossing points. It a practical method, yet lacks a legal basis and legal guarantee. –Author's note.

only approximately 30–50 intermarrying illegal immigrants (among 10 households) there. We visited three families, and their neighbors who saw their acquaintances among the visitors also joined us for "fun" or "a quick visit." We chose seven people to represent seven families for the interview, and one more person we came across on the way to the village (intermarrying illegal immigrants). Therefore, we interviewed eight families in total, which accounted for approximately 80% of illegal immigrant families in Laoaochang. In seven of the families, both husband and wife are illegal immigrants, and in one family, the woman is raising two children, with her husband having "gone somewhere else."

We held face-to-face interviews with them and asked them the questions in Questionnaire 2, along with some others. Below is what I learned from the interviews.

All eight families came from Vietnam, both husbands and wives in seven of the families came from Vietnamese ethnic groups, and the husband of one family came from the Kinh group (Vietnam's majority group). They could not remember exactly in which year they came to China. Two families said they came here in the 1980s, another two said in the 1990s, and the remaining four said it had been many years and they could not remember. Only one family said they came to China with border resident certificates to join families and friends in China and did not go back to Vietnam. The remaining seven families did not understand the meaning of "smuggling" and said they came (via unauthorized crossing points) by foot, boat or motorcycle. For the reasons to come to China, eight families said, "the life here (in China) is better."[68] Moreover, they all acknowledged that they "speak the same languages and share similar lifestyles" with the locals, and "they belong to the same ethnic group, which makes it easier to have life together," "the transportation is convenient, and does not cost (much) money," and "it is easy to pass the borders, there is nothing to worry about even if we get caught."[69] They previously had only spoken Vietnamese and the languages of their ethnic groups. After they came to China, it was easy to communicate with locals with the languages of their own ethnic groups, and they were able to speak and understand Chinese. In addition, they did not receive much education, three families said they did not go to school (six people), four families said they went to school for several years (primary school: eight people), the wife of one family said her husband went to junior high school, while she did not go to school (junior high school: one person, never went to school: one person). These eight families have low educational levels; 15 people had gone to primary school or had not gone to school at all, and only one person had gone to junior high school.

They live in bunkhouses they built themselves or at relatives' homes and make a living by working for others, doing small businesses, or farming on leased land.

---

[68] There is a saying in Vietnam, "Paradise is too far away, and China is too close (or China is very close)." This can be understood in two aspects: China has become a threat to Vietnam and impeded the Vietnamese from going to paradise; or China is a paradise.

[69] Under further inquiries, they explained that "it is easy to pass the borders, there is nothing to worry about even if we get caught" meant it was easy to cross the borders via unauthorized crossing points. When one of them is blocked, they can choose other ones. Even if they are caught, they will either pay fines or be admonished (lectured) if they did not have any money.

They could not obtain IDs or household registration booklets at relevant departments[70] or marriage certificates for marriage among themselves (marriage among illegal immigrants). Therefore, their children could not obtain household registration due to the lack of these three certificates. They wishe to reside in China, obtain Chinese citizenship and become Chinese citizens, and they feel sad and embarrassed for their status of not belonging to any group, i.e., Chinese citizens, Vietnamese citizens or refugees. During the interviews, they stressed numerous times that they could not go back to Vietnam, and they hoped they could obtain IDs, household registration booklets and a piece of land from relevant departments. They knew that they were either already married (marriage among illegal immigrants) or too old, so they could not marry Chinese citizens to change their status. Moreover, they were more concerned about the education and employment of their children.

When asked about related Chinese laws and regulations, they either kept silent or said they did not know about them or stated it was a matter of the government (the Chinese government).

3. **Illegal Immigrants Who Married People of Other Status**

The number of illegal immigrants who married people of other status in Hekou County has been relatively stable. According to the statistics provided by relevant departments, as of June 2011, there were 568 illegal immigrants (two males and 566 females) in Hekou County. Most of them were Vietnamese, and the rest came from Myanmar and Laos. They mainly lived in the villages along the Honghe River and the Nanxi River and border villages such as Qiaotou Township. A total of 19–30 illegal immigrants married refugees (3–5% of illegal marriages), and at least 95% of the illegal marriages were between illegal immigrants and Chinese citizens (border residents).[71]

The inquiries regarding this type of illegal immigrant were made cooperatively: I visited Hekou County and the refugee settlement area in Chahe, while my two graduate students visited border villages under the company of local friends. The inquiry results were taken down during family visits. I visited two couples between illegal immigrants and Chinese citizens (border residents) in Hekou County and two couples between illegal immigrants and refugees in the refugee settlement area in Chahe. In addition, one team visited Laoaochang and Longbao in Nanxi Town, collected 21 valid questionnaires regarding marriage between illegal immigrants and Chinese citizens (border residents), while another team visited Laojiezi

[70] According to relevant departments, they issued IDs and household registration booklets for this type of illegal immigrants who had lived in China for a long time, and treated them as refugees in practice. However, this kind of practice cannot become a written rule; otherwise, it would encourage the influx of more illegal immigrants.

[71] The data were drawn from logical reasoning: according to the statistics of the Civil Affairs Bureau of Hekou County, as of June 2011, there were 19 married couples between refugees under the jurisdiction of the county and Vietnamese illegal immigrants. There were 2,659 refugees under the jurisdiction of the county and 3,929 refugees under the jurisdiction of farms, 1.47 times the former. Therefore, it can be assumed that there were approximately 30 refugees under the jurisdiction of these farms who married Vietnamese illegal immigrants (1.47 times 19).

Village and Xiawanzi Village in Qiaotou Township, and collected 20 valid questionnaires. In the end, we collected a total of 43 valid questionnaires regarding marriage between illegal immigrants and Chinese citizens (border residents)[72] and two questionnaires regarding marriage between illegal immigrants and refugees. We obtained the following information by analyzing the questionnaires and the notes taken during the interviews.

1. Marriage between Illegal Immigrants and Refugees

I paid a visit to a village in the refugee settlement area in Chahe of Hekou County and met a Vietnamese woman named Afang who had come to China illegally from Vietnam and had the following conversation with her:

Me: Would you like to tell me something about you?

Afang: Yes, I have been approached by other people before.

Me: When did you come here and why?

Afang: I have been here for five or six years. I used to come here for work (to harvest sugar cane). Later, I met my husband through a friend and moved here after we got married.

Me: Who else do you have in your family? Did they agree with your decision to marry someone in China? Do you still have contact with them?

Afang: My parents, two sisters, and one brother. They did not say anything about me moving here after marriage. They also visited me and said they thought my life here was better. I often contact them, I visit them regularly and they come here to see me, too.

Me: Do you have an ID card? Is it easy for you to cross the borders?

Afang: It is easy to go there by boat. My family often came to pick me up.

Me: Do you belong to a ethnic group?

Afang: Yes, my husband and I are Yao people.

Me: How is your life here? Do you have any thoughts or requests?

Afang: It is hard to say. I have been here for many years. This is my life. I do not have any thoughts. It would be better if I could get an ID card and household registration. My child cannot get household registration either. It is fine for us, but I do not know what my child will do without it.

...

I learned that her husband is a Vietnamese refugee and that they have a three- or four-year-old child. The entire family has lived in the village for five or six years. Afang and her husband had met when she came to work in Hekou, and they held a wedding ceremony in the village. They did not register their marriage because of their status, and their child could not obtain household registration without the three certificates (marriage certificate, birth certificate and birth permit). The regulatory department in charge of refugee affairs asked her to go through formalities in Vietnam (to obtain an identification document, single status certificate, and other documents),

[72] There are two requirements for a "valid questionnaire": the interviewee's identity must be confirmed; and illegal immigrants themselves must be present. It is necessary to note that the questionnaire was just an interview outline, while the content of the interview was altered as needed.

but she did not want to, out of fear that the Vietnamese government had revoked her citizenship and that it may cost many money to complete these tasks. However, she seemed quite happy about her current life and was holding her child with a smiling face when I took a photo of them. Her husband was a second-generation refugee (child of first-generation refugees) and had gone away from home for work.

The second couple seems younger, and the husband is also a second-generation refugee. They had first met each other at a market fair in China, and later they held a wedding ceremony (a wedding banquet) in the opposite (Vietnamese) village, and now had two children together. The husband was watching Hunan TV and said they had just visited his wife's parents via an unauthorized crossing point a couple of days ago, and no one was there for border-crossing control. He had an ID card, so he could do some small business in Hekou County. Their elderly child was at primary school, while the younger child was taken care of by his parents (first-generation refugees). His two children cannot obtain household registration without three certificates. When asked about his suggestions, the husband was confused about his refugee status, even though he was born and raised in China. He was also bewildered about why his children (also born and raised in China) could not obtain refugee status, just because his wife had come here illegally (being an illegal immigrant).

I asked the relevant departments about this question, and the explanation I received is as follows:

When first-generation refugees come to China, if they are a married couple with children, both the couple and their children are granted refugee status. If they are unmarried when entering China, when they later marry Chinese citizens (they could not register the marriage in the past, but now they can renew or register their marriage after policy reform), then their children are able to obtain Chinese citizenship.[73] When first-generation refugees enter China unmarried, after they marry refugees or illegal immigrants, they can renew or register their marriage and obtain their IDs and household registration booklets based on their long residence in China, although they could not do so before the policy reform. Their children can also obtain IDs and household registration booklets, but they did not qualify for Chinese citizenship due to the lack of a legal basis and related documents issued by the Ministry of Public Security or the government. Therefore, their children are regarded as refugees and referred to as second-generation refugees. Second-generation refugees can register their marriage and obtain Chinese citizenship for their children if they marry Chinese citizens.

Two questions remain: First, when a second-generation refugee marries another refugee of the same status and they register their marriage, can their children obtain Chinese citizenship? Second, when a second-generation refugee marries an illegal immigrant (such as in the case of the two families I interviewed), they cannot register their marriage according to current policies, and their children cannot obtain household registration without three certificates. How can we resolve these problems? Are

[73] Article 4 of the *Nationality Law* stipulates that "any person born in China whose parents are both Chinese nationals shall have Chinese nationality.".

the current practices legal? Can they help solve the problem of illegal immigration? All these questions will be discussed in later chapters.

2. Marriage between Illegal Immigrants and Chinese Citizens (Border Residents)

After analyzing 43 valid returned questionnaires and inquiry notes, we found that all 43 illegal immigrants were women, of which 42 came from Vietnam, and the other came from Myanmar. The length of their marriages with border residents ranged from six months to over ten years. All of them had children, except two families. The youngest woman was 20 years old (according to her neighbors, she was 17 or 18 at most), while the oldest was almost 40. When asked if they had registered their marriages, one woman said they were going through the process, and one woman said they had, although she could not find the marriage certificate. The remaining 41 families admitted that they had not registered their marriages for various reasons, such as "we could not because the government did not allow it," "it does not matter, we already held the (wedding) banquet," and "it is troublesome and it costs money." Among these 43 families, nine families have no children, 19 families have one child, 11 families have two children, and four families have more (three families have three children, and one family has four children). Therefore, there are 54 children in 43 families.

These women were not worried about the citizenship of their children in that they may obtain Chinese nationality in theory, as the father was Chinese. After the reform of the household registration system, children can choose to inherit either their mother's or father's registration location. Theoretically, there should be no problem with their children's household registration. However, since three certificates were required, they may not be registered because their parents' marriages were not legal without marriage registration. In practice, local departments and officials still issued household registration booklets for their children based on "de facto marriage," although there were no solid legal grounds.

When asked about their sources of income, they gave similar answers: their husband owned some land, so most of them worked in the field, took care of children at home, worked for others, or ran small businesses. Most of them were poorly educated: 34 women had received primary schooling or below (79%), seven women had gone to junior high school (16.3%), and only two had gone to high school (4.3%). Meanwhile, they barely knew related laws and regulations. When asked "Do you know the relevant Chinese laws and regulations?", all of them answered "I do not know them" or "I am not sure." They did not understand concepts such as "illegal immigration" or "smuggling" and stated that they had easily crossed borders by foot, boat or car. It was not economical to pass through border crossings, as they had to take detours and pay fees.

They shared the same views as the illegal immigrants mentioned above regarding the reasons for coming to China. For example, "the life here (in China) is better," "we speak the same languages and share similar lifestyles with the locals," "we belong to the same ethnic group which makes it easier to have life together," "the transportation is convenient, and does not cost (much) money," and "it is easy to pass the borders, there is nothing to worry about even if we get caught." In addition, they had another reason, to "marry someone in China."

They were embarrassed about their identity and knew that they could not and did not want to go back to where they came from, i.e., Vietnam. However, China did not approve their naturalization or issue ID cards or household registration booklets, which made it difficult for them to find jobs.

It had been a long time since the beginning of refugee issues in Hekou County. In the late 1970s, especially after 1978, a large number of refugees swarmed into China from Yunnan and Guangxi. Most of them came from the three countries of the Indochinese Peninsula (Vietnam, Laos and Cambodia), and the majority were Vietnamese, which was why they were called "Indochinese refugees." Yunnan is one of the host provinces for Indochinese refugees who came to China for three reasons[74]:

First, the anti-Chinese protests in Vietnam. Yunnan shares borders (mostly land boundaries) with Myanmar, Vietnam and Laos, without natural barriers. Many Chinese citizens living in border areas moved to Vietnam, Laos, Myanmar and other Southeast Asian countries for residence or business and later became citizens of these countries. After 1978, when China-Vietnam relations intensified, the Vietnamese authorities promoted anti-Chinese and purification policies; many overseas Chinese people living in Vietnam, Cambodia and Laos and some people of Miao, Yao, Hani, Yi, Zhuang and other ethnic groups living on the Vietnam side along the borders were driven into China. Second, the China-Vietnam War. Some Vietnamese border residents fled to China in fear of retaliation because of their provision of intelligence information and assistance for China during the China-Vietnam War. Third, family reasons. Some Chinese people living in Vietnam, Myanmar and Laos moved back to China for family reasons, immigration or to join their families.

Professor Lu Gang argues that the issue of Vietnamese refugees is the result of deteriorated China-Vietnam relations in the late 1970s and is one of the historical legacies (1979–1988) of the China-Vietnam War. The influx of Vietnamese refugees can be divided into three periods. First, in 1978–1979, at the dawn of the China-Vietnam War, overseas Chinese were expelled back to China under the anti-Chinese campaign of the Vietnamese government. Second, at the beginning of the war in February 1979, Vietnamese border residents followed the Chinese troops back to China after withdrawal from the northern part of Vietnam. Third, during the following years, when Vietnamese border residents entered China, most of them claimed persecution by the Vietnamese government.[75]

---

[74] Liang (2009), pp. 269–270.

[75] Lu and Li (2007).

Scholars Wu Xi and Liang Jinyun classify Vietnamese refugees in Hekou into three types. First, refugees do not obtain identification documents when waiting for repatriation. Second, refugees do not apply for identification documents. Third, refugees are under the minimum age to apply for identification documents.[76]

I believe the first two types of Indochinese refugees listed by Professor Liang Shuying are consistent with the situation of those refugees in Hekou. However, the third type of refugee (the same cases in Hekou County) shall be classified as "returned immigrants,"[77] rather than refugees, as they are overseas Chinese who have previously lived in Vietnam, Myanmar or Laos. Professor Lu Gang regards the outbreak of the China-Vietnam War as the entry point. The first two types can be regarded as war refugees, while the third type is Vietnamese border residents who entered China after the war, most of whom claimed the persecution of their government. Scrupulous assessment of refugee status is needed. In recent years, the rapid economic development in China has become a "pull factor" for Vietnamese border residents, in addition to the improvement of China-Vietnam relations. Some Vietnamese border residents who entered China may claim "the persecution by the Vietnamese government" to seek refugee status. Nonetheless, they shall still be deemed regular *sanfei* or illegal immigrants. The classification of the Vietnamese refugees in Hekou as per identification documents proposed by Wu Xi and Liang Jinyun is just a specific classification based on the acknowledgment of their refugee status.

According to the statistics of the Civil Affairs Bureau of Hekou County, from 1978 to the end of 1995, there were over 50,000 Vietnamese refugees who had entered China from Hekou, and over 4,000 of them had settled there. As of June 2011, there were 6,588 Vietnamese refugees (1,527 households) in Hekou County (3,128 males and 3,460 females). In addition, 2,659 Vietnamese refugees (557 households) had settled in Hekou County (119 males and 1,460 females), among which 1,427 refugees (265 households) had settled in the refugee settlement area in Chahe, 86 refugees (24 households) in No.12 Brigade in Nanping, 432 refugees (88 households) in Laoaochang, 367 refugees (94 households) in Qiaotou Township, and 367 refugees (86 households) in Nanxi Town. Finally, 3,929 refugees (970 households) settled in farms, among which 1,806 refugees (363 households) had settled in Nanxi Farm, 810 refugees (271 households) in Mahuangbao Farm, 1,062 refugees (251 households) in Basa Farm, and 251 refugees (85 households) in Hekou Farm.

Hekou County has made serious efforts in refugee settlement to fully guarantee their basic rights to survival. 1. Beginning in 2003, impoverished refugees were included in the urban subsistence allowance program to ensure their basic living standard.[78] 2. Beginning in 2008, refugees were provided with basic medical insurance

[76] Wu and Liang (2010).

[77] Returned refugees refer to the refugees who have returned to their country of citizenship or birth after residing in other countries after a certain period of time. Luyi (2011), p. 20.

[78] As of June 2011, 1,625 refugees (699 households) in Hekou County were included in the urban subsistence allowance program, which accounted for 24.67% of the total number of refugees. The monthly subsistence allowance was 196,655 yuan.

for urban residents and medical assistance to ensure basic medical support for them.[79] 3. Beginning in November 2006 and March 2010, refugees issued second-generation ID cards and household registration booklets, respectively.[80] 4. Beginning in 2004, marriage registration was restored for refugees, after which 385 couples registered marriage, and 18 couples registered divorce.[81] 5. Primary schools were set up for refugees to increase access to the education of their children.[82]

Following numerous years of efforts, refugees in Hekou County can now enjoy "quasi-citizen treatment,", i.e., basically the same political and legal rights as Chinese nationals, except for the rights to vote and be elected and to join the civil service or army.[83] Of course, they still face problems such as limited land, housing difficulties and restricted development[84] and are in need of further support from the government.

[79] As of June 2011, 1,520 refugees (250 households) in Hekou County were provided with urban medical insurance, among which 1,050 refugees (124 households) were provided with basic medical insurance for urban residents, and 470 refugees (126 households) were provided with new rural cooperative medical insurance.

[80] As of June 2011, Hekou County had issued second-generation ID cards for 4,900 refugees and household registration booklets for 1,407 households, which effectively solved the difficulties faced by refugees (especially second- and third-generation refugees) while living, traveling, working, and studying in China. The issuance of ID cards and household registration booklets was based on the *Notice by Yunnan Provincial Public Security Bureau of Issuing the Work Plan for Granting Indochinese Refugees ID cards (GZ No. 99 [2005])*, and the *Notice by Yunnan Provincial Public Security Bureau and Yunnan Provincial Civil Affairs Bureau of Issuing the Work Plan for Granting Indochinese (Vietnamese) Refugees Household Registration Booklets (GZ No. 259 [2009])*.

[81] Refugee marriage refers to the marriage and divorce between refugees, and between refugees and Chinese citizens (primarily border residents). The marriages between illegal immigrants and refugees were illegal, thus their marriages and divorces were not registered.

[82] According to the Office of Refugee Affairs, there were four primary schools for refugees in Hekou County, namely, No. 189 Primary School, Basa Primary School, Dananxi Primary School and Longbao Primary School, with 538 refugee students and 45 faculties. After graduation from primary school, refugee students can attend township high schools and take the university entrance exam. One refugee student is working in Chengdu, Sichuan after graduating from university.

[83] According to relevant departments, the refugees in Hekou were granted ID cards with unique numbers that can be recognized of their status by specialists. However, these refugees were not able to hold Chinese passports for international travel without Chinese nationality. Since 2000, the Chinese government has seen increasing petitions of naturalization by Vietnamese refugees. In 2003, there were eight petitions by Vietnamese refugees for naturalization and household registration at provincial, prefecture and county governments, with over 30 petitioners each time. The most prominent one took place in August 2003, when 869 refugees signed the petition letter and raised over 30,000 yuan (35 yuan per person) for the visits at prefecture, provincial or even central governments. The CPC county committee and government paid utmost attention to it and made a visit to mediate the disputes and stop them from intensifying. With their urgent calls for naturalization, these refugees may make new petitions. See Wu and Liang (2010), p. 100.

[84] According to the Office of Refugee Affairs of Hekou County, as of June 2011, the average housing space per household of the refugees in Hekou County was 24 m^2, and the average land per person was 0.43 mu (286.67 m^2). In addition, 500 Indochinese refugee households were included in the 2010 renovation plan of run-down village houses for the first time, and provided with a renovation fund of 10,000 yuan per household, in conformity with the government document regarding solving their housing difficulties. The total funds provided amounted to five million yuan. The renovation projects are currently in progress. See "Indochinese refugees included in the renovation of run-down

From the perspective of illegal immigration governance, it is difficult to manage refugee settlement areas. The marriage between illegal immigrants and refugees is persistent, as they share the same languages and cultural backgrounds. As of June 2011, there were 19 couples of refugees under the jurisdiction of Hekou County and Vietnamese illegal immigrants, most of whom had children. Marriage between refugees and illegal immigrants led to greater difficulties in illegal immigration governance.

References

Castles, S. International migration at the beginning of the twenty-first century: Global trends and issues. *International Social Science Journal (Chinese Edition)*, (3).

Dictionary of the Social Sciences. (1973). *Dictionary of the Social Sciences*. The Commercial Press.

Encyclopedia Americana. (1994). *Encyclopedia Americana*. Foreign Languages Press.

Encyclopedia of China (1991). *Encyclopedia of China*. The Encyclopedia of China Publishing House

He, D. (2009). *The research on cross-border ethnic problems from the perspective of frontier governance: A case study of Southeast China's cross-border ethnic groups*. MA diss., Yunnan University

Liang, X. (2000). *International law* (2nd ed.). Wuhan University Press.

Li, M. (2005). The study of international migration: Its scope, frameworks and significance. *Journal of Xiamen University*, (3).

Liang S. (2008). Principles of dealing with illegal entry refugees. *Law Science Magazine*, (6).

Liang, S. (2009). *International Refugee Law*. Intellectual Property Press.

Lu, G. (2011).*Social harmony and stability in border areas*. Social Sciences Academic Press.

Lu, G., & Li, S. (2007). The research on the current situation, problems and countermeasures of cross-border movement of people in the yunnan border areas. *Journal of Humanities*, Lu, G. (eds.) Yunnan University Press.

Luyi, H. (2011). *EU legal regime of international migration research*. People's Publishing House.

Practical Chinese Dictionary. (2008). *Practical Chinese Dictionary*. The Commercial Press.

Qiao, W. (2002). Global governance and its institutionalization. *Europe* (6)..

The Commission on Global Governance. (1995). *Our global neighborhood*. Oxford University Press.

Tian, Y. (2010). *Immigrants and National Security: The Research on the Derivation of Threats and Their Conditions*. World Affairs Press.

Wang, T. (1995). *International law*. Law Press China, pp. 89–90.

Wen, F. (2010). *The research on European Union's governance on illegal immigration*. Jinan University.

Wu, Q. (2004). The concept of contemporary international migration and its globalized characteristics. *Contemporary International Relations* (8).

Wu, X., & Liang, J. "The Refugee Issue as the Cause Affecting the Stability of China's Border Areas: Research Report on the Refugee Issue in Hekou County of Yunnan Province," *Journal of Yunnan Police Officer Academy*, no. 1 (2010).

Xu, J. (2005). *The study on the problems of legal control of illegal immigration*. PhD diss., Wuhan University.

village houses for the first time," source: Honghe Daily, January 8, 2011. Cited from http://www.hh.cn/news_1/xw01/201101/t20110108_335650.html . Accessed October 19, 2011.

Zhou, J. (2008). *On peaceful cross-border dwelling models: A study of the peaceful cross-border dwelling model of South China and mainland Southeast Asia*. Ethnic Publishing House.
Zhou, P. (2008a). Historical evolution of the concept of frontier in China. *Journal of Yunnan Administration College* (4).
Zhou, P. (2008b). The research on China's frontier governance. *Academic Exploration*, (2).

Chapter 3
Causes of Illegal Immigration in Yunnan Border Areas with a High Concentration of Ethnic Minorities

1 Current Theories of the Causes of Illegal Immigration

Now that we have defined illegal immigration and the other core concepts, let us take Hekou County as an example to examine the current situation and issues of illegal immigration in the Yunnan border areas with a high concentration of ethnic minorities. For the purpose of governance, and particularly to tackle both the symptoms and root causes, we must analyze the reasons for illegal immigration to develop a more targeted governance approach. Illegal immigration is a problem faced by all countries around the world. With China opening wider to the outside world in recent years and increased interaction between the Yunnan frontier areas and other countries and regions, we should analyze and account for the reasons for illegal immigration in these areas based on relevant theories proposed by Chinese and overseas scholars. Meanwhile, we must also consider the impact of relevant factors of Yunnan's neighboring countries, specific geographic locations and natural endowment of these areas, as well as various cross-border ethnic groups residing there, to further analyze the complicated and specific causes of illegal immigration in local areas.

1.1 Overseas Theories Regarding the Causes of Illegal Immigration and Their Limitations

As stated earlier, the term "illegal immigration" was not strictly defined until the 1970s and 80 s. As it was not easy to give it a precise definition, the study of illegal immigration was often included in immigration research for quite a long time. Overseas theories regarding the reasons for international migration were fairly instructive in explaining the reasons for illegal immigration in the Yunnan border areas with a high concentration of ethnic minorities. However, there are questions that cannot be easily explained by these theories. Perhaps it may justify the application

G. Luo, *The Issues of Illegal Immigration and its Solutions in the Minority-Border Regions in Yunnan Province, China*, https://doi.org/10.1007/978-981-19-1249-8_3

scope of every theory. As Professor Chen Ruihua put it, "Only by knowing exactly in what circumstances one particular theory is not applicable can we get rid of our blind faith in it. Defining the circumstances in which this theory is applicable allows us to make theoretical research as objective as possible."[1]

American sociologist E.G. Ravenstein, the founder of push–pull theory and neoclassical economic equilibrium theory, believes that differences in economic development, chiefly differences in wages among countries, are the main causes of immigration. His theories highlight the impact of differences in economic development and wages on immigration causes; however, this is only one of the critical factors. This factor can explain immigration from developing countries to developed countries in general but not immigration among developed countries and developing countries. This factor can also explain the immigration from Yunnan's neighboring countries to China from a certain perspective (better economic development and higher wages in China). However, this cannot fully explain why these immigrants mainly choose to live in Yunnan border areas with a high concentration of ethnic minorities rather than moving to interior China, the eastern coastal areas, or tier-one cities in China featuring better economic performance and higher wages.

Deeply influenced by Karl Marx's thoughts of capital and capitalist mode of production, historical-structuralist theory holds that immigration stems from colonialism, wars and imbalanced political and economic development among regions. The growing infiltration and expansion of capitalism from core countries to peripheral countries produce a rootless proletarian class that is prepared to go abroad. They are lured to work in core countries' economic sectors as cheap laborers at any time, and the enormous profits they earn end up in the pockets of others. However, this theory cannot explain the immigration from Yunnan's neighboring countries to China, as China is not a "core country" that infiltrates and expands to peripheral countries. Moreover, the immigrants moving to China (especially the Yunnan border areas with a high concentration of ethnic minorities) are not rootless proletarian workers who create substantial profits for others.

The prerequisite of the dual-labor market theory is "developed countries." It argues that local workers of developed countries prefer high-end sectors with higher wages, superior security and better working environments, while low-end sectors with lower wages, inferior security and poorer working environments require external labor forces. Therefore, this practical internal demand prompts cross-border immigration. This is the first theory to consider the reasons for international migration from the internal factors of immigrant-receiving countries and is in fact the application of push–pull theory. However, from what we have learned during our investigation,

[1] Chen Ruihua, *On Research Methods of Jurisprudence* (Beijing: Peking University Press, 2009), 125. On page 121, it reads: When doing research, we shall avoid looking for theories at the very beginning. We need to look into previous cases and legislative issues, determine questions from experience and facts, and then propose theoretical hypotheses. If existing theories can explain these questions, we must give them up immediately because they are not real questions. The current theories of the reasons for illegal immigration cannot fully explain this phenomenon in the Yunnan border areas with a high concentration of ethnic minorities. That is why this book has its research values.

the immigrants residing in the Yunnan border areas with a high concentration of ethnic minorities make a living by "farming," "working for others," or "running small businesses," which are the same as the local residents. At the very least, there are no internal needs for external labor forces in low-end sectors with lower wages, inferior security and poorer working environments. This theory is thus not applicable in the specific research area of this book.

World systems theory asserts that immigration is the direct result of economic globalization and considers the catalytic role of the movement of products, capital, information and the labor force in immigration. It concludes that the expansion of capitalism stimulates the international flows of products, capital, information and labor force, and unequal international relations make the labor force of underdeveloped countries the target of depredation by developed countries. Yunnan's neighboring countries are indeed underdeveloped, but China is also a developing country. Logically, it may raise the question of an "unqualified subject" if we apply this theory to explain immigration into China.[2] Furthermore, it does not consider the factors of individual immigrants when they choose to move to another country. These individual factors are complicated and variable, and they may not be spurred by the movement of products, capital, information and labor force. Taking Hekou County as an example, the main reason for the influx of illegal immigrants here is the difficulty male border residents in Yunnan face finding wives. Apparently, we cannot use this theory to explain the idea of "marrying someone in China for a better life" that motivates illegal immigrants to enter these border areas.

The migration network theory and migration systems theory proposed by overseas scholars are useful for explaining immigration from Yunnan's neighboring countries to border areas with a high concentration of ethnic minorities. These two theories will be discussed further below.

1.2 Explanations and Implications of the Theories on the Causes of Illegal Immigration Proposed by Chinese Scholars

Chinese scholars have published numerous research papers on the reasons for illegal immigration, among which I selected the papers of Wang Xianfeng and Xu Junhua for analysis.

Wang Xianfeng divides the reasons for illegal immigration into "international reasons for illegal immigration" and "China's reasons for illegal immigration," i.e., international reasons and domestic reasons. It must be noted that the domestic reasons he proposes are based on China's illegal immigration in the coastal areas of Fujian

[2] Of course, it can be further described as the immigration from more underdeveloped countries to underdeveloped countries, or the immigration from developed countries to more developed countries. However, this will only make the matter more complicated. –Author's note.

occurring since the 1990s. His research object is the reasons for illegal Chinese immigrants to other countries.

Wang Xianfeng argues that as sovereignty and citizenship identification continue to grow stronger in modern nation-states, each state has built a set of complex and rigorous legal systems and management mechanisms governing sovereignty and citizenship to place a strict limit on free movement across borders. Illegal immigration occurs when risk-takers manage to break movement limitations imposed by modern nation-states. In my opinion, we can make the following hypothesis based on his theory: illegal immigration is contrary to the respect of a modern nation-state's sovereignty and citizenship identification. Both illegal immigrants and their acts constitute a violation of a nation-state's sovereignty. Moreover, they abandon or reduce their citizenship identification. In the case of the research object of this book, there must be one or more factors that are more attractive to most illegal immigrants who have entered China, resulting in immigrants ignoring national sovereignty (a country's management over entering and leaving its territories) and abandoning or reducing the identification of their citizenship.

The question remains, just what are these more attractive factors? There are two noteworthy points in his research. First, uneven global distribution of wealth and job opportunities are essential drivers of illegal immigration. Illegal immigrants seek the illegal side of the international economic structure in economic globalization, i.e., the black or underground economy. The first point is consistent with our investigation results. Illegal immigrants often come to China mainly for the following reasons: "getting a job," "doing business," "it is easier to make money here" or "the life here is better." However, we must differentiate specific circumstances regarding the notion of illegal immigrants seeking after the "black or underground economy." According to our investigation, regular *sanfei* do participate in illegal and criminal activities such as prostitution, smuggling, money laundry or drug trafficking, i.e., the so-called "black or underground economy." Meanwhile, most illegal immigrants who married border residents in the Yunnan border areas with a high concentration of ethnic minorities work in legal economic sectors, such as "farming," "working" and "doing business." Second, cultural factors such as the convergence of national characteristics and religious beliefs. It should be noted that so-called "national characteristics" were proposed from the macroscopic view of nation-states. For example, the national characteristics of China refer to the characteristics of the Chinese nation. In this book, they refer to the national characteristics of ethnic groups residing outside of their state boundaries in the Yunnan border areas. These characteristics were developed over the long course of living together in the same region, thus resulting in the same lifestyles, languages or religious beliefs. These characteristics can be used to distinguish ethnic groups and to develop mutual dependency and trust among members of the same ethnic groups. Ethnic self-identification in this sense is one of the essential factors that appeal to immigrants (including illegal immigrants) from neighboring countries to the Yunnan border areas.

According to Xu Junhua, illegal immigration can be attributed to economic, policy, legal and individual reasons. Some reasons on the policy level proposed by him are very instructive for this book.[3]

First, restrictive immigration policies. He takes EU member states (Germany, the UK and France) and the US as examples to indicate that their restrictive immigration policies have to some extent contributed to the increase in illegal immigration. More generous immigration policies may have reduced the number of illegal immigrants and their growth rate. I believe that, as a highly populated country, China should strictly control the entry of immigrants now and in the future. If its border control gives rise to illegal immigration, China should implement more rigorous policies to stop illegal immigrants from entering the country and repatriate them to the extent permitted by law.

Second, differences in immigration policies. "Differences" here refer to different immigration policies (including policies targeted at illegal immigration) implemented at different times by the same country. Xu Junhua lists the immigrant legalization policies enacted in the US and some Western European countries since the 1980s, which granted long-term residence to immigrants who had already stayed in these countries. In my opinion, these policies were very appealing to the people of developing countries who desired to move to those countries and made illegal immigrants believe their status would finally be legalized if they continued to stay there.

Does the same problem exist in Yunnan border areas with a high concentration of ethnic minorities? As previously mentioned, according to our investigation, relevant departments issued ID cards and household registration booklets to illegal immigrants who had lived in China for a long time by treating them as refugees. In contrast, for illegal immigrants who recently came to China, these departments followed the principle of not recognizing their status, not issuing ID cards and household registration booklets, and repatriation when possible. However, in practice, only a small portion of newly arrived illegal immigrants, especially those who married Chinese citizens, were repatriated. It impeded the governance of illegal immigration in these areas and became a significant cause of the entry of illegal immigrants and their "refusal to leave."

2 Complicated and Special Causes of Illegal Immigration in Yunnan Border Areas with a High Concentration of Ethnic Minorities

Neither Chinese nor overseas theories regarding the reasons for illegal immigration described above can fully explain this phenomenon in Yunnan border areas with a high concentration of ethnic minorities. Some reasons even contradict the real situations in these areas. The unique locations and geological environment, as well

[3] Xu Junhua (2005).

as ethnic groups residing across the borders, gradually created the micro- or regional environment that appeals to illegal immigrants. The microenvironment is the result of long-term integration and the interaction of historical, cultural, economic and ethnic factors, eventually leading to complicated reasons for illegal immigration. Of course, this complexity originated from distinctive regional characteristics of these areas or their specialty.

2.1 Rapid Economic and Social Development as Major Pull Factors

In addition to rapid improvement of the overall economic and social situations of these areas under tremendous government support and the hard work of locals, China's stable political environment and its increasing prominence as a major country have become a powerful appeal to the residents of Yunnan's neighboring countries, especially their border residents. That is more than subjective feelings of immigrants who "vote with their feet," but solid benefits that they enjoy. For example, they can make more money by working or doing business and have a better life by marrying someone in China. Different interviewees responded with almost the same answers: "the life here (in China) is better," "to earn money by doing business," and "to work and make money." These are the best explanations for this appeal.

However, I found that there were other reasons for the appeal from on-site investigation. For example, China's lack of labor force has given leeway to regular *sanfei* or illegal immigrants. Most local youths seek working opportunities in more developed regions, resulting in a labor shortage, and their farmland at home is unattended. Therefore, many families hired workers from Vietnam at lower costs, especially in spring and autumn, for sowing and harvest.

Moreover, during the investigation in Hekou County, we found that local villagers who married Vietnamese women were mostly "poorly qualified" (old, divorced, not attractive, etc.), or "not capable" (did not earn much money, not skilled at doing business, etc.). The local women they knew either married more eligible local folks or outlanders, worked or ran business in other places with no intention to move back. Meanwhile, we also found that there were financial reasons why they might choose to marry Vietnamese women. It costs tens of thousands of yuan or even more to marry a local woman. However, marrying a Vietnamese wife according to legal procedures (legally registered interracial marriage) costs much more money and effort. Some villagers said, "anyone who gets a Vietnamese wife like that must be out of his mind." Formal (legal) procedures of marrying a Vietnamese wife have been scorned. Local bachelors only marry Vietnamese women when they have "no other choices," even if doing so may bring many trouble. Their families and friends can usually understand their situation and accept their "Vietnamese wives," and local villagers and officials also believe there is nothing wrong with it, which creates a relaxed environment for these women to integrate into local communities. With the spread of news and feedback via various channels, this relaxed environment has become the appeal of "marrying someone there (in China) for a better life."

In addition, the opening up and the rapid economic and social development in these areas are also related factors. Therefore, theoretically, China's attraction or pull factors for immigrants, including illegal immigrants, should be something to be proud of. However, if we look closer at the specific aspects, we may determine that the reasons for this attraction may not be positive and legal, nor something to take pride in.

2.2 *Easy Illegal Border Crossing Due to Unique Geological Environment and Lax Border Management*

The Yunnan border areas with a high concentration of ethnic minorities share borders with Vietnam, Laos and Myanmar and are adjacent to Thailand, Cambodia, India and Bangladesh. There are 4,060 km of borderlines in these areas, composed of the 1,353 km China-Vietnam border, the 710 km China-Laos border, and the 1,997 km China-Myanmar border. Aside from the 13 national category-1 ports and seven category-2 ports, there are numerous temporary crossing paths for border residents. According to the statistics of the Office for Port Services of Yunnan Provincial Department of Commerce, there are 90 border trade paths and 103 border trade points along the borderlines,[4] as well as countless unauthorized crossing points. In addition, with no natural barriers in between, the territories on both sides of the borderlines are linked by mountains and rivers. Some villages of the two countries are even connected,[5] making it very easy for border residents to cross the borders.

Such situations make it convenient for border residents to cross borders but extremely difficult for authorities to manage border crossings. This book uses the word "lax" to describe the management of border crossing in Yunnan. Is this the reality in these areas? During the discussions with relevant departments of Hekou County, when asked about their thoughts of the management of border crossing along the borderlines (boundaries) between Yunnan and neighboring countries, they replied with similar words: "there are difficulties in border control."

What they meant is that the land boundaries between China and Vietnam, Laos and Myanmar are delineated, and all countries manage the border crossing in accordance with their laws, regulations and bilateral treaties and agreements. However, in practice, this is quite challenging due to the reasons mentioned above. In particular, numerous unauthorized crossing points connecting these countries are out of reach for the border control authorities because of limited human, material and financial resources. I believe that "difficulties in border control" may be the reality. This is

[4] *An Overview of the Ports in Yunnan*, source: Yunnan Provincial Department of Commerce website: http://www.bofcom.gov.cn/bofcom/432345564227567616/index.html. Accessed June 15, 2011.

[5] An example is Yinjing Village in Ruili, Dehong Prefecture divided by a boundary marker as the borderline between China and Myanmar. –Author's note.

distinct from "no border to control," "absence of border control" or "no control over the border" in nature. However, unlike "strict border control," the current management leaves loopholes for illegal border crossing. Therefore, I believe "lax" to be the most suitable word to describe the situation.

What are the reasons for "difficulties in border control"? Are there other reasons besides those mentioned above? Shall we impose strict border control? These questions will be discussed further below. Regarding the causes of illegal immigration, "lax" border management is by no means an attraction with negative impacts. During our inquiries in Hekou County, the answer of "it is easy to pass the borders, there is nothing to worry about even if we get caught" is the best illustration of "lax" management.

2.3 *Optimal Immigration: Costs and Risks of Immigration*

Immigration costs are the costs that one must pay for immigration (including illegal immigration), usually referring to economic cost, time cost, and opportunity cost.[6] Immigration risks are foreseeable or unforeseeable risks and consequences that one must face for immigration (including illegal immigration). Intentionally or otherwise, and whether it is from one's own investigation or from families and friends, when considering whether to immigrate or the destination of immigration, the would-be immigrates always desire the greatest attraction of the receiving country and the lowest costs and risks. This is described as "optimal immigration" in this book.

Residents of Yunnan's neighboring countries usually consider the following questions when thinking about immigration: Should I immigrate (stay in my home country or not)? Which country should I move to (including the specific location of the country)? How should I immigrate (legal or illegal immigration)? There are two measurements: attraction of the destination and costs and risks of immigration. The best option is the greatest attraction of the destination and the lowest costs and risks of immigration, i.e., optimal immigration, as shown in Fig. 1.

Taking Hekou County as an example, when making the decision to move to China, immigrants from Vietnam and other neighboring countries regarded Hekou County as the epitome of China. Therefore, the attraction of Hekou County was the attraction of the Yunnan border areas with a high concentration of ethnic minorities, as well as the attraction of China. As mentioned before, Vietnamese citizens, especially border residents keeping close contact with China, believe that "paradise is too far away, and China is so close." China is enormously attractive to them, and they need to consider, what are the costs and risks of moving to China? In addition, what are the

[6] Opportunity cost is the maximum value one must forgo in order to obtain something. It is a widely used term in economics. In this book, it refers to the opportunity of staying in one's country of citizenship or the opportunity of moving to other countries when he or she decides to immigrate to a particular country. –Author's note.

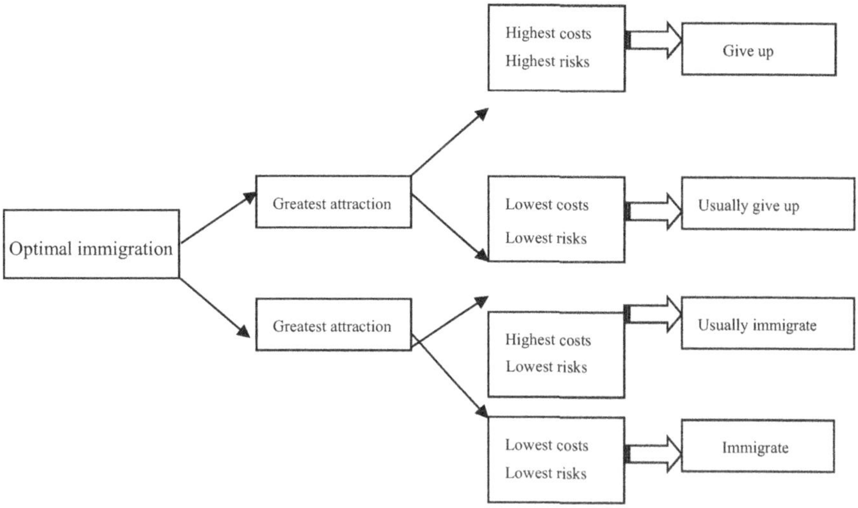

Fig. 1 Optimal immigration

possibilities and costs and risks of legal immigration? What about the possibilities and costs and risks of illegal immigration?

During our investigation in Hekou County, I reached out to several families who had legally registered marriage with Chinese citizens. However, the relevant departments did not pay sufficient attention because of the small number of these cases. It is rather difficult to immigrate to China by legal means. According to the *Nationality Law*, foreigners can apply for Chinese nationality in theory. However, this is not easy to do so for common residents (especially border residents) of Yunnan's neighboring countries, and the chance of success is quite slim. Foreigners are less likely to obtain Chinese nationality or permanent residence in China. Article 47 of the *Exit-Entry Administration Law of the People's Republic of China* reads, "foreigners who have made a remarkable contribution to China's economic and social development or meet other conditions for permanent residence in China may obtain permanent residence status upon application approved by the Ministry of Public Security." However, it is difficult or impossible for most foreigners (especially common residents of Yunnan's neighboring countries) to obtain "green cards." In other words, the costs and risks are too high. Therefore, illegal immigration to China is a helpless option and is proven highly viable.

An important question remains: since they chose illegal immigration, why did they choose Yunnan Province, which is relatively lagging in economic and social development, rather than better-off regions in eastern China, or large- or medium-sized cities? Why are underdeveloped Yunnan border areas with a high concentration of ethnic minorities?

As previously indicated, network theory holds that migrant networks are, in fact, sets of interpersonal ties that connect migrants, home-coming migrants, and their families and fellows through ties of kinship, friendship and shared community origin. They provide various assistance, such as information, economic support, job opportunities and accommodation, to lower the costs and risks of migration to a great extent, thus promoting migratory movements. Migration systems theory also claims that migration systems are a sort of space that comprises a group of relatively stable connections between receiving countries and sending regions. Moreover, this kind of connection is established through migratory movements based on various bonds. These "various bonds" are actually microlevel structures, i.e., chain migration, which makes the migration process safer and more reliable and helps new migrants know more about the countries they move into, find new jobs, and become accustomed to the new environment as soon as possible. Families and communities play critical roles in chain migration. Once the chain is established, it will be self-perpetuating. There are similarities between these two theories, as they both point out that the reasons for sustained immigration (including illegal immigration) to an immigrant-receiving country (including one particular region of the country) are these "ties" or "chains." They can be kinship, friendship and shared origin, or families and communities. They can provide information, economic support, job opportunities and accommodations to help new immigrants find new jobs, become accustomed to the new environment as soon as possible, and make the immigration process safer and more reliable, thus lowering the costs and risks of immigration.

When searching for the reasons for immigration in these areas, we found that answers such as "having similar languages and lifestyles" and "belonging to the same ethnic group makes it easier to live together" revealed the "ties" or "chains" specific to the Yunnan border areas with a high concentration of ethnic minorities. Similar to other similar areas, Hekou County is home to Yao, Miao and other cross-border ethnic groups who share the same languages, cultures, lifestyles and religious beliefs. Moreover, many of them are related to new immigrants and try to provide them with various types of assistance to reduce their immigration costs and risks as much as possible. According to the investigation of other scholars, refugees who have settled in Hekou County are mainly of Han, Miao, Dai, Zhuang, Yao, Buyi, Yi and Jing ethnicities. They have lived in the border areas between China and Vietnam for generations and have maintained marriage or blood relations with China's ethnic groups. They are typical cross-border ethnic groups who share the same cultural origins and languages and similar customs with those ethnic groups on China's side. As a vulnerable group among cross-border ethnic groups, Vietnamese refugees are bound to receive empathy and assistance from other groups due to their situation.[7]

Of course, the decisive factors of the lowest immigration costs and risks include lighter punishment for violating China's laws and regulations, convenient transportation, and lax border management systems. After taking stock of all the costs and risks, immigrants will make decisions such as whether to immigrate or not; by which means

[7] Wu Xi and Liang Jinyun (2010).

(legal or illegal); what kind of countries to move to (developed or developing countries); and which areas in the destination country (developed or developing areas). That is, their final choice must be the optimal option after they take all factors into consideration.

2.4 *Current Conditions and Policies in Yunnan's Neighboring Countries as Push Factors*

China's strong appeal and the consideration of costs and risks are not adequate for the residents of Yunnan's neighboring countries to move to China and live therein as illegal immigrants. The economic and social conditions and domestic policies and laws of countries of origin are also drivers of illegal immigration. This book takes Vietnam as an example, as most illegal immigrants in Hekou County come from Vietnam.

After Vietnam's reunification in 1976, the new national government faced urgent tasks of rebuilding its economy. However, its postwar economic development was halted due to inappropriate economic policies. At the beginning of 1978, agricultural collectivization took place in the southern part of the country when various agricultural cooperatives were established. However, under the wide opposition of farmers, the Vietnamese government had to abolish collectivization in 1980. Unpopular policies exacerbated the general public's subsistence crisis, as food production was 4.5% less than expected, totaling merely 12.9 million tons in 1978. The portioned food for farmers was barely sufficient for subsistence. Before its domestic economy was recovered, the Vietnamese government squandered limited expenditures on the war, which worsened its economic conditions. At the end of 1978, Vietnam's invasion of Cambodia resulted in the suspension of economic assistance from Western Europe and Japan, the US ban against bilateral trade with it, and China's cancellation of all assistance projects. The postwar reconstruction was basically at a standstill. Despite the economic and military assistance provided by the former Soviet Union and its satellite states, it was impossible to finance Vietnam's enormous financial deficit. To cope with this situation, the government resorted to excessive issuance of banknotes, substantial external debt, and a large increase in tax rates. In September 1985, the government's attempted currency devaluation caused spiral inflation, with an increase in the inflation index from 700 to 1,000% and an unemployment rate of 20% in the next few years.[8]

Since its economic reform in 1986, Vietnam has witnessed a rapid increase in economic development, although still lagging behind China.[9] However, the Five-year Plan (1986–1990) did not substantially change the Vietnamese people's lives,

---

[8] Chen Xiaoying, "The Study on Vietnamese Refugees and Boat People in Hong Kong" (MA diss., East China Normal University), 7.

[9] Even though (Vietnam's) GDP in 2010 exceeded 100 billion US dollars for the first time, its overall economic output was less than that of Shenzhen. Ye Weimin, "Vietnam: Paradise is too far away,

and the government admitted that farmers were still facing a daily struggle for subsistence. In 1987, over 60% of the residents in Ho Chi Minh City (Saigon) depended on remittances from their families abroad.[10] More importantly, Vietnam's economic development was apparently uneven among regions, with a wide gap between northwestern mountain areas next to Yunnan Province and the well-off southeastern region. In 2004, the annual income per capita of the richest provinces and cities in the southeastern region was 628 US dollars, while that in the northwest, the poorest region, was 206 US dollars, less than one-third that of the former. Even within the same region, the eastern part was 10.4 times richer than the northern part.[11] According to Vietnam's *Economic Times*, the country's monthly income per capita was 1.38 million Vietnamese dong (or 68 US dollars) in 2010, an increase of 39.4% compared with 2008, and the poverty rate dropped to 10.7%. However, the wealth gap became increasingly wider. The income of the richest southeastern region was 2.6 times that of the poorest areas, namely, the central and northern mountain areas. The richest people mainly lived in large cities, with a monthly income of 3.4 million Vietnamese dong (or 166 US dollars), while the income per capita of the poorest people in remote areas inhabited by ethnic groups and rural areas was 369,000 Vietnamese dong (or 18 US dollars), approximately one tenth that of the former. The monthly expenditure per capita was 1.21 million Vietnamese dong (or 60 US dollars), an increase of 52.8% over 2008, and the monthly expenditure of the richest was 4.7 times that of the poorest. Finally, the richest people spent 7.5 times more than the poorest on services other than food.[12]

During the 11th Five-year Plan period, Yunnan farmers' annual income increased at rates higher than the national average. Their net income per capita was 3,952 yuan in 2010, and the actual annual growth rateH reached 9.9%. This was the period when farmers' income enjoyed the fastest growth since the implementation of the household contract responsibility system. Yunnan Province's economic figures in 2011 were as follows: 875.095 billion yuan of GDP, an increase of 13.7%; 710.97 billion yuan of total investment in fixed assets, up 27.4%; 225.82 billion yuan of total revenues, increased by 24.8%; 111.08 billion yuan of local revenues in general public budget, an increase of 27.5%; and 300.01 billion yuan of retail sales of national social consumer goods, an increase of 20%. The annual disposable income of urban and rural residents per capita reached 18,576 yuan, an actual increase of 10.3%, and farmers' net income per capita amounted to 4,722 yuan, an increase of 13.9%.[13]

---

and China is so close." Source: Southern Weekly, http://www.infzm.com/content/62315. Accessed September 13, 2011.

[10] Cited from Chen Xiaoying, "The Study on Vietnamese Refugees and Boat People in Hong Kong" (MA diss., East China Normal University), 7.

[11] Wang Longhu (2005).

[12] "A Widening Gap between Rich and Poor in Vietnam," source: China's Ministry of Commerce website: http://www.mofcom.gov.cn/aarticle/i/jyjl/j/201.107/20110707645378.html. Accessed October 8, 2011.

[13] Report on the Work of the Yunnan Provincial People's Government 2012, source: China's Central Government website: http://www.gov.cn/test/2012-02/20/content_2071269.htm. Accessed May 15, 2012.

These striking income gaps in adjacent regions on both sides of the China-Vietnam borderlines prompted immigration from Vietnam's northwestern mountain areas to China and other neighboring countries.

Additionally, Vietnam's birth rate increased rapidly after the war. In 2007, its total population was nearly 87 million (49.2% males and 50.8% females).[14] The sex ratio imbalance in Vietnam is related to its lengthy period of war. In 2005, its sex ratio was 99.66 males per 100 females. In 1992, the sex ratio of the age group of 20–39 years was 83.09 males per 100 females. Gender imbalance in Vietnam's marriageable population made it difficult for women to find husbands, thereby prompting them to seek international marriage to some extent.[15]

In addition, according to relevant departments of Hekou County, it was difficult to send regular *sanfei* and illegal immigrants back to Vietnam. The Vietnamese authorities did not respond to China's notification within the time limit laid out in the minutes of bilateral meetings, which impeded the transfer and repatriation of illegal immigrants. Moreover, the Vietnamese government did not cooperate in accepting the *sanfei* and illegal immigrants repatriated by China. The Vietnamese government also denied the identity of those who crossed the border illegally and revoked their nationality and household registration. Finally, it also took counter-repatriation measures that stipulated that Vietnamese citizens who moved to China after 1975 shall not be identified as Vietnamese and organized interception against these people.[16] This noncooperative policy is another driver of Vietnamese citizens' illegal residence in China.

References

Jing, D. (2010). *The study on illegal interracial marriage and immigration along the China-Vietnam border: A case study of seven villages in Longzhou county*. Jinan University.

Jianxin, Z. (2008). *On peaceful cross-border dwelling models: A study of the peaceful cross-border dwelling model of south China and Mainland southeast Asia*. Ethnic Publishing House.

Wang Longhu. (2005). The income of vietnamese Urban and Rural residents in recent years. *Around Southeast Asia*, 12.

Wu Xi, & Liang Jinyun. (2010). The refugee issue as the cause affecting the stability of China's border areas: Research report on the refugee issue in Hekou county of Yunnan province. *Journal of Yunnan Police Officer Academy*, 1.

Xu Junhua. (2005). The study on the problems of legal control of illegal immigration. PhD diss., Wuhan University.

[14] "Vietnamese population," source: Wikipedia: http://zh.wikipedia.org/wiki/%E8%B6%8A%E5%8D%97%E4%BA%BA%E5%8F%A3. Accessed September 13, 2011.

[15] Dang Jing (2010), 30.

[16] Zhou Jianxin (2008).

Chapter 4
Impact of Illegal Immigration in Yunnan Border Areas with a High Concentration of Ethnic Minorities

We have now completed examining the current situation and reasons for illegal immigration in the Yunnan border areas with a high concentration of ethnic minorities. Next, let us analyze its negative impact so that we may lay a theoretical foundation for the governance of illegal immigration in these areas. In other words, why do we need to control it? Of course, we may draw from our inquiries that illegal immigrants have also had a positive impact on local societies, such as improving exchanges and communication among border residents of different countries, solving the difficulties faced by some border residents (mainly male residents) in terms of aspects such as finding spouses, and replenishing laborers in some industries. However, illegal immigration itself is against the law. It undermines and damages national laws and regulations, and its negative impact is profound and widespread.

The impact of illegal immigration proposed by overseas scholars has mainly focused on four aspects: the impact on border security and control; on the politics, economy and society of receiving countries; on international security and relations; and on national security. The studies of Chinese scholars have also been based on these four aspects, yet they have scarcely mentioned the impact of illegal immigration, specifically on the Yunnan border areas with a high concentration of ethnic minorities.

I believe that illegal immigration is a typical nontraditional security issue that must be examined from the perspective of nontraditional security. Within the vast territory of China, circumstances among regions vary considerably, as do the symptoms and severity of nontraditional issues. Therefore, when formulating countermeasures and prioritizing these issues, we must align our holistic thinking with the local conditions.[1] The political, economic and social impacts of illegal immigration on the Yunnan border areas are the primary factors affecting national stability and security. I will first analyze this aspect in this section. In addition, the research regarding nontraditional security emphasizes a people-centered approach, i.e., "to integrate national security with individual security," or "to take individual security as a basis and starting

[1] Wang Yizhou (2010), 21.

G. Luo, *The Issues of Illegal Immigration and its Solutions in the Minority-Border Regions in Yunnan Province, China*, https://doi.org/10.1007/978-981-19-1249-8_4

point of overall security."[2] Therefore, this book will examine the issue of population security caused by illegal immigration. Second, considering ethnic self-identification as one of the reasons for illegal immigration and considering the complex relationship between ethnic self-identification and national self-identification, this book will explore the relationship between ethnic and national self-identification regarding illegal immigration. Finally, immigration itself is a transnational or international issue. Illegal immigration will undoubtedly change the relations among related countries, and its governance cannot be performed by any country alone. Therefore, this book will also focus on the impact of illegal immigration on China-Vietnam relations.

1 Political, Economic and Social Impact

The political, economic and social impacts of illegal immigration in the Yunnan border areas with a high concentration of ethnic minorities also impact national stability and security. Stable frontier areas are the foundation of national security. The stability and security of frontier areas are significant guarantees of national stability and security. As mentioned earlier, illegal immigrants are *sanfei* with a certain time limit or with an additional condition of a time limit. Most of China's laws, regulations, rules and practices regarding the management of *sanfei* can be applied in illegal immigration governance. In contrast, the study on the impact of illegal immigration must include the impact of regular *sanfei*. Furthermore, this book will also discuss the political, economic and social impacts of refugees in Hekou County on these areas.

1.1 Disrupting Border Security

Borderlines and boundaries are the legal basis of border demarcation, thus having obvious implications for a sovereign country. Strict border management by law is the manifestation of a country's sovereignty. As mentioned above, the unique geological conditions and lax border control in the Yunnan border areas with a high concentration of ethnicgroups render the province prone to illegal border crossing, in turn leading to difficulties in border control. I previously performed investigations at two locations in Hekou County, and after witnessing how easy and convenient it was to illegally cross the border, I wondered whether the true problem was that there were "difficulties in border control" or simply that there was an "absence of border control." As previously stated, the repatriation of "three illegals" (*sanfei*, namely, illegal entry, illegal residence and illegal employment) and illegal immigrants was ineffective for the following reasons: (1) A lack of cooperation and poor efficiency on the Vietnamese side, along with their strict scrutiny and severe punishment toward

[2] Ibid., 17.

people repatriated by China. This has resulted in the "three illegals" and illegal immigrants of Vietnamese nationality not wishing or not daring to return home, in turn leading to the pattern of repeated repatriation and return. (2) An excessive number of routes and "free" access to China have undermined the deterrence of repatriation and thus seriously disrupted the order of China's border control.

In addition, illegal border crossing facilitates smuggling, money laundry, drug and human trafficking and other criminal acts, thereby seriously threatening the stability and security of frontier areas, which will be illustrated in the following two cases.

Case 1: Drug trafficking by Xiang Azhou.[3]

On May 28, 2009, Xiang Azhou (male, Miao ethnicity, Vietnamese nationality) purchased two bars of heroin (696 g) from Vietnam's Dien Bien County and stored them in a shed, having planned a drug deal in Coc Leu, Lao Cai Province. At approximately 18:00 on June 2, Xiang Azhou carried the heroin as he rode a motorcycle to search for potential buyers in Coc Leu, Lao Cai Province. While there, he met a man named Yang A're (male, Miao ethnicity, Chinese nationality), who also spoke the Miao language. After their conversation in Miao, Xiang Azhou brought the heroin and took a boat with Yang A're to smuggle into Hekou, China for the trade. After having dinner in Hekou, he checked room 304 at Xinli Hotel, wrapped the heroin with his clothes, and hid the bundle under a blanket in the closet. He was arrested at approximately 12:00 on June 3.

This was a cross-border drug trafficking crime characterized by convenient border crossing by illegal means.

Case 2: Illegal arms trade by Zhong Kaifa.[4]

On July 9, 2009, Zhong Kaifa (male, Chinese) purchased a military revolver and three military bullets at the price of 15,000 yuan from a Vietnamese seller (a male from Trung Chai, Vietnam, nicknamed Xiaobao) at the junction between Trung Chai of Vietnam and Lengshuigou, Qiaotou Township of China. He hid the revolver and bullets at home and planned to sell them to interior China. On July 10, the Chinese authorities arrested Zhong Kaifa at the passenger station of Qiaotou Township for the suspected crime of illegal arms trade.

This was a cross-border arms trade crime, also characterized by convenient border crossing by illegal means.

Illegal border crossing seriously impacts China's border management and challenges China's border control mechanisms and its national sovereignty. In addition to smuggling, the Yunnan border areas with a high concentration of ethnic minorities have also become one of the "best routes" for Chinese criminals fleeing from the country.[5] During our investigation, relevant departments stated that related groups of the "three forces" also took advantage of illegal border crossing in these areas for the

[3] Editorial Office of Hekou Yearbook: *2010 Yearbook of Hekou Yao Autonomous County*, 165–166.

[4] Editorial Office of Hekou Yearbook: *2010 Yearbook of Hekou Yao Autonomous County*, 166–167.

[5] According to incomplete statistics, since the 1990s, apart from better-off coastal areas, southeastern provinces, such as Yunnan and Guangxi, have become the shelters favored by fleeing

movement of core members and supplies to send religious figures for infiltration and criminal purposes, thus posing considerable threats to frontier stability and security.

Established boundaries (borders) represent a country's sovereignty over its territory. Without borders, a country will be unable to exert internal control by means of passport and visa.[6] The persisting phenomenon of illegal border crossing will damage China's image, gradually reduce Chinese citizens' (especially border residents') national identity and legal awareness, and even raise questions regarding the government's governance capabilities and the authority of China's laws.

In my personal opinion, this will weaken not only China's border management but also legal awareness in people's minds, which in turn will further damage border management in China.

1.2 Threatening Public Safety

Due to their special status, illegal immigrants face difficulties in obtaining land, houses, healthcare and employment after entering China. They face limited job opportunities, as they do not have ID cards or household registration, thus leading to tremendous life pressure, inferior social status and various forms of discrimination. All of these factors will trigger their discontent with society and lead to the frequent occurrence of alcoholism, violence and offensive actions.

During my family visits in Hekou County, illegal immigrants were not as evasive, indifferent or uncooperative as I had imagined. In contrast, they were eager to speak out their wishes. When we were paying a visit to one family, three to five people living nearby dropped in and participated in our conversation. When asked about their suggestions and requests, they gave us similar answers, namely, they hoped that the local government could improve their livelihood because their lives were "not very good, but [they] cannot go back." Their marriage with refugees or local residents could not change their status as illegal refugees and instead brought troubles for administrative tasks such as household registration, demographic census, family planning, social relief, civil assistance and medical insurance. Taking family planning as an example, most illegal marriages are "de facto marriages" that developed from illegal cohabitation. People participating in this kind of marriage violated China's laws and regulations regarding family planning for bearing children without birth permits. According to China's current exit-entry administration laws and regulations, foreigners who illegally reside in China shall be penalized and deported.[7] However, most people participating in illegal marriage have had children and integrated into

---

corrupted officials. Numerous mountain roads and paths and unique geological location have facilitated their escape. See "Secrets: why fleeing corrupted officials swarmed to Yunnan and their four escape routes." Source: http://news.xinhuanet.com/legal/2007-02/14/content_5737279.htm. Accessed September 13, 2011.

[6] [U.K.] David Held et al. *Global Transformation: Politics, Economics and Culture*, trans. Yang Xuedong et al. (Beijing: Social Sciences Academic Press, 2010), 448–449.

[7] *Exit-Entry Administration Law of the People's Republic of China*, Articles 40 and 42.

local societies. Forced deportation of these people will destroy their families and may trigger resentment from themselves, their family and others against the government or even lead to mass incidents that may cause additional public security issues.

1.3 Triggering Criminal Activities

Due to life pressure and lack of livelihood skills, illegal immigrants are prone to committing criminal activities such as prostitution,[8] theft, robbery and murder. For example, an illegal immigrant named Tao (a Vietnamese citizen from Lao Cai) entered China illegally and cohabited with someone named Xiang (a Chinese citizen from Miechang Township, Maguan County), then relocated to Maoping Village, Dulong Town to cohabit with another person, named Xiong. Later, Xiong murdered Xiang.[9] Illegal immigrants are prone to committing or participating in cross-border crimes, such as money laundry, smuggling, and human and drug trafficking.

According to relevant departments of Hekou County, from January 2010 to September 2011, there were two criminal cases committed by illegal immigrants and five cases committed by refugees. The following case is provided as an example[10]:

Case: Robbery and attempted human trafficking committed by Yang Tingrong and Liang Shishang.

At approximately 23:00 on June 6, 2010, the suspect Yang Tingrong, together with Liang Shishang (Xiang Guangxue's girlfriend, a Vietnamese illegal immigrant), Xiang Guangxue, Tao Yunjin, Li Qing (a fugitive suspect), and "Xiaohuang" (an unnamed fugitive suspect) coaxed Dong Pinping (female, born in 1983, a Vietnamese regular *sanfei*, address: Guangling Street and Zaodian Street, Hekou County) and Luo Gonghuan (female, born in 1994, a Vietnamese regular *sanfei*, address: Guangling Street and Zaodian Street, Hekou County) to arrive at crossroads on Xinhe Highway, Hekou County, under the guise of dining out. They robbed the victims and forced them to go to Bazhai Town, Maguan County. At approximately 14:00 on June 8, Yang Tingrong and several of the others mentioned above, in an attempt to take the victims to Wenshan County and sell them to a person whom they referred to simply as "Sister Zhen" for 16,000 yuan, were arrested by the police officers of the Public Security Bureau of Wenshan County when passing by Pingba Town.

---

[8] The second and third floor of a Vietnamese market located in the downtown of Hekou County, have become a typical "red-light district" where over 100 Vietnamese women have committed prostitution. See Wu Xi and Liang Jinyun, "The Refugee Issue as the Cause Affecting the Stability of China's Border Areas: Research Report on the Refugee Issue in Hekou County of Yunnan Province," *Journal of Yunnan Police Officer Academy*, no. 1 (2010). According to relevant departments, these women were of various backgrounds, including regular *sanfei*, illegal immigrants and people of legal entry and residence.

[9] Yang Shuhua, Li Lianfen and Zhang Mengmeng, "Yunnan: door-to-door inspection of *sanfei*," source: http://www.cpd.com.cn/gb/newspaper/2010-02/06/content_1284288.htm. Accessed September 15, 2011.

[10] I extend my deep gratitude to the relevant departments of Hekou County for providing this case.

In this case, the suspects were illegal immigrants and Chinese citizens, while the victims were illegal *sanfei*. In addition, the suspects in this case were illegal immigrants and Chinese citizens, while the victims were regular *sanfei*. Aside from criminal offenses, relevant departments of Hekou County have dealt with more than ten crimes endangering national security in recent years according to law. In addition, refugee settlement areas closely related to illegal immigrants in Hekou County have also become crime-prone areas. Some refugees, without sources of income, make a living by stealing, robbing and kidnapping. Other refugees collude with criminal groups and gangs and commit crimes such as selling stolen cattle, kidnapping, and drug and arms trafficking. Bickering and fighting frequently occur among refugees and with their neighbors and farm workers. Serious drug addiction and the increase in crimes caused by drug use also affect public safety and stability.[11]

2 Impact on Population Security

There are two issues regarding China's population security: controlling its population and improving the general competence of the population. Next, this book will analyze the impact of illegal immigration on the population size and general competence of the population.

2.1 Population Size

The movement of illegal immigrants to the Yunnan border areas with a high concentration of ethnic minorities has caused drastic increases in the population and competition over resources of production and life with local residents. More importantly, the children of illegal immigrants, illegal immigrants and refugees and illegal immigrants and local residents (illegal marriage) have increased the local population, impacted China's population management, and seriously affected the implementation of laws and regulations, such as the *Constitution* and the *Law on Population and Family Planning*.

Article 20 of the *Yunnan Provincial Amended Regulations on Population and Family Planning* stipulates that a rural farmer couple of any ethnic group within the jurisdiction of the border village committee is permitted to have a second child upon the approval of the county-level family planning administrative department. That is, border residents are able to have two children when the above requirement is met. During our investigation, we found that some officials and villagers believed that marriage (marriage between illegal immigrants, illegal immigrants and refugees

[11] "Thoughts on Stabilizing Local Communities in the Border Areas Inhabited by Ethnic Groups in Yunnan under the New Circumstances," source: Guangming Online, cited from http://www.xjkunlun.cn/tzgz/llyj/2011/2181948.htm. Accessed October 19, 2011.

and illegal immigrants and Chinese citizens) was a type of "de facto marriage" and should be treated as such. However, this does not seem right. According to China's current laws, regulations and judicial interpretations, after February 1, 1994, without marriage registration, such a relationship shall not be treated as de facto marriage unless both sides apply for remedial marriage registration. If they fail to do so, then their legal spousal rights shall not be protected by law. This signifies that after February 1, 1994, illegal immigrants living in China had to apply for remedial marriage registration to obtain legal marital status regardless of whether they married illegal immigrants, refugees, or Chinese citizens.

If that is the case, then how can they apply for remedial marriage registration? Suppose an illegal immigrant retains his or her citizenship. In that case, he or she must provide the following documents and materials to apply for remedial marriage registration with a Chinese citizen: (1) a valid passport or other international travel documents; and (2) a certificate of no spouse issued by the notary office or the authoritative agency in his/her home country and authenticated by the embassy (consulate) of the People's Republic of China in that country or home country's embassy (consulate) in China; or a certificate of no spouse issued by the embassy (consulate) of the applicant's home country in China.[12] Clearly, it is difficult for illegal immigrants to meet these requirements.

Let us now take a step back and suppose that both the illegal immigrant and the Chinese citizen are border residents. According to Article 3 of the *Interim Measures for Administration of Marriage Registration for Residents in Border Areas of China and Neighboring Countries* enacted by the Ministry of Civil Affairs of the People's Republic of China on February 17, 1995, if a Chinese resident and a foreign resident in border areas apply for marriage, divorce or remarriage registration, then these measures shall apply.[13] Nevertheless, Article 9 stipulates that a border resident who has illegally entered China shall be denied marriage registration. Therefore, for the "marriage" concluded between a Chinese citizen and an illegal immigrant (both of who are border residents) after February 17, 1995, if they cohabit in the name of the husband and wife before reaching the legally marriageable age, or if they conform to the marriage conditions yet cohabit in the name of the husband and wife without marriage registration, then their marriage relationship shall be null and void and outside the protection of law.[14] The measures in fact deny the "de facto" marriage. If a couple of border residents cohabited before February 17, 1995 (before the implementation of the *Interim Measures*), then they must apply for marriage registration

---

[12] See Article 5 of *China's Regulation on Marriage Registration* that came into force beginning October 1, 2003.

[13] Article 3 of the *Interim Measures for Administration of Marriage Registration for Inhabitants in Border Areas of China and Neighboring Countries* enacted by the Ministry of Civil Affairs of the People's Republic of China reads, "if a Chinese inhabitant and a foreign inhabitant in border areas apply for marriage, divorce or remarriage registration, these Measures shall apply. If one of the parties is not an inhabitant in border areas, the regulations on marriage registration by a Chinese citizen and a foreigner shall apply."

[14] Article 14 of the *Interim Measures for Administration of Marriage Registration for Inhabitants in Border Areas of China and Neighboring Countries.*

to the marriage registration authority according to the *measures*. Accordingly, if the proposed marriage is found to conform with the provisions of the *Measures*, then the couple shall be permitted to register and issued marriage certificates.[15] That is, people can apply for remedial registration for this kind of "marriage." However, the problem remains that there are two barriers to marriage registration between an illegal immigrant (border resident of neighboring countries) and a Chinese citizen (Chinese border resident). First, anyone who has illegally entered China shall be denied marriage registration (Article 9). Second, if a resident in border areas applies for marriage registration or remedial marriage registration, then he or she shall have to present the following documents and certificates: (1) the passport issued by his or her country, or the entry and exit certificate for border areas used in place of the passport and confirmed by both countries through diplomatic channels; (2) the valid identity card issued by his or her own country; (3) the marital status certificate and the certificate showing the approval of the resident's application for marriage with a Chinese citizen, provided by the governmental department of the border country (city or district) of his or her own country, and notarized by a notary office; and (4) the premarital health certificate by the hospital designated by the border county (city or district) of China.[16]

Vietnamese immigrants residing in Hekou County are unlikely to move back to their home country, except for short home visits via unauthorized crossing points. For most of them, their household registration or even nationality has been revoked, and they cannot provide the requested certificates and documents for remedial marriage registration. Therefore, after February 1, 1994, the marriages of most illegal immigrants were considered illegal (illegal cohabitation in terms of law); thus, their legal marital rights were not protected by China's laws. The children they bear are born out of wedlock. Even if having one child is against China's laws and regulations, they are not allowed to have a second child according to *Yunnan Provincial Amended Regulations on Population and Family Planning*. Among the 43 families composed of illegal immigrants and Chinese citizens (border residents) in our investigation, there were nine families without children, 19 families with one child, 11 families with two children, and four families with more children (three families with three, and one with four), totaling 54 children. In addition, in eight families composed of illegal immigrants (intermarrying illegal immigrants), there were 12 children in eight families. The birth of these 66 children caused an increase in the population in Hekou County and impacted and undermined China's laws and regulations. Scholars have also observed in their inquiries that Vietnamese refugees still believe that "having more children means greater blessings" under the influence of traditional Vietnamese family values. Due to language barriers and the difficulties in imposing family planning on refugees, it has been a prominent phenomenon that Vietnamese women tend

[15] Article 17 of the *Interim Measures for Administration of Marriage Registration for Inhabitants in Border Areas of China and Neighboring Countries*.

[16] Article 6 of the *Interim Measures for Administration of Marriage Registration for Inhabitants in Border Areas of China and Neighboring Countries*.

to have larger numbers of children, in some families more than 10. This lawless behavior occurring in China has seriously affected the implementation of China's laws and regulations on family planning.[17]

2.2 General Competence of the Population

General competence of the population, also referred to as the quality of the population, refers to the overall quality of a specific population, which includes ethical, cultural and physical qualities. Ethical quality is the consciousness that determines people's behavior, cultural quality denotes people's abilities to understand and reconstruct the world, and physical quality is the natural condition and basis of population quality. The quality and quantity of the population are interrelated and mutually constrained. Under certain circumstances, controlling the population size helps improve its quality, while improving population quality is conducive to controlling the population size. China's *Law on Population and Family Planning* aims to take comprehensive measures to control China's population size while at the same time improving the general competence of the population.

The cultural quality of illegal immigrants in Hekou County can be analyzed based on their level of education.[18] As we did not investigate regular Sanfei's level of education, and we only visited two families composed of illegal immigrants and refugees, we will take eight families composed of illegal immigrants (the couples were all illegal immigrants, 16 people in total) and 43 families composed of illegal immigrants and Chinese citizens (border residents; the wives were illegal immigrants, 43 people, and the husbands were Chinese citizens) for the analysis.[19] Therefore, we have 51 illegal immigrant families (one or both parties are illegal immigrants) and 59 illegal immigrants as our samples. The level of education of these 59 illegal immigrants is shown in Fig. 1.

A total of 49 people (83%) had undergone primary school schooling or below, eight people (14%) had gone to junior high school, and only two people (3%) had attended high school. As they had not received much education themselves, they could not help with their children's studies. In addition, most of their children went to nearby primary schools with inferior teaching quality, which reduced their opportunities for further education. Due to their poor level of education, these illegal immigrants are poorly informed about state events, guidelines, policies, laws and regulations.

---

[17] Wu Xi and Liang Jinyun (2010).

[18] The refugees' level of education was previously discussed. Most of the first-generation refugees in Hekou County did not receive much education. The government had set up four primary schools for refugee children, but their teaching methods were not very effective. Over all these years, only one refugee child received university education, and it is something that many of these people still relish today. This gives an idea of the poor level of education of the first and second generations of refugees.

[19] Here we are discussing the level of education of illegal immigrants themselves. Some of their children are still in school, so it is hard to reflect the level of education of their children.

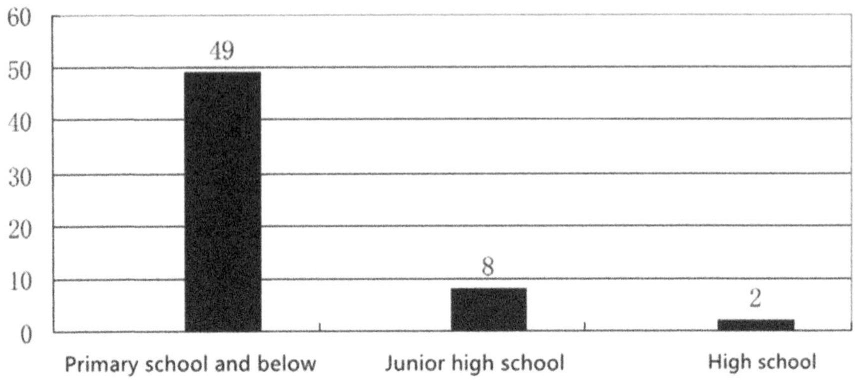

Fig. 1 Illegal immigrants' level of education

Furthermore, they have fewer job opportunities, as they do not possess ID cards or household registration. The result is that they must do farm work or run small businesses near the village. Similar to refugees, they do not have basic political rights, and they have little interest in social and political activities, such as township elections.

Rural medical insurance has played a significant role in ensuring the health of the rural population. The new rural cooperative medical insurance in the Yunnan border areas with a high concentration of ethnic minorities has been particularly constructive.[20] In 2008, the *New Rural Cooperative Medical Insurance Plan* was carried out in Hekou County. According to Article 8 of the *Plan*, rural residents with their household registered in the county were covered by the new rural cooperative medical insurance, meaning that only people with local household registration were covered.[21] The article excluded illegal immigrants without household registration who had to cover medical expenses on their own when they fell sick.

According to the statistics in recent years, the crime incidence in the refugee settlement areas of Hekou County has been higher than in other areas. Drug abuse among refugees was particularly serious. There were 36 drug addicts in the refugee settlement area in the No. 12 Brigade of Nanping Village, accounting for 26% of the entire county's drug addicts. Drug abuse not only triggers criminal activities and destabilizes social and security orders but also reduces the quality of the population and labor force.[22]

[20] The *New Rural Cooperative Medical Insurance* is a cooperative medical scheme for the rural population with multiple funding sources from individuals, units and local governments to cover the treatment costs of critical illnesses. Rural residents are encouraged to participate in the scheme voluntarily under the organization, guidance and support of governments. This has played a significant role in ensuring the rural population's access to basic health care services and alleviating their financial difficulties due to their illnesses. - author's note.

[21] The 2008 New Rural Cooperative Medical Insurance Plan of Hekou County, source: http://www.ynf.gov.cn/canton_model21/newsview.aspx?id=83546. Accessed September 16, 2011.

[22] Wu Xi and Liang Jinyun, (2010).

3 Impact on National Self-Identification

3.1 *Theoretical Hypotheses*

As previously stated, when investigating the reasons for illegal immigration, we discovered that reasons such as "speaking the same languages and sharing similar lifestyles" and "belonging to the same ethnic group, which makes it easier to have life together" can be understood from different perspectives. These are the "bonds" and "chains" of specific regional characteristics, which give immigrants a sense of affection, security and belonging to help them integrate into local communities. At the same time, families, local villagers and government officials also feel close to illegal immigrants and accept them as people who belong to the same ethnic group, thus providing them with as much assistance as possible to minimize their immigration costs and risks.

The sense of mutual identification based on shared ethnic origin has been critical in marriage among people of the same ethnic group. The question remains: does ethnic self-identification reduce or weaken national self-identification? Additionally, does it impact the social stability and security of the border areas?[23]

One representative position on the relationship between ethnic self-identification and national self-identification is that ethnic self-identification and national self-identification coexist. They are not isolated but closely related and interactive. However, these two are not positively correlated, as they do not reinforce but constrict each other. On the one hand, national self-identification is a sort of constraint on ethnic self-identification: increasingly consolidated national self-identification will inhibit ethnic self-identification. On the other hand, the latter will result in structural restraint on the former. Diversified ethnic self-identification and its enhancement will eventually offset national self-identification, thus leading to erosion thereof. Consequently, the degree of national self-identification depends on how effectively one can balance his or her national identity and ethnic identity.[24] According to this mild viewpoint of their correlation, these two can interact and affect each other. Meanwhile, they are mutually restraining, but not excessively, simply "inhibiting" or "eroding" each other to "a certain extent." Another viewpoint argues that national self-identification and

---

[23] "Ethnic self-identification" as described in this book refers to the identification with ethnic groups in China's frontier areas. It is the identification or confirmation of the members of a ethnic group of the group that they belong to. It is also a process of the members' acceptance of their ethnic group. It can be reflected as their sense of belonging, emotional attachment, political allegiance, sense of responsibility, identification and praise of ethnic culture, celebration of ethnic spirit, protection of ethnic image, and real actions for the interests of his or her ethnic group. See Zhou Ping, "Self-identification in the Perspective of Frontier Governance." *Journal of Yunnan Normal University (Philosophy and Social Sciences)*, no. 1 (2009): 11. National self-identification refers to the identification with the country by ethnic groups in China's frontier areas. It is the confirmation of their relations with the country by ethnic groups, and is represented by their sense of belonging, political allegiance, sense of responsibility, national pride and patriotism. See Zhou Ping, "On the Building of China's National Self-Identification." *Academic Exploration*, no. 6 (2009): 37.

[24] Zhou Ping (2009).

ethnic self-identification are complementary and mutually reinforcing and confrontational at the same time to a greater extent. They are in a competing relationship, as the former focuses on the ethnic group, while the latter focuses on the entire nation. The increase in the sense of belonging to and acceptance of a particular ethnic group leads to decreased acceptance of a nation-state, and vice versa.[25]

I believe that if the theory of the relationship between ethnic self-identification and national self-identification is tenable, then it will be applicable to illegal immigrants' ethnic and national self-identification when moving to China.

Taking "Vietnamese wives" as an example, the main reasons for marrying someone from the same ethnic group are "speaking the same languages and sharing similar lifestyles" and "belonging to the same ethnic group, which makes it easier to have life together." This strong sense of belonging and identification with their ethnic group should reduce identification with their country of birth (country of nationality), i.e., the identification with their original nation-state. Furthermore, aside from these reasons, are there other reasons that their Chinese husbands married them? Is their ethnic self-identification contradictory to the national self-identification of China? Based on the information gathered from our investigation, this book will perform analyses from the perspectives of both the Vietnamese wives and their husbands.

3.2 Conclusion

(1) **Vietnamese Wives' Ethnic and National Self-Identification**

Upon reviewing the inquiry notes about the 43 couples between illegal immigrants and Chinese citizens (border residents), I realized that the relationship between ethnic and national self-identification was extremely complicated and inconsistent with the theory mentioned above.

Among the 43 respondents of our questionnaire, 42 came from Vietnam. Ethnic self-identification was a critical reason for their decision to marry someone in China. Their willingness to marry a husband of the same ethnic group indicates strong ethnic self-identification. When answering "Which country do you think you belong to now?", 36 out of 42 respondents (85.7%) said "Vietnam," five people (11.9%) said "None, I am stateless," and one respondent (2.4%) said "Not sure." Over 80% of these women still believed they were Vietnamese after having lived in China for several years. The answers were out of my expectation.

I believe it represents their strong sense of ethnic pride and extended identification with their country of birth. That is, their ethnic self-identification of having the same ethnic origin as their husbands did not impact or offset their national identification with their home country. This may have resulted from two reasons. First, their ethnic self-identification is simply a sense of security and belonging of marrying someone of the same ethnic origin. It is one of the considerations of lowering immigration costs

[25] He Danpeng (2009).

and risks. The stronger self-identification they have, the greater their sense of security and belonging will be. At the same time, their strong ethnic self-identification is not contradictory to their identification with their home country. Second, most of them were adults of deep identification with their birth country when they came to China. Aside from ethnic self-identification, they had other reasons for coming to China, such as pursuing a better livelihood and a satisfying love life. However, these reasons or factors are not in direct conflict with their national self-identification.

On the other hand, another factor may be dissatisfaction with their current status in China. Their marriages are not legally recognized in China. It is unlikely that they will obtain remedial marriage registration or Chinese citizenship. However, without Chinese citizenship, they could not obtain ID cards or household registration; thus, they could not enjoy the same welfare benefits and job opportunities as local villagers. They felt inferior and disappointed due to these differentiated treatments and believed they were still Vietnamese instead of Chinese, or they replied, "None, I am stateless."

Supposing the hypothesis holds up, that is to say, their ethnic self-identification does not directly impact or offset the identification with their home country, then it reveals that ethnic self-identification and national self-identification are not "competing." Another question remains, does their ethnic self-identification impact or offset the identification with their country of residence (i.e., China)? When answering the question "Do you want to obtain Chinese citizenship (become a Chinese citizen)," all these women replied "Yes" and expressed their willingness to become Chinese citizens. Although their answers were not unexpected, I was still bewildered.

As these Vietnamese wives maintained identification with their home country, why did they want to obtain Chinese citizenship and become Chinese citizens? Does this willingness indicate the identification with their country of residence (i.e., China)? Is it possible to identify with two countries at the same time? What is the relationship between their identification with China and that with their ethnic groups?

After reviewing the questionnaire and the notes I had taken, I concluded three reasons for their wish to obtain Chinese citizenship. First, real feelings in daily life. They believed that obtaining Chinese citizenship could solve many practical problems, such as ID cards, household registration and welfare benefits. Second, helpless and pessimistic thoughts, such as little possibility of moving back to Vietnam. As their household registration or even citizenship had been revoked, it was impossible for them to return, and their husbands and children would not go to Vietnam. Third, through home visits by illegal border crossing and contact with family members, they knew about the living standards of Vietnam, and after comparison, they realized that life in China was more appealing. However, their inner conflict made their answers contradictory. Their willingness or wishes to obtain Chinese citizenship indicated their identification with their country of residence (China), yet this self-identification was held down by the unsatisfactory current situation. Supposing they successfully obtained Chinese citizenship and the issues that made them feel inferior and disappointed were resolved, then their identification with China would be intensified and strengthened, while their identification with their home country would be gradually weakened and decreased.

However, the key point remains: the factor that weakens or offsets their national self-identification, or inactivates or enhances it, does not constitute their ethnic self-identification. When they undergo drastic changes in national self-identification, factors other than ethnic self-identification play a role.

(2) **Ethnic Self-Identification and National Self-Identification of Chinese Husbands**

During my inquiries from the husbands of 34 Vietnamese women about why they married Vietnamese wives, they were hesitant to answer the question. Most of them said, "they speak the same languages and share similar lifestyles" and "they belong to the same ethnic group, which makes it easier to have life together." However, they were reluctant to mention other reasons. Only a few (two) people said, "I cannot find a [local] wife" or "it is difficult to find a [local] wife."

As indicated previously, local villagers who marry foreign women are generally considered "poorly qualified" to be husbands. There are also financial reasons why one might choose to marry a foreign woman (it costs tens of thousands of yuan or even more to marry a local woman). Marrying a foreign woman illegally is always a "last resort". Their families and friends can usually understand their situation and accept their "foreign wives" with whom they share the same ethnic origin. For local villagers and government officials, it is not a major problem either. As one local official put it, "there is not much we can do about it."

It is thus clear that ethnic self-identification is one important reason why local bachelors marry "foreign wives." However, it is not the decisive factor. The decisive factors are the "difficulties in finding a wife," the parental pressure to marry and bear children, and economic hardship. They do not believe that ethnic self-identification is in direct conflict with national self-identification. In contrast, they realize that, whether consciously or unconsciously, the fact that their native country is more prosperous and developed makes them attractive in the eyes of their foreign wives. In other words, marrying a foreign wife can enhance their national self-identification. Of course, if we look at this dialectically, we may find that they are weak in legal and civic awareness by marrying illegal immigrants. Therefore, when their wives and children face differentiated treatment in employment, education and welfare, it may have what Professor Zhou Ping referred to as "a corrosive effect on national self-identification, which can lead to its erosion.". The offsetting impacts on national self-identification are not, or at least not mainly, based on ethnic self-identification but dissatisfaction with the real social and living environment.

The American scholar Samuel Huntington believes that the crisis of national identity posed serious threats to national security. In the book *Who Are We?: The Challenges to America's National Identity*, he proposes his views about national security featuring the threat posed by immigration.[26] He holds that the dual identity, allegiance and citizenship caused by immigration have blurred national identity and caused fragmented America's national identity. According to Huntington, nothing is

[26] Like other overseas scholars, Samuel Huntington included both legal and illegal immigrants in his theory. –Author's note.

more important than national identity.[27] He believes the reasons for the weak national identity of the immigrant-receiving country are dual identity and allegiance to both the home country and country of residence and dual citizenship of immigrants. The realities of these Vietnamese wives are not fully consistent with Huntington's views because they do not possess dual citizenship. Furthermore, Huntington holds that the reasons for weak national identity are dual identity, allegiance and citizenship, but he does not mention ethnic self-identification or the competing relationship between national and ethnic self-identification.

In Huntington's theory, the term "immigrants" refers to both legal and illegal immigrants. However, illegal immigrants cannot obtain dual citizenship within a short time, as China's laws do not recognize dual citizenship. Vietnamese wives developed fragmented national identity toward their home country and the country of residence, as well as due to lengthy stateless status. However, the fundamental reason for fragmented national identity is not the competing relationship between national and ethnic self-identification, their dual identity, allegiance or citizenship, but instinctive response to the uncomfortable reality they must face.

Therefore, in my personal opinion, the prevailing ethnic self-identification among Vietnamese wives is not directly or necessarily related to weakened or blurred national self-identification. Ethnic self-identification is merely one essential factor for marrying someone in China. The practical problems that remain unresolved are the reasons for weakened or blurred self-identification with the country of residence (China) of themselves and their families. However, their problems cannot be addressed under China's current laws and regulations. These persistent and unresolved problems will become significant factors affecting the stability and security of China's border areas. Chinese scholar Tian Yuan wrote in the conclusion part of his book *Immigrants and National Security: Research on the Derivation of Threats and Their Conditions*," systematic discrimination against immigrants[28] and their ethnic groups[29] in the immigrant-receiving country will prevent immigrants and their ethnic groups from building loyalty and trust toward it and provide motives for their rebellion to directly undermine their interests.[30]

Similarly, the Chinese husbands of these Vietnamese women will also weaken or blur their national self-identification with China for the same reasons. Fragmented national self-identification will gradually hurt their pride in the country for marrying "a foreign wife," which will in turn harm their national self-identification.

---

[27] [United States] Samuel Huntington, (2005).

[28] Tian Yuan held that illegal immigrants were categorized as immigrants, and thus they should be included in relevant arguments about immigrants. Tian Yuan, *Immigrants and National Security: Research on the Derivation of Threats and Their Conditions* (Beijing: World Affairs Press, 2010), 15.

[29] In my personal opinion, a nation is a group defined in a political sphere. It carries the meaning of a country and a nation, i.e., a group under a country or government. In contrast, an ethnic group is a group defined from the kinship and cultural spheres. It is a group that distinguishes itself from others by language, appearance, and customs. Illegal immigrants are such a particular group.

[30] Tian Yuan (2010).

4 Impact on International Relations

4.1 Illegal Immigration Has Significant Implications for International Relations

Illegal immigration is a cross-border and international phenomenon in nature; therefore, it has significant implications for international relations, particularly the relationship between a sending country and a receiving country. I believe that immigration (especially illegal immigration) has an interactive relationship with international relations, especially between a sending country and a receiving country. This interaction can be either a virtuous cycle or a vicious one. The immigration issue, if effectively resolved, will maintain and promote friendly exchanges among countries. Countries maintaining cordial relations based on equality and mutual benefits may properly cope with illegal immigration through coordination and cooperation. On the other hand, if not handled properly, the immigration issue will damage or exacerbate normal bilateral relations. Countries that do not enjoy normal relations will find it challenging to communicate and cooperate regarding this issue and may even provoke disputes or conflicts under this pretext. In short, illegal immigration is a critical factor that must not be ignored, although it is not the only factor affecting international relations.

The UK scholar David Held draws the following conclusions on the impact of immigration in the globalization era on nation-states' autonomy and sovereignty. First, illegal migratory movements indicate that many nation-states have limited capacities to protect their boundaries. Second, it is difficult to end illegal immigration through border monitoring. Third, it is imperative to control and adjust immigration policies and carry out cross-border cooperation. Fourth, immigration has substantial implications for the internal affairs of developed capitalist countries.[31] David Held points out clearly that illegal immigration inevitably affects the relations among countries. It is impossible to protect state boundaries or stop the movement of illegal immigrants by any country on its own. Countries must adjust their immigration policies and enhance international cooperation, since illegal immigration has significantly influenced the internal affairs of developed capitalist countries.

There are numerous examples of the implications of international migration, especially illegal immigration, on international relations. Taking the US as an example, due to historical and ideological reasons, the US and Cuba have been hostile against each other for many years, and the Cuban missile crisis in the 1960s increased the tensions between the two countries. To overthrow the socialist regime in Cuba, the US government accepted Cuban citizens who managed to enter the country by any means and arranged settlements for them. This policy was implemented until 1994, when the US began to impose certain restrictions on immigration from Cuba. Despite this,

[31] [U.K.] David Held et al. (2001).

under the "wet feet, dry feet policy," Cuban immigrants enjoyed preferential treatments compared with immigrants from other countries.[32] In the 1960s and 1970s, the US accepted and settled over 800,000 Cuban refugees, most of whom were illegal immigrants, and treated them as strategic tools to bring down the regime. In the end, it led to the Bay of Pigs Invasion in 1961. After the end of the Cold War, the relations between the US and Cuba improved but had not yet normalized. The Elián González incident[33] was the best illustration of the vicious circle of immigration (especially illegal immigration) and international relations (especially the relationship between the sending country and the receiving country).

In contrast, the US's solution to illegal immigration from Mexico achieved different results.[34] At the beginning of the twenty-first century, an average of 170,000 Mexican immigrants swarmed to the US every year and caused frequent arguments between the two countries over immigration, especially illegal immigration.[35] On October 26, 2006, President George W. Bush signed an Act to authorize the federal government to build walls and install cameras, moving object detectors and other barriers along the 1,100 km of US-Mexico borders to prevent illegal immigrants from entering the US. These measures were objected by Mexican officials. However, no large-scale conflict has ever occurred between the two countries due to immigration issues. This was because the US, on the one hand, reduced or exempted some of the Mexican government's debts to help promote its economic development. On the other hand, it enacted immigration reform to accept some immigrants from Mexico while at the same time providing a path to legal status for illegal immigrants. In addition, led by the US, the two countries carried out continuous negotiations regarding immigration. They managed to bring tranquility to border areas and harmonize bilateral relations, setting an example of a virtuous cycle of immigration (especially illegal immigration) and international relations (especially the relationship between the sending country and the receiving country).

---

[32] America and Cuba reached an agreement in 1995 to jointly resolve the illegal immigration from Cuba. According to the agreement, the US implemented the so-called "wet feet, dry feet policy" toward Cuban immigrants. Wet feet referred to the Cuban immigrants caught on the water, who would be sent back to their home country. However, those who made it to shore (dry feet) had a chance to obtain legal status in the US. Li Fangtian, "The Research on International Immigration and Immigration Policies" (PhD diss., Nankai University, 2009), 59.

[33] On November 22, 1999, a 7-year-old boy named Elián González was brought to the US by his mother, who had attempted to sneak into the country. A total of 11 illegal immigrants, including his mother, were found dead on the beach. Elián González was handed over to his paternal great-uncle Lázaro González in Miami. With the support of Cuban authorities, his father Juan González demanded that Elián González be returned to Cuba. However, this request was obstructed by the anti-Cuba forces in Miami, which made it a political issue. Under the decision of an American court, Elián González returned to Cuba. Source: http://www.people.com.cn/GB/channel2/17/20000629/123236.html. Cited from Xu Junhua, "The Study on the Problems of Legal Control of Illegal Immigration" (PhD diss., Wuhan University, 2005), 37.

[34] The materials about America's settlement of the persistent illegal immigration issue with Mexico were cited from Li Fangtian, "The Research on International Immigration and Immigration Policies" (PhD diss., Nankai University, 2009), 135–136.

[35] Zhou Yu'e and Bai Qingzhe, "International Immigration and Contemporary International Security: Impulses, Interactions and Challenges," *Around Southeast Asia*, no. 1 (2006).

4.2 Illegal Immigration and China-Vietnam Relations

China, traditionally an immigrant-sending country, has faced immigrant influx in recent years. The immigration issue in Yunnan is particularly prominent, as the province is at the forefront of China's opening-up along its southwestern borders. The governance of illegal immigration in Yunnan border areas with a high concentration of ethnic minorities will influence the stability and security of China's border areas and its relations with neighboring countries to its southeast.[36]

Let us take Vietnam, the country adjacent to Hekou County, as an example. China-Vietnam relations have gone through numerous twists and turns. Among the various factors affecting their bilateral relations, the protracted immigration (especially illegal immigration) issue was particularly prominent. On June 9, 1978, China's Ministry of Foreign Affairs issued the *Statement on the Expulsion of Chinese Residents by Vietnam*, in which it pointed out that, in early 1977, the Vietnamese side implemented the policy of "clearing up the border areas" in the provinces sharing borders with China, and in October 1977, it began to expel Chinese residents from the northern part. The statement strongly protested the massive anti-Chinese campaign launched in April 1978, stating that it was an incorrect step to blindly follow the Soviet Union's anti-Chinese campaign and undermine China-Vietnam relations. By the end of May 1978, over 100,000 Chinese residents had been driven back to China.[37] Vietnam's anti-Chinese campaign was one of the main reasons for the 1979 war between the two countries.

In the 1990s, China and Vietnam began to gradually repair their relations. The General Secretaries of the Communist Party of China (CPC) and the Communist Party of Vietnam (CPV) established future-oriented guidelines for ensuring long-term stability, good-neighbor friendship and all-round cooperation in China-Vietnam relations in the twenty-first century. The improvement of bilateral relations under the guidelines has laid a foundation for solving the persistent immigration issue between the two countries. China and Vietnam cosigned the *1991 Interim Agreement on Handling Border Issues between the People's Republic of China and the Socialist Republic of Vietnam* through negotiation and thus reached agreement on relevant border issues. Specific regulations on personnel exchanges in border areas were included in the *Interim Agreement*.[38]

The normalization of China-Vietnam relations has played a significant role in solving illegal immigration between the two countries. Competent authorities on both

---

[36] According to relevant departments, many Chinese citizens who had illegally entered Myanmar's border areas obtained border resident IDs of Myanmar, and called themselves "Cambodian Chinese." They lived in Myanmar, found jobs and married "by legal means." They retained their Chinese citizenship at the same time, and some of them still held Chinese ID cards. Their behavior was against the mandatory requirement of no dual citizenship in China's *Nationality Law*, and affected the normal relations between China and Myanmar.

[37] The Chronology of the Communist Party of China (1978), source: http://www.cnr.cn/zhuanti1/jd/zgdsj/200606/t20060620_504227075.html. Accessed September 18, 2011.

[38] Chapter III of the *Interim Agreement on Handling Border Issues between the People's Republic of China and the Socialist Republic of Vietnam.*

sides enhanced cooperation on illegal immigration control by establishing the mechanism of working meetings. Taking Honghe Prefecture as an example, the Public Security Bureau of Honghe Prefecture and Lai Chau Provincial Police Department of Vietnam held the third working meeting in Mengzi City, China, on October 26, 2010. To better solve the problem, the two sides made the following decisions: (1) strictly implement the agreements reached between the two governments and the Ministries of Public Security, increase the public awareness of laws and regulations, vigorously combat illegal border crossing, and prevent people from entering the other country for illegal residence and employment; (2) further increase public awareness of border management regulations, permit the border crossing of legal certificate holders only, and prevent and reduce the occurrence of illegal border crossing; (3) uphold the equivalent and favorable principle of personnel exchanges, earnestly implement the *Interim Agreement on Handling Border Issues between the People's Republic of China and Socialist Republic of Vietnam*, allow the access of border residents holding illegal entry and exit certificates to the border areas of the other country for family visits, medical treatment and business; and (4) educate or penalize them dorongton for illegal employment, exit certificates to the border areas according to the other country for family visits, or over their business.[39]

Despite the issues in implementing these decisions, the mechanism of working meetings between the two sides shall be fully recognized due to its role in resolving illegal immigration. At the same time, we must remain attentive to the measures taken by the Vietnamese side. For example, the Vietnamese government issued *Paper No. 135* (*Programme 135*) in 1997, which included the aspects of stabilizing ethnic groups, increasing productivity, accelerating the development of the socialist course, and infrastructure construction. The Vietnamese government also carried out a series of preferential policies and measures regarding border areas and border residents according to this paper. Taking Lao Cai Province next to Hekou County as an example, it made full use of preferential policies provided by the central government while exerting its advantages to make comprehensive plans and take various measures to improve the construction of border economic zones. At the end of 2002, the provincial government issued the decision of granting preferential policies of building four key economic zones (*Paper No. 496/QD-UB*), which stipulated that "stabilizing policies toward border areas and border residents" and "tax refund policies" were to be included among the "economic and social policies." Time will tell if these policies will increase the "pull factors" or "attraction" to China's citizens (particularly border residents), and if they will encourage illegal Vietnamese immigrants to move back, or possibly even attract the border residents of Hekou County to relocate to Vietnam. In the meantime, we must pay close attention to the effects of these policies.

[39] "Policemen from Honghe Prefecture and Lai Chau Province Join Hands in Cracking down Crimes," source: http://honghehanizuyizu.mofcom.gov.cn/aarticle/gaikuang/201010/20101007217472.html. Accessed October 8, 2011.

References

He Danpeng. (2009). The research on cross-border ethnic problems from the perspective of frontier governance: A case study of southeast China's cross-border ethnic groups. MA diss., Yunnan University.

[U.K.] Held, David et al. (2001). *Global Transformation: Politics, Economics and Culture*. Translated by Yang Xuedong et al. Beijing: Social Sciences Academic Press.

[United States] Huntington, Samuel. (2005). *Who Are We?: The Challenges to America's National Identity*. Translated by Cheng Kexiong. Beijing: Xinhua Publishing House.

Wang Yizhou. (2010). On non-traditional security: based on the analysis of the relations between state and society. In The Center for Non-Traditional Security and Peaceful Development Studies of Zhejiang University ed. *Non-Traditional Security Studies*, no. 1. Beijing: Intellectual Property Publishing House.

Wu Xi, & Liang Jinyun. (2010). The refugee issue as the cause affecting the stability of China's border areas: Research report on the refugee issue in Hekou county of Yunnan Province. *Journal of Yunnan Police Officer Academy*, 1.

Yuan, T. (2010). *Immigrants and national security: The research on the derivation of threats and their conditions*. World Affairs Press.

Zhou Ping. (2009). On the building of China's national self-identification. *Academic Exploration*, 6.

Chapter 5
Practices of Illegal Immigration Governance in Yunnan Border Areas with a High Concentration of Ethnic Minorities

As stated earlier, this book identifies four elements of governance: who (subject), why (reasons), how (methods) and effects (comprehensive assessment). The previous chapter discussed the impact of illegal immigration in the Yunnan border areas with a high concentration of ethnic minorities and answered the question of "why" (negative impacts on the local society). The current situation of illegal immigration in these areas was also described to illustrate the governance effects. Now, we will explore the questions of who governs and how. This chapter will analyze how illegal immigration governance has actually been carried out, and the following chapter will elaborate on how, ideally, it should be carried out. In other words, we will analyze the illegal immigration governance in this area both as it is and as it ought to be.

1 The Governing Bodies

The governing bodies are those organs and institutions charged with illegal immigration governance. Among various standards of classification, this book adopts two of them: vertical classification, which divides the subjects into international organizations, states and local governments, and horizontal classification, namely, into the military, public security and judicial authorities.

1.1 Vertical Structure of Governing Bodies

The vertical structure refers to the relationship among different governing bodies in an administrative hierarchy. The vertical structure of illegal immigration governance can be divided into international organizations, states and local governments. It should be noted that by becoming a member of an international organization, a country transfers part of its sovereign rights to this organization and thus assumes the corresponding

G. Luo, *The Issues of Illegal Immigration and its Solutions in the Minority-Border Regions in Yunnan Province, China*, https://doi.org/10.1007/978-981-19-1249-8_5

obligations while enjoying its rights. The organization has the right to handle the breach or default of its charter by any member state in accordance with the provisions therein. In other words, the organization is in a vertical supervisory or managerial relationship with its member states. In the same vein, whether in a federal state or a unitary state, local governments are hierarchically supervised or managed by the central government.

(1) International Organizations—Supranational Governance

An international organization refers to a standing body established by a treaty by governments, civil society or individuals from two or more countries for the purpose of specific international cooperation. The following definition is adopted in this book: it is an intergovernmental organization, i.e., a standing body established by an international treaty by two or more state governments to seek cooperation and serve their common interests.[1] International organizations can be divided into global and regional organizations according to their geological coverage. Global organizations are open to all countries without limitations regarding the scope of activities. Regional organizations are organizations and groups composed of countries in the same region or countries with the same goal of safeguarding regional interests, although not within the same region.[2] Based on the research requirements of this book, I select the UN and IOM as examples of global organizations and the Shanghai Cooperation Organization (SCO) and Association of Southeast Asian Nations (ASEAN) as representative regional organizations.

1. United Nations

The UN has provided a definition of immigrants[3] but not illegal immigrants. Due to the considerable differences in the understanding of illegal immigrants among states, it is difficult for the UN to draft a unified definition through coordinated consultations. Therefore, in terms of illegal immigration governance, the UN has focused on the main forms of illegal immigration, i.e., smuggling and related offenses, instead of illegal immigrants, and has reserved the right to deal with illegal stay to individual states according to their domestic laws. Xu Junhua acknowledges this fact but argues that the reason for it is that it is under the sovereignty of states to deal with illegal immigrants after their entry into the destination country, and it is inappropriate to apply international law at the current stage. However, as the repatriation of illegal immigrants involves both the country of destination and the country of origin, this issue is often resolved via negotiations or bilateral treaties. It depends on the future circumstances as to whether a unified definition is required by referring to relevant international legal documents.[4]

---

[1] Shao Jin, (2000).

[2] Ibid., 247.

[3] The UN definition of international immigrants is individuals who have resided in a country other than their country of origin for more than one year, except diplomats residing in other countries and military personnel of peacekeeping troops stationed in other countries. See Li Minghuan, (2005).

[4] Xu Junhua, (2005).

Regardless of the reason, the UN chose combating the smuggling of illegal immigrants and related activities as the starting point in illegal immigration governance. Within this mindset, the UN enacted the *International Convention Relating to Stowaways* in 1957. In December 2000, 118 countries and regions signed the *United Nations Convention against Transnational Organized Crime and the Protocols* thereto (the *Protocol against the Smuggling of Migrants by Land, Sea and Air and Protocol to Prevent, Suppress and Punish Trafficking in Persons, Especially Women and Children*). China's Vice Foreign Minister Wang Guangya signed the Convention on behalf of the Chinese government and later deposited the instrument of ratification to UN Secretary General Kofi Annan on September 23, 2003. The United Nations *Convention against Transnational Organized Crime* is significant in being the first international instrument in the battle against transnational organized crime. It has established the goal of better preventing and combating transnational organized crime through international cooperation and thus provided the legal foundation for such cooperation among countries. It includes the provisions of confiscating the proceeds of cross-border migrant smuggling and related crimes and the provisions of criminal jurisdiction, extradition and international cooperation regarding such crimes, thereby setting out the legal basis for combatting crimes related to illegal immigration.

2. International Organization for Migration

The IOM currently includes 122 member states, and in June 2001, China became an observer state. On September 5, 2006, Ambassador Sha Zukang, Permanent Representative of the People's Republic of China to the United Nations Office at Geneva and other international organizations in Switzerland, signed the *Agreement on the Establishment of an IOM Liaison Office between the People's Republic of China* and the International Organization for Migration with the IOM Director General, Brunson McKinley.

The functions of the organization are as follows: (1) Make arrangements for the organized transfer of migrants, for whom existing facilities are inadequate or who would not otherwise be able to relocate, without special assistance, to countries offering opportunities for orderly migration; (2) Oversee the organized transfer of refugees, displaced persons and other individuals in need of international migration services for whom arrangements may be made between the organization and the states concerned, including those states undertaking to receive them; (3) Provide, at the request of and in agreement with the states concerned, migration services such as recruitment, selection, processing, language training, orientation activities, medical examination, placement, activities facilitating reception and integration, advisory services on migration questions, and other assistance as is in accord with the aims of the organization; (4) Provide similar services as requested by states, or in cooperation with other interested international organizations, for voluntary return migration, including voluntary repatriation; and (5) Provide a practical forum of solutions to the international and other organizations views for the coordination of international reputations, including cooperation and other issues on and return migration issues to develop a forum.[5]

Beginning in the 1990s, the IOM shifted its focus on cooperation with governments in acquiring and providing information on illegal migration. It has made prominent contributions to combating illegal migration through the international conferences convened at its initiative and the declarations concluded thereof.[6]

3. Shanghai Cooperation Organization

The SCO's purposes and mandates are to safeguard and enhance regional peace, security and stability and to jointly combat terrorism, separatism, extremism, drug and illicit arms trafficking, and other cross-border crimes. It is written in its declaration that it will "work out corresponding documents of multinational cooperation in a bid to curb illegal arms smuggling, drug trafficking, illegal migration, and other criminal activities." By integrating illegal immigration governance with combating three forces (of separatism, extremism and terrorism), the SCO has made illegal immigration governance more critical in national security strategies and has established a more effective platform for promoting China's international cooperation in illegal immigration governance.

4. Association of Southeast Asian Nations

On November 4, 2002, the 6th ASEAN-China Summit was held in Cambodia's capital, Phnom Penh. The Summit culminated in the signing of the *Framework Agreement on Comprehensive Economic Cooperation between the People's Republic of China and the Association of Southeast Asian Nations*, including the decision to establish an ASEAN-China Free Trade Area by 2010. Chinese and ASEAN leaders signed the *Joint Declaration of ASEAN and China on Cooperation in the Field of Non-Traditional Security Issues*. The Declaration stated that they were deeply concerned over the increasingly serious nature of nontraditional security issues such as trafficking in illegal drugs, people-smuggling including trafficking of women and children, sea piracy, terrorism, arms-smuggling, money-laundering, international economic crime and cybercrime, which have become major factors of uncertainty affecting regional and international security and are posing new challenges to regional and international peace and stability.

With the completion of the ASEAN-China Free Trade Area, there will be more frequent personnel, material and financial exchanges between the two sides, thus posing severe challenges to border management orders and, as a result, causing cross-border immigrant smuggling and related crimes to become increasingly prominent. Increased cooperation is the only way to tackle these challenges altogether.

[5] Article 1, paragraph 1 of the *IOM Constitution*.

[6] Regarding the significance of these international conferences and their contribution to illegal immigration governance, see Xu Junhua, (2005).

(2) National Governance

Countries are the subject of illegal immigration governance, and their roles differ internally and externally. Externally, they join international organizations, international conventions or bilateral treaties on an equal and voluntary basis and communicate with other countries on illegal immigration governance to seek common grounds and coordinated responses while setting aside differences. Internally, based on the highest jurisdiction, they exercise legislative, enforcement and administrative rights to formulate and implement relevant policies and to coordinate with relevant departments and governments to implement comprehensive illegal immigration governance. The differentiated roles stem from two fundamental features of sovereignty, i.e., the right to independence (external) and the highest right (internal).

Let us take China as an example. Based on the "five principles of peaceful coexistence," China has made independent and autonomous decisions in joining the international organizations and conventions that it has deemed appropriate and has signed bilateral treaties on preventing illegal immigration and enhancing border management with many countries.[7]

In terms of domestic legislation, China's legislature has adopted a series of laws and regulations, including the *Exit-Entry Administration Law* (effective since July 1, 2013), which was approved on June 30, 2012, at the 27th session of the Standing Committee of the 11th National People's Congress. It used the expression of "illegal entry, illegal residence and illegal employment," but not "illegal immigration," and merely stipulated the measures to address *sanfei*. Meanwhile, in criminal legislation, violation of China's exit and entry management rules was criminalized in the *1979 Criminal Law*. On March 5, 1994, *Supplementary Provisions on Severely Cracking Down on the Crime of Organizing People to Illegally Cross National Borders (Frontiers) or of Illegally Shipping People Across National Borders (Frontiers)* were adopted by the Standing Committee of the 8th National People's Congress. The clauses of such crimes were added to the *1997 Criminal Law* based on its 1979 edition and its *Supplementary Provisions*.

(3) Local Governments—Subnational Governance

According to China's *Constitution*, local people's governments at all levels are the executive organs of the local state organs of power at their respective levels; they are the local state administrative organs at their respective levels. Therefore, local people's governments at all levels are the bodies directly in charge of illegal immigration governance. It is their responsibility to implement relevant CPC and state guidelines and policies and exercise their administrative and enforcement rights.

According to Article 11 of the *Interim Agreement on Handling Border Issues between the People's Republic of China and the Socialist Republic of Vietnam* (signed

[7] For example, China signed the *Interim Agreement on Handling Border Issues between the People's Republic of China and Socialist Republic of Vietnam*, the *Boundary Treaty between the People's Republic of China and People's Democratic Republic of Laos* and the *Agreement between the Government of the People's Republic of China and Government of the Union of Myanmar on the China-Myanmar Border Areas Management and Cooperation* with Vietnam, Laos and Myanmar.

on and effective as of November 7, 1991), local governments in the border areas, provincial governments of Yunnan and Vietnam's Lai Chau, Lao Cai and Ha Giang have established a counterpart liaison system. Local governments from both sides are responsible for carrying out the following activities related to the Interim Agreement: 1. Implementation of the instructions issued by their respective governments; 2. Management, inspection and maintenance of the boundary lines and markers under each country's jurisdiction; 3. Civil issues in the border areas (including production and business activities, marriage and relocation, traditional networking events and daily exchanges); 4. Public security issues in the border areas (including cooperation and coordination on public security management and the fight against drugs and smuggling); 5. Other issues to be handled by local governments under the approval of the two governments. This signifies that the provincial government of Yunnan is authorized to cooperate with Vietnamese local governments regarding border issues, including illegal immigration governance. Meanwhile, the Provincial Government of Yunnan also formulated corresponding local regulations[8] to regulate exit and entry in border areas, which has been vital for the governance of illegal immigration.

Hekou County is an area with a high concentration of ethnic populations and is under autonomous rule. According to China's *Constitution*, the organs of self-government of areas under autonomous rule are the people's congresses and people's governments of autonomous regions, autonomous prefectures and autonomous counties.[9] People's congresses of areas under autonomous rule possess the power to enact regulations on the exercise of autonomy and other separate regulations in light of the political, economic and cultural characteristics of the nationality or nationalities in the areas concerned.[10] The *Law of the People's Republic of China on Regional Ethnic Autonomy* entails a provision regarding separate regulations of the people's congresses of ethnic autonomous areas of the same wording.[11] In addition, it states that "If a resolution, decision, order or instruction of a State organ at a higher level does not suit the conditions in an ethnic autonomous area, the organ of self-government of the area may either implement it with certain alterations or cease implementing it after reporting to and receiving the approval of the State organ at a higher level; the said State organ shall give a reply within 60 days from the date of receipt of the report."[12]

No provisions regarding illegal immigration are to be found in either the *1986 Autonomous Regulations of Honghe Hani & Yi Autonomous Prefecture* or the *1990 Autonomous Regulations of Hekou Yao Autonomous Prefecture.* I also observed from the inquiries of various sources that there were no separate regulations regarding

[8] *Regulations of Yunnan Province on Border Management, Yunnan Province Administrative Rules for Entry-Exit of External Border Residents in the Chinese-Myanmar Border Areas, Yunnan Province Provisional Administrative Rules for Entry-Exit of Chinese Citizens in the China-Myanmar Border Areas*, and *Yunnan Province Administrative Rules for Entry-Exit in the China-Vietnam and China-Myanmar Border Areas.*

[9] Article 112 of the *Constitution of the People's Republic of China.*

[10] Article 116 of the *Constitution of the People's Republic of China.*

[11] Article 19 of the *Law of the People's Republic of China on Regional National Autonomy.*

[12] Article 20 of the Law of the People's Republic of China on Regional National Autonomy.

illegal immigration of Honghe Prefecture and Hekou County, nor any reply or report of a resolution, decision, order or instruction of a State organ at a higher level which needed to be implemented with certain alterations or ceased. Therefore, the legal grounds of illegal immigration governance in Hekou County are (1) relevant national laws, regulations and policies and (2) resolutions, decisions, orders or instructions of a state organ at a higher level.

1.2 Horizontal Structure of Governing Bodies

The horizontal structure includes three distinct branches: the army (military and armed police forces), public security authorities (public security and state security), and judicial authorities (courts, procuratorates and the Ministry of Justice).[13] Although they do not form a chain of command, they are closely related to one another. For example, procuratorates have the right to supervise the investigative activities of public security authorities. In fact, horizontal subjects of illegal immigration governance also include foreign affairs, customs, inspection and quarantine and civil affairs authorities. In this book, we only look at the military, public security and judicial authorities, which are closely related to illegal immigration governance.

(1) **Military Authorities**

According to the *National Defense Law of the People's Republic of China*, the active forces of the People's Liberation Army (PLA) are the standing forces of China, which are responsible for combating the defense of the motherland and helping to maintain social order when necessary. This signifies that the PLA is mainly tasked with defense operations, which were also the purpose of their border patrol over the borders (frontiers). They have the right to suppress the acts or crimes of illegal border (frontier) crossing related to illegal immigration but do not possess the corresponding enforcement powers.

The armed police forces undertake the national mandates of security protection, defensive operations, disaster relief and economic development. From 0:00 January 1, 2018, the People's Armed Police Force ("PAPF") was under centralized and unified leadership of the CPC Central Committee and the Central Military Commission (CMC) and established a CMC-PAPF-Troops leadership and management system. The functions of the armed police forces have remained unchanged and were not included in the PLA sequence. Based on the principle of separating military, police and civilian forces, the active armed police units listed in the armed forces sequence under the management of the State Council were withdrawn from armed police registration. Maritime police forces, which were previously under the leadership of the State Oceanic Administration, began to serve their duties as armed police forces. Additionally, armed police forces who previously answered civil-related duties,

[13] As part of the People's government, China's public security and state security organs are administrative but not judicial organs.

including gold, forestry and hydropower troops, were transferred to state institutions accordingly and were no longer in military service. The guarding forces with the country's customs were also withdrawn. Therefore, following the reform, the managing and commanding relationship in the armed police forces was completely rationalized.

(2) **Public Security Authorities**

China's public security and state security authorities are state administrative organs with distinctive divisions of labor and separate mandates from the perspective of illegal immigration governance.

Among the wide-ranging responsibilities of the public security authorities, two of them are closely associated with illegal immigration governance: first, to manage household registration, nationality and exit and entry matters and the matters of foreigners' residence and travel in China; and second, to safeguard public security and order in border (frontier) areas. The exit-entry administration bureaus are responsible for the management of exit and entry, while the frontier inspection stations at ports opening to foreign countries are responsible for frontier inspection. The frontier inspection station shall exercise the following functions: (1) carry out the frontier inspection on exit-entry passengers and their luggage, means of transport and the goods carried; (2) carry out supervision on the exit-entry means of transport in accordance with the provisions set by the state; (3) take precautionary measures within the specified areas of ports and safeguard the public order of exit from or entry into the country; and (4) exercise the functions authorized by the competent authorities and tasks specified by other laws and administrative regulations.[14]

Article 4 of the *Exit-Entry Administration Law of the People's Republic of China* states that "the Ministry of Public Security and the Ministry of Foreign Affairs shall, within the scope of their respective responsibilities, be responsible for administering exit and entry affairs. Embassies and consulates of the People's Republic of China and other institutions stationed abroad entrusted by the Ministry of Foreign Affairs (hereinafter referred to as "the visa-issuing authorities abroad") shall be responsible for the issuance of entry visas to foreigners. Exit and entry border inspection authorities shall be responsible for carrying out exit and entry border inspection. Public security organs under local people's governments at or above the county level and their exit and entry administrations shall be responsible for the administration of the stay and residence of foreigners. The Ministry of Public Security and the Ministry of Foreign Affairs may, within the scope of their respective responsibilities, entrust exit and entry administrations of public security organs or foreign affairs departments under local people's governments at or above the county level to accept foreigners' applications for entry, stay and residence in China. In the administration of exit and entry affairs, the Ministry of Public Security and the Ministry of Foreign Affairs shall strengthen communication and cooperation, cooperate closely with relevant departments under the State Council, and exercise functions and powers and bear liabilities

[14] Article 4 of the *Regulations of the People's Republic of China on Frontier Inspection of Exit from or Entry into the Country*.

within the scope of their respective responsibilities in accordance with the law." In addition, Article 6 details that "the State shall establish exit and entry border inspection authorities at the ports open to foreign countries. Chinese citizens, foreigners and transport vehicles shall exit or enter China via ports open to foreign countries or via places approved by the State Council or by departments authorized by the State Council under special circumstances. Personnel and transport vehicles that exit or enter China should be subject to exit and entry border inspection. Exit and entry border inspection authorities shall be responsible for relevant administration work in the restricted zones of ports. On the basis of the need for safeguarding national security and maintaining the order of exit and entry administration, exit and entry border inspection authorities may conduct border inspection on the belongings of the persons who exit or enter China. When necessary, exit and entry border inspection authorities may conduct border inspection on the goods carried by transport vehicles that exit or enter China. However, exit and entry border inspection authorities shall notify the Customs of such inspections."

China's state security bodies are responsible for investigating activities that endanger national security that are ostensibly irrelevant to illegal immigration governance. During the inquiries I made in Hekou County, I observed that the Hekou County Bureau of State Security had been established. This is related to the status of Hekou County as a port city, and the activities endangering China's national security *sanfei* and illegal immigrants have engaged in, with the help of their special status and the convenience of border crossing.

(3) **Judiciary Authorities**

Courts are judicial entities that exercise judicial power independently in accordance with the provisions of law and shall not be subject to interference by any administrative organ, public organization or individual. By exercising judicial power, they hear cases regarding illegal immigration to exert their roles in this regard.

The crime of arranging for or transporting another person to cross the national border (frontier) illegally was included in the *1997 Criminal Law of the People's Republic of China*. Since this time, the people's courts in the Yunnan border areas with a high concentration of ethnic minorities have heard numerous cases. For example, the People's Court of Menghai County of Xishuangbanna Prefecture tried a case of smuggling people across the national border (frontier) illegally in the first trial. The accused, surnamed Yu, and her husband, surnamed Yan, smuggled 58 Xinjiang residents to Thailand within a period of three months (March to June 2010), for which they received criminal proceeds totaling 383,100 yuan. For this crime, the two were sentenced to eight years of imprisonment with a penalty of 10,000 yuan and five years of imprisonment with a penalty of 3,000 yuan.[15]

Procuratorates are state organs for legal supervision that exercise procuratorial power independently, in accordance with the provisions of law, and are not subject to interference by any administrative organ, public organization or individual. For illegal

[15] Source: http://www.gy.yn.gov.cn/Article/Print.asp?ArticleID=23079. Accessed September 21, 2011.

immigration cases, procuratorates possess the right to examine the cases scheduled for investigation by public security organs and determine whether a suspect should be arrested or not and whether a case should be prosecuted or exempt from prosecution. They also supervise the investigation undertaken by public security organs and lodge public prosecution and oversee activities in people's courts.

The Ministry of Justice is a state organ in charge of judicial administration. Among its functions most relevant to illegal immigration governance are to "formulate publicity and education plans about the rule of law, and organize the publicity of the rule of law." During our investigation in Hekou County, I discovered that the lack of legal awareness among border residents was a key factor hindering illegal immigration governance. As Mr. Su Li had already suggested "bringing the law to the countryside,"[16] border areas with a high concentration of ethnic minorities should be the focus of such activities.

The Hekou County Bureau of Justice conducted its legal awareness campaign with distinctive local characteristics by targeting refugees, officials and staff concerning foreign affairs and Vietnamese bus drivers traveling between Hekou and Vietnam, which has played an active role in illegal immigration governance.

2 Governing Methods

We have analyzed the subjects of illegal immigration governance and determined who is in charge of governance. Now it is time to discuss governing methods, i.e., how to deal with governance. There are two issues involved: the basis of governance and how to resolve the difficulties in governance. Without the basis, there is a lack of legality and legitimacy. In terms of resolving the difficulties in governance, instead of simply implementing relevant laws, regulations and policies, we shall explore the governing methods that are both effective and conform to China's laws, regulations and policies.

2.1 Basis of Governance

The primary basis of illegal immigration governance is relevant laws, rules, regulations and policies. As part of the laws (international and domestic law), international law refers to the aggregate of legally binding principles, rules and systems governing the relations among nations (the subjects of international law). International law mainly includes international treaties and customs, such as the *United Nations Convention against Transnational Organized Crime* and the *Interim Agreement on Handling Border Issues between the People's Republic of China and the*

---

[16] Su Li, *Bringing the Law to the Countryside: A Study on the Grassroots Judicial System in China* (Beijing: China University of Political Science and Law Press, 2000).

Socialist Republic of Vietnam mentioned above. Domestic law is the internal law of a state that aims to regulate the behavior of individuals and other organizations within its jurisdiction.

China's existing law includes statutory law and unwritten law; the former is the law referred to in this book. Statutory law signifies legal documents formulated and released according to legal procedures of state organs, including China's *Constitution*, laws, administrative rules, local rules, autonomous rules, administrative regulations and the laws of Special Administrative Regions. "Unwritten law" refers to the behavioral norms formulated and released not according to the legal procedures of state organs. It is a supplement to statutory law and includes policies and customs.

Policies are the guidelines formulated by a state or a political party to fulfill the aggregate tasks of a certain period.[17] The Communist Party of China (CPC) is China's ruling party, and its policies are consistent with China's national policies. Meanwhile, the CPC's policies and China's laws are highly consistent in terms of class nature, economic foundation, guidelines, fundamental principles and social objectives.[18] Policies and laws have their respective advantages in state governance.[19] Whether to regulate a social relationship or a social issue by policies or by law depends on its nature and characteristics. Similarly, whether to rule a state by policies or by law depends on its development phase and historical tasks.[20] At the 15th National Congress of the CPC, it was proposed to "govern the country by law and build a socialist country under the rule of law" as China's strategic guideline. China's current *Constitution* stipulates that "the People's Republic of China practices ruling the country in accordance with the law and building a socialist country of law," "the state upholds the uniformity and dignity of the socialist legal system," and "all state organs, the armed forces, all political parties and public organizations and all enterprises and institutions must abide by the *Constitution* and the law."[21] This fully demonstrates that China has entered a new phase of regulating social relations and handling social issues by law.

"Custom," as a verb, means "to adapt to new circumstances," and as a noun means "an established and entrenched behavior or social norm."[22] A "custom," as a behavior or social norm, can be assessed by different standards. For example, it can be classified as a "good custom" or a "bad custom" according to people's values and concepts regarding life. In my personal opinion, a custom can also be classified as a "legal custom" or an "illegal custom" by the provisions of existing laws and regulations. The word "norm" refers to the general appearance, habit and manner developed over

---

17 Practical Chinese Dictionary (2008).

18 Zhang Wenxian, (1999).

19 Policies are highly flexible, and can be adjusted according to the changes of situation. In contrast, laws are highly stable and authoritative because of a whole set of implementing agencies. –Author's note.

20 Zhang Wenxian, (1999)

21 Article 5 of the *Constitution*.

22 Practical Chinese Dictionary (2008).

time.[23] Sharing similar meanings, they are usually referred to altogether as "customs and norms." A concept closely related to custom is "customary law."[24] Mr. Liang Zhiping defines "customary law" as "a set of local regulations developed in the long course of life and production. It is used to distribute rights and obligations among villagers, adjust and resolve their interest conflicts, and is implemented in a set of relationship networks."[25]

Contrary to customary law, customs as unwritten law are the primary original source of law. Customary law carries special meanings and is of particular contemporary value in the history of law. There are two ways in which customs become law: to generally acknowledge the basis of its legal application in a particular setting or to regard customs as the source of legislation and enshrine them in written law. Additionally, there are two modes of existence of customary law in the legal system: the coexistence of law and customary law; and, in the application of specific legal provisions, customs become the customary law as the basis of the specific case and event.[26]

The ethnic groups in the Yunnan border areas have developed the customs and norms of distinctive ethnic features in the long course of life and production that are referred to as ethnic customs and norms.[27] The CPC and the state have implemented consistent policies of respecting ethnic groups' customs and norms and acknowledging and insisting on their freedom to preserve or reform their customs and norms. This can be comprehended from two aspects. First, respecting their customs and norms means acknowledging the equality of all ethnic groups and acknowledging and respecting their autonomy in customs and norms. Other ethnic groups must not judge, interfere in or even discriminate or insult the customs and norms of a particular group, even when some of them are stereotypical or harmful.[28] To prevent ethnic customs and norms from violating, Article 4 of China's *Constitution* reads, "all nationalities have the freedom to use and develop their own spoken and written languages and to preserve or reform their own folkways and customs." In addition, Article 251 of China's *Criminal Law* reads, "workers of state organs who illegally deprive citizens' right to religious beliefs or who encroach on ethnic groups' customs or habits, if the case is serious, are to be sentenced to two years or fewer in prison or put under criminal detention." On the other hand, members of ethnic groups must take a dialectical view of their ethnic customs and norms by refraining from an ethnic nihilistic attitude or an absolutely certain and constant attitude. This is because ethnic

---

[23] Practical Chinese Dictionary (2008).

[24] In fact, there is another concept closely related to customs, i.e., folk law. Regarding the definition and analysis of the customary law and the folk law, see Wang Qiliang, (2010).

[25] Liang Zhiping, (1996).

[26] Hu Xingdong, (2011).

[27] Ethnic customs and norms refer to the long-standing behavioral psychology and behavioral patterns of the people of one particular ethnic group developed under the influence of prevailing values of the group in a particular life setting during the activities in all spheres to meet the needs of subsistence and production. Jin Binggao, (2007).

[28] Jin Binggao, (2007).

customs and norms are relatively stable, but the times continue to evolve.[29] Therefore, these customs and norms may change over time.

ethnic groups residing on both sides of the China-Vietnam borders for generations have developed their own customs and norms that became a crucial part of their culture in the lengthy process of life and production. Some of them are now outdated and run counter to China's current laws and regulations and the development of these groups. First, when illegal immigrants marry border residents belonging to the same ethnic group, they hold wedding ceremonies by following their own customs, without marriage registration according to law. This kind of "de facto" marriage unprotected by law will lead to many problems. In addition, the local people's and some officials' acceptance of "de facto" marriage has seriously hindered the governance of illegal immigration. Second, Chinese and Vietnamese border residents belonging to ethnic groups have formed the habit of cross-border farming, grazing and family visits through unauthorized crossing points. They did not realize that this behavior violated China's laws and regulations or understood or cooperated when they were prevented or penalized by the relevant departments.

I believe this issue can be resolved in terms of the following two aspects.

First, by resolving conflicts in jurisprudence. As unwritten law supplements statutory law, customs should be used to maintain social order and regulate social relations. However, the customs mentioned above have become behavior against statutory law or illegal behavior. I believe that the status of customs as the unwritten law has not changed. Just as there are just laws and unjust laws, there are "good customs" and "bad customs." Good customs supplement the statutory law, while bad customs undermine it. In addition, there are legal customs and illegal customs. The former can be retained and can evolve, while the latter shall be held accountable, at least *mutatis mutandis*, so that these illegal customs will be gradually rectified and become legalized.

Second, to deal with the undermining and negative impact of "bad customs."

According to the CPC and the state's consistent policies toward ethnic customs and norms, i.e., respecting ethnic groups' customs and norms and acknowledging and insisting on their freedom to preserve or reform their customs and norms. That is, theoretically speaking, some outdated ethnic customs and norms that run against the development of ethnic groups or the dignity of the state and its laws must be reformed and gradually rectified for their legalization. However, it depends on the ethnic groups' conscious efforts to undertake the reform, i.e., they may decide whether and how to reform.

It is a gradual process for ethnic groups to reform some of their customs and norms, yet this does not signify that the government shall do nothing about it. The government can promote this reform by accelerating the economic and social development of these areas and by strengthening the publicity of the rule of law. In fact, the state has fully understood the longevity and complexity of this reform and applied its theoretical awareness to concrete measures. For example, China's *Criminal Law*

[29] About the necessity of reforming ethnic customs and norms, reform methods and notable principles, see Jin Binggao, (2007).

focuses on the crime of arranging for or transporting another person to cross the national border (frontier) illegally. This does not apply to the general offenses of crossing the national border (frontier) illegally, and the perpetrators are not held criminally responsible. Only when the circumstances are serious will the perpetrators be subject to light criminal punishment.

2.2 *Difficulties in Governance*

Now that we have discussed the basis of governance, let us analyze the practical application of relevant laws, regulations and policies. This book elaborates on the difficulties in governance in three cases: illegal entry, repatriation and illegal residence. Only by facing existing issues can we determine their solutions.

(1) **Illegal Border Crossing**

Why does the perennial phenomenon of illegal border crossing in Hekou County still exist, despite years of implementation of relevant laws and regulations and years of governance practices? How do we resolve the difficulties involved? There must be more significant and determining factors, aside from objective reasons, such as long state borders, numerous unauthorized crossing points, a lack of natural barriers on both sides of the borderlines, and the fact that the lands are connected by shared mountains and rivers.

1. Issues in China's Current Law and Regulations[30]

Border crossing management in Yunnan border areas with a high concentration of ethnic minorities aims to regulate this behavior according to relevant policies and manage it according to laws and regulations based on the actual situation in different segments of borders at different times. Beginning in the 1990s, Yunnan Province formulated the *Yunnan Province Administrative Rules for Entry-Exit of External Border Residents in the Chinese-Myanmar Border Areas*, *Yunnan Province Provisional Administrative Rules for Entry-Exit of Chinese Citizens in the China-Myanmar Border Areas*, and *Yunnan Province Administrative Rules for Entry-Exit in the China-Vietnam and China-Myanmar Border Areas* (hereafter referred to as the "three rules"), based on the actual situation in three segments of borders and the bilateral treaties signed between China and neighboring countries.

Considering China's ethnic policies and the particular situation in the Yunnan border areas, and to stabilize border areas, promote economic and trade exchanges with neighboring countries, safeguard productive activities of border residents and respect their living habits, China has adopted specific management measures on temporary border crossing of border residents, established two fundamental principles and included them in the current entry and exit laws and regulations. The

[30] I extend my deep gratitude to Mr. Xiao Zhenyu with the Exit and Entry Administration Bureau of Yunnan Public Security Bureau for his considerable assistance with the writing of this part.

principles are to (1) take different approaches to border crossing of border residents from neighboring countries and (2) apply international treaties in the border crossing management of border residents from neighboring countries first or China's domestic laws in the absence of these treaties. Following a comprehensive analysis of China's current laws and regulations, I have observed the presence of the following issues.

(i) Disorganized Legal Rules

In terms of current laws and regulations, China's legal system of border management is sound yet unsystematic, complex and diversified, and it involves numerous types of laws, supplementary rules, implementation guidelines and regulations. There are legal documents specifically formulated for almost all specific matters. However, the legal rules of temporary border crossing management of border residents are disorganized, and the primary basis is normative documents, such as local rules and local government regulations developed by the provincial government of Yunnan.

(ii) Outdated Laws and Regulations

The border crossing realities in the Yunnan border areas changed since the 1980s and 90s when the "three rules" were enacted; thus, some laws and regulations have since become outdated, which leads to differences among local regulations in terms of the level and scope of border crossing management. In addition, the "three rules" are unable to meet the evolving needs of border crossing in these areas. For example, the *Yunnan Province Administrative Rules for Entry-Exit of External Border Residents in the Chinese-Myanmar Border Areas*, established by the Yunnan Provincial Government in 1990, stipulated the management of entry and exit of Myanmar's residents based on China's unilateral management of this issue by taking into consideration the actual situation of Myanmar's border control.[31] In 1997, the two governments signed the *Agreement Between the Government of the People's Republic of China and the Government of the Union of Myanmar on China-Myanmar Border Areas Management and Cooperation*, which included the fundamental principles of border management between China and Myanmar. The *1990 Administrative Rules*, although now outdated, have yet to be amended.

(iii) Inconsistent Laws and Penalties and Inadequate Punishment

In regard to illegal border crossing, Article 322 of China's *Criminal Law* states that "whoever, in violation of the laws or regulations on the administration of the national border (frontier), illegally crosses the national border (frontier), if the circumstances are serious, shall be sentenced to fixed-term imprisonment of no more

[31] The northern part of Myanmar, adjacent to Dehong Prefecture of Yunnan Province, is plagued by complex political circumstances and numerous militia groups. In addition to the government troops, immigration offices and police offices, there are the Kachin Independence Army, Shan militia and Lisu ethnic militia of Namhkan and other ethnic militia groups. The Agreement was never implemented, due to the limited border management capabilities of the Myanmar government, which has led to major differences in the issuance of exit and entry permits for border residents and inspection between the two countries. The result was that the responsibility of cooperatively managing the exit and entry between China and Myanmar was undertaken by China on its own.

than one year, criminal detention or public surveillance and shall also be fined," while Article 30 of the *Regulations of Yunnan Province on Border Management*, Article 29 of *Yunnan Province Administrative Rules for Entry-Exit of External Border Residents in the Chinese-Myanmar Border Areas*, Article 11 of the *Yunnan Province Provisional Administrative Rules for Entry-Exit of Chinese Citizens in the China-Myanmar Border Areas*, and Article 19 of the *Yunnan Province Administrative Rules for Myanmar Exit-Exit of Chinese Cinam and Mymarmarmar Border Areas*, and Article 19. However, the amount of penalty and duration of detention are different from one another. This will cause people to cast doubt on the authority and impartiality of China's enforcement agencies and the unity of China's laws. In particular, according to the "three rules," any border resident who illegally crosses the national border shall be given a warning and fined a penalty of different amounts, ranging from 10 yuan to 50 to 100 yuan. Furthermore, the punishment is too inadequate to prevent any future occurrence of the same behavior. See Table 1 for detail:

The penalties for illegal border crossing in the *Exit-Entry Administration Law* (effective on July 1, 2013) were adjusted as follows: Article 71 reads, "Persons who commit any of the following acts shall be fined no less than 1,000 yuan but no more than 5,000 yuan; where circumstances are serious, such persons shall be detained for no less than five days but no more than ten days, and may also be fined no less than 2,000 yuan but no more than 10,000 yuan: (1) Exit or enter China with forged, altered or fraudulently obtained exit-entry documents; (2) Exit or enter China using others' exit-entry documents; (3) Evade exit-entry border inspection; or (4) Illegally exit or enter China in any other way." Finally, Article 72 reads, "Persons who assist others in illegally exiting or entering China shall be fined no less than 2,000 yuan but no more than 10,000 yuan; where circumstances are serious, they shall be detained for no less than 10 days but no more than 15 days and shall also be fined no less than 5,000 yuan and no more than 20,000 yuan, and the illegal gains, if any, shall be confiscated. Entities engaging in any of the acts prescribed in the preceding paragraph shall be fined no less than 10,000 yuan and no more than 50,000 yuan, with the illegal gains confiscated if there are any; and the persons in charge of the entities who are directly responsible and other persons directly responsible shall be punished in accordance with the provisions in the preceding paragraph."

The penalties for illegal border crossing have clearly increased in China's current *Exit-Entry Administration Law*, which summarized previous practices and experience and adapted to the inevitable trend of China's rapid economic and social development. The provinces and autonomous regions sharing borders with neighboring countries must, taking into account perennial problems in local exit and entry management, re-establish or amend local rules and local government regulations regarding interpersonal exchanges in border areas, based on the relevant provisions of the *Exit-Entry Administration Law* and existing border management agreements signed between China and other countries. The abovementioned three rules that are inconsistent with the needs of local exit and entry management must be amended. Alternatively, efforts must be made to establish and implement the *Administrative Rules of the Entry and Exit of Personnel and Materials in the China-Vietnam, China-Laos and China-Myanmar Border Areas* to aggregate the penalties for illegal border

Table 1 Punishment for Illegal Border Crossing according to Different Laws and Regulations

Number	Laws and regulations	Punishment
1	Article 322 of the *Criminal Law*	Whoever, in violation of the laws or regulations on the administration of the national border (frontier), illegally crosses the national border (frontier), if the circumstances are serious, shall be sentenced to fixed-term imprisonment of no more than one year, criminal detention or public surveillance and shall also be fined
2	Article 30 of the *Regulations of Yunnan Province on Border Management*	Whoever, in violation of Article 13 of the *Regulations*, holds valid documents but does not exit or enter China through designated ports and paths, shall be given a warning and fined 50 yuan. Whoever evades border inspection and holds forged, altered or fraudulently obtained exit and entry documents or uses others' exit and entry documents, shall be given a warning and fined 100 to 300 yuan. Moreover, his or her documents shall be confiscated. Whoever helps or transports others to illegally cross the border or facilitates such behavior, shall be fined 2,000 to 5,000 yuan, or 5,000 to 10,000 yuan if the circumstances are serious
3	Article 29 of *Yunnan Province Administrative Rules for Entry-Exit of External Border Residents in the Chinese-Myanmar Border Areas*	Any external border resident, in violation of Articles 5, 6, 7, 8 and 9 of the *Rules*, illegally exits or enters China's border counties (cities), shall be given a warning and fined 10 to 100 yuan
4	Article 11 of the *Yunnan Province Provisional Administrative Rules for Entry-Exit of Chinese Citizens in the China-Myanmar Border Areas*	Whoever, in violation of the Rules, illegally exits or enters China shall be given a warning, fined 10 to 100 yuan, or detained for a maximum of 10 days. When the circumstances are serious and constitute a crime, the perpetrator shall be held criminally responsible
5	Article 19 of the *Yunnan Province Administrative Rules for Entry-Exit in the China-Vietnam and China-Myanmar Border Areas*	Whoever, in violation of the *Rules*, illegally exits or enters China's border counties (cities) without exit/entry permit, shall be given a warning and fined 50 to 100 yuan

crossing, clarify the enforcement authorities and their functions, and coordinate the relations between superior legislation and inferior legislation. Otherwise, the issues of inconsistent laws and penalties and inadequate punishment cannot be resolved.

(iv) Various Exit-Entry Permits

The exit and entry documents held by border residents vary according to different laws and regulations. Chinese border residents use the Yunnan Provincial Exit-Entry

Permit in the China-Vietnam (Laos and Myanmar) Border Areas issued by China's armed police and frontier defense departments. The documents used by the border residents from neighboring countries include: The Exit-Entry Permit in the Vietnam-China Border Areas and the Exit-Entry Permit of the Socialist Republic of Vietnam issued by Vietnam; and the Exit-Entry Permit in the Laos-China Border Areas and the Temporary Transit Permit issued by Laos. In the China-Myanmar border areas under unilateral border management of the Chinese side, people who live outside the Chinese territory use the entry cards issued by China's armed police and frontier defense departments or the Exit-Entry Permit for Extra-Territorial Border Residents in the Yunnan Border Areas. Extraterritorial border residents, after entering China's border areas, issued the Exit-Entry and Stay Permit for Extraterritorial Border Residents in the Yunnan Border Areas, the Temporary Stay Permit for Extraterritorial Border Residents in the Yunnan Border Areas and the Exit-Entry Permit for Foreigners. All of these documents, which are difficult to confirm and distinguish from one another, are used simultaneously, which leads to difficulties in border management and control.

(v) Overlapping Legal Responsibilities

There are numerous border management authorities with overlapping responsibilities based on different laws and regulations. The inconsistent understanding of border management, unreasonable exercise of powers, and unclear division of mandates among public security, armed police, foreign affairs, customs, inspection and quarantine and civil affairs authorities has rendered it difficult to pursue collective efforts. For example, the management of exit and entry is shared by three different departments. The immigration departments of China's public security authorities oversee the approval and permit issuance for Chinese citizens' border (frontier) crossing for nonofficial business and the management of entry-exit permits, residence permits and visas for people entering China. The active forces of public security and frontier defense oversee the inspection of border-crossing personnel and permit issuance for border residents. Finally, the management of border-crossing vehicles is undertaken by traffic police departments. These inconsistent systems, overlapping mandates, inadequate management and control, and lack of sharing resources have caused a fragmented approach to border management and control among the three police units.

Unfortunately, the current *Exit-Entry Administration Law* has not substantially resolved this problem, and the situation of comanagement and overlapping responsibilities continues to exist. I suggest addressing this issue in the *Rules for the Implementation of the Exit-Entry Administration Law* to be enacted.

(2) **Repatriation**

The original meaning of "repatriation" is "the act of sending somebody back to their own country."[32] I believe that, from the perspective of jurisprudence, repatriation signifies the act of sending people who enter a country illegally, or are not entitled

[32] Practical Chinese Dictionary (2008).

to residence, back to their country of origin or residence by the destination country, based on the international conventions to which the country is a party, or based on bilateral treaties that the country has signed. Repatriation can also be simply defined as the system under which the destination country's government forcibly sends illegal immigrants who do not obtain entry permits or overstay their visas back to their country of origin.[33] The prerequisite of repatriation is an agreement signed by two countries or regions to mutually accept repatriated personnel. That is, when one party wishes to repatriate these people, the other side shall be willing to accept them. The two parties must also establish a system related to repatriation on this basis. Article 62 of the *Exit-Entry Administration Law* reads as follows: "Under any of the following circumstances, foreigners may be repatriated: (1) They are ordered to exit China within a prescribed time limit but fail to do so; (2) They are involved in circumstances in which they are not allowed to enter China; (3) They illegally reside or work in China; or (4) They must be repatriated for violation of this Law or other laws or administrative regulations. Other overseas personnel who fall under any of the circumstances prescribed in the preceding paragraph may be repatriated in accordance with the law. Repatriated persons shall not be permitted to enter China for one to five years, as calculated from the date of repatriation." It must be noted that this provision, although falling outside the scope of illegal immigration mentioned in this book, can be regarded as the legal basis of China's repatriation of illegal immigrants.

The repatriation mechanism, which is of great importance to illegal immigration governance, has been adopted by many countries. If there is no such mechanism between a sending country and a receiving country of illegal immigrants or if the two countries cannot cooperate even though such a mechanism has been established, thus leading to the failure of repatriation, it will bring many troubles to the residence country of illegal immigrants and directly impact the governance of illegal immigration.

Let us once again take Hekou County as an example. Local authorities there are responsible for repatriating regular *sanfei* and illegal immigrants within their jurisdiction, as well as Vietnamese regular *sanfei* and illegal immigrants transferred by provincial and municipal government departments in the interior parts of China. We learned from the inquiries that two problems exist in repatriation. First, there was insufficient cooperation from Vietnamese counterparts. According to the minutes of working meetings between the two sides, the Vietnamese side shall first confirm the identities of repatriated personnel and then receive them at the designated port as scheduled. However, the Vietnamese side's nonresponse or refusal to receive repatriated personnel for not being able to confirm their identities has hobbled the repatriation. Second, ineffective repatriation. Repatriated personnel can easily return to China by illegally crossing the border through unauthorized crossing points, which has led to the vicious cycle of "having issued repatriation order without actual return," "return soon after repatriation" followed by "repeated repatriation and return." The same problem of ineffective repatriation of Vietnamese regular *sanfei* and illegal

[33] Xu Junhua, (2005).

immigrants also exists in Maguan County, a Yunnan border county with a high concentration of ethnic minorities.

(3) **Illegal Residence**

Illegal immigrants residing in China can be classified into three types: intermarrying illegal immigrants (unmarried or divorced illegal immigrants, or illegal immigrants who married people of the same status); illegal immigrants who married refugees; and illegal immigrants who married Chinese citizens. The latter two types are referred to as illegal immigrants who married people of other status. Different problems occur in the management of illegal immigrants of various types.

1. Intermarrying Illegal Immigrants

Theoretically speaking, the ideal way to handle this type of illegal immigrant is to send them back to their home country. However, based on my investigation in Hekou County, repatriation of such people is neither easy nor effective, even if the two preconditions of repatriation have been ostensibly met. It appears that substantive departments cannot determine superior ways to deal with immigrants who should have been repatriated. Moreover, it is very challenging to deal with cases where both parents are illegal immigrants. They are born as "people without legal status" or "people without household registration," as one's parents are something that one cannot choose. In addition to discrimination due to their status at an early age, they also face difficulties in education and employment or even limited opportunities to find employment elsewhere when they reach adulthood.

All of these issues would be resolved if these people could obtain Chinese nationality and become Chinese citizens. It is also their common wish to do so. The question is, how can they be naturalized as Chinese nationals?

There are rare cases of foreigners acquiring citizenship in China due to China's specific national conditions. The naturalization of George Hatem, the first foreigner granted Chinese citizenship since the founding of the PRC,[34] was an exception in a special period in history. Article 7 of the *Nationality Law of the People's Republic of China* enacted on September 10, 1980 reads: "Foreign nationals or stateless persons who are willing to abide by China's *Constitution* and laws and who meet one of the following conditions may be naturalized upon approval of their applications: (1) they are near relatives of Chinese nationals; (2) they have settled in China; or (3) they have other legitimate reasons." Therefore, anyone who wishes to be naturalized must meet these requirements and follow designated procedures according to the Law. Being near relatives of Chinese nationals means that they must be either spouses, parents

[34] George Hatem (USA) was born in upstate New York in 1910. After receiving his doctoral degree in Medicine in the summer of 1933, he began to practice medicine in China in November of the same year. In June 1936, accompanied by Edgar Snow, George Hatem traveled to the northern part of Shaanxi Province with the help of Soong Ching-ling and decided to stay there after Edgar Snow had completed his interviews and departed. In 1937, upon his arrival in Yan'an, George Hatem requested to be naturalized as a Chinese national. After the founding of the People's Republic of China, Zhou Enlai personally approved his naturalization application, making him the first foreigner granted Chinese citizenship since the founding of the PRC.

or children of Chinese nationals. That is, foreign nationals or stateless persons are eligible if they have a legal marriage relationship with Chinese nationals or a legal parental relationship with their children or parents who are Chinese nationals. Foreign nationals or stateless persons who have settled in China mean that they have settled within the territory of China (mainland China) for a certain period of time. "Having settled" is a mandatory requirement, which means they must have plans of long-term residence and have resided there for a long time. The legal requirements for the settlement duration vary among countries, and it is not indicated in China's *Nationality Law*.[35]

Therefore, intermarrying illegal immigrants can only apply for Chinese citizenship on the ground of "having settled in China," as they are usually not "near relatives of Chinese nationals." They are ostensibly eligible for having settled in China for a sufficiently long period of time. The question remains, how do they prove their status as "foreign nationals or stateless persons"? To prove that they are foreign nationals, they must provide their passports or permanent resident cards of another country, which of course are not available for those who enter China illegally. The next question is how do they prove they are stateless persons? The identification of their stateless status by local officials and villagers cannot be taken as proof, and their lack of Chinese citizenship, although residing in China, requires no proof. This leads to the issue of how to prove that the Vietnamese government has revoked their citizenship. Without supporting documents from the Vietnamese government, they are not able to prove their stateless status and are thus not eligible to apply for naturalization.

My analysis has been confirmed by the official documents of competent authorities. The application requirements, stipulated in the *Announcement on the Naturalization as a Chinese National issued by the Ministry of Public Security* on May 13, 2008, are identical to those in the *Nationality Law*, while the former requests a foreign national or stateless person applying for naturalization to provide the following: (1) a photocopy of the applicant's passport; (2) a photocopy of the applicant's permanent resident card; (3) documents to prove the applicant has acquired foreign citizenship at birth if one or both parents are Chinese nationals; and (4) other documents deemed by the authorities that are responsible for accepting the application to be relevant to the application for naturalization as a Chinese national.[36]

Next, are the children of illegal immigrants able to apply for Chinese nationality? According to Article 6 of the *Nationality Law*, any person born in China whose parents are stateless or of uncertain nationality and who has settled in China shall possess Chinese nationality. It is difficult to prove the stateless status of illegal immigrant parents, yet they can be deemed people of uncertain nationality. Furthermore, their residence in China can be confirmed by local villagers' committees, neighborhood

---

[35] China's current *Nationality Law* was established 30 years ago, but at present no supplementary *Rules for Implementation* have been formulated. It is imperative to release detailed implementation rules and provide elaborative and authoritative explanations to issues regarding citizenship. –Author's note.

[36] *Announcement on the Naturalization as a Chinese National*, source: http://www.mps.gov.cn/n16/n84147/n84211/n84334/n399132/1275624.html. Accessed September 23, 2011.

committees or police offices. Although their children can obtain Chinese nationality without problems, a birth certificate is the only means to prove that the children were born in China. A birth certificate is also called a medical certificate of childbirth. According to Article 23 of the *Law on Maternal and Infant Health Care* enacted on June 1, 1995, "Medical and health institutions and midwives engaged in at-home delivery shall, as prescribed by the administrative department of public health under the State Council, issue uniformly prepared medical certificates for childbirth." This acts as regulated medical proof of an infant's condition at birth and his or her parents, as well as a proof for nationality and household registration application. To acquire a birth certificate, the infant's parents must provide the maternity and child healthcare hospital seated in the same jurisdiction in which the mother's household registration is registered with their ID cards or identification documents issued by the Ministry of Public Security and the medical record of birth issued by the hospital where the infant was born. This signifies that to obtain the childbirth medical certificate to prove that the applicant was born in China, ID cards, household registration booklets or identification documents of their parents issued by the Ministry of Public Security must be provided. What does this mean for illegal immigrant parents who do not possess marriage certificates, ID cards or household registration booklets?

The management of these illegal immigrants becomes obscured, as they cannot be effectively repatriated, and the chance of their naturalization is slim.

2. Illegal immigrants Who Married Refugees

China attaches importance to the protection of refugees. After acceding into the *1951 UN Convention relating to the Status of Refugees* and its *1967 Protocol relating to the Status of Refugees* in 1982, China used the provisions in the *1951 Convention* as a reference for the definition of refugees. There are two principles of refugee protection under international law: nonrefoulement and international cooperation.

The "nonrefoulement principle" means that states shall not expel or return a refugee in any matter to the territories where his or her life or freedom would be threatened unless they have reasonable grounds to believe that the refugee is a danger to national security or may cause other severe circumstances. Professor Liang Shuying argues that the principle of "no denied access at the border" is included in the "nonrefoulement principle" established by the *1951 Convention.* No denied access at the border means states should not deny access to their territories or the entry of a refugee in case of emergency. Even if states may not provide asylum for long, they must not expel a refugee to the territories where their life or freedom would be threatened, regardless if they enter legally, or are confirmed as a refugee.[37] The "nonrefoulement principle" is very important, as James C. Hathaway points out that "Perhaps the most important innovation of the *1951 Refugee Convention* is its commitment to the protection of refugees who travel to a state party without authorization. For the first time, the duty of nonrefoulement was conceived as the entitlement of all refugees, including those who arrive without permission to enter the territory of an asylum country. The decision to grant protection against refoulement to all refugees,

[37] Liang Shuying, (2008).

whether authorized or unauthorized, closed the most critical protection gap that had initially prompted the drafting of a specific duty of nonpenalization. Because even irregular refugees are now shielded from return in any manner whatsoever to a place in which they are at risk, Article 33 can be relied upon to counter penalties which raise the prospect."[38]

The international cooperation principle means that all states shall share the expenditures of receiving, accommodating, aiding and protecting refugees and the responsibilities of jointly eradicating or decreasing the root causes of refugee flows.[39] Refugees are a group of people who are disconnected from their home country and caught in between states. Without the protection of their rights established by international law as a legal obligation, they will certainly become outcasts of the world. The international community must work together to protect their rights. The obligation to resettle refugees and to care for them pending resettlement must be accepted as the common responsibility to be met by common action.[40]

The Yunnan provincial government also developed the policy of equal treatment, nondiscrimination, and equal remuneration for equal work regarding refugee settlement, including providing basic livelihood protection and necessary employment opportunities for refugees, assisting and encouraging them to participate in productive activities, improving their self-sustaining capabilities, supporting their integration into local economic and social life, and facilitating the voluntary return of refugees who are ready for family reunification.[41]

As mentioned previously, after years of efforts, refugees in Hekou County now enjoy "quasi-national treatment." Aside from Chinese nationality and related political rights, they have obtained ID cards and household registration booklets, their housing and land problems have been resolved and their basic livelihood guaranteed. However, there are no provisions regarding the naturalization of refugees in China's *Nationality Law*; thus, this issue has yet to be resolved.[42]

Compared with the difficulties in the naturalization of refugees, the naturalization of illegal immigrants is even more intractable. The marriage between a refugee and an illegal immigrant is illegal due to the latter's status. Although acknowledged as a de facto marriage, their relationship is not protected by China's laws, and their child is deemed as having been born out of wedlock. Even if one refugee parent

[38] James C. Hathaway, (2005).

[39] Li Fangtian, (2009).

[40] [United States] Louis Henkin, (1997).

[41] Yunnan Provincial Department of Finance, (1977).

[42] The universally accepted approach to refugee settlement is as follows: After the war or emergency has ended, the host country shall repatriate refugees on a voluntary basis, or accept them as citizens, or resettle them in a third country. The Chinese and Laotian governments signed the Agreement on the Repatriation of Laos Refugees in China. According to this Agreement, between 1991 and 1997, over 3,000 Laotian refugees returned to their home country in 17 batches. China is now drafting a refugee law under the persistent help of the Office of the United Nations High Commissioner for Refugees (UNHCR). See "The Investigation on the 200,000 Laos Refugees in China: Not Chinese Nationals However," source: http://news.china.com/zh_cn/domestic/945/20070524/14118275_4.html. Accessed October 23, 2011.

has obtained an ID card and household registration, their child cannot obtain a birth certificate because they cannot provide ID cards and household registration for both parents. The result is that their child cannot obtain Chinese nationality, ID card or household registration.

Therefore, it is even more difficult to determine the identities of such children. They are certainly not a Chinese national or a refugee (refugees are granted ID cards and household registration). It is erroneous to call them illegal immigrants because they did not cross the border illegally. In that case, where shall we send them to if we opt for repatriation? However, if we do not, what is their status? This is a problematic and complex situation that China must face.

3. Illegal Immigrants Who Married Chinese Citizens

In comparison, the situation of illegal immigrants who married Chinese citizens is somewhat better. Although their de facto marriages are unprotected by law and there is little hope for remedial marriage registration, their children can still obtain Chinese nationality by law.[43] Legally speaking, there are two prerequisites: first, one or both parents are Chinese nationals; second, the child is born in China (which requires a birth certificate). However, the ID cards and household registration booklets of both parents are required to obtain such a certificate. Theoretically speaking, the child cannot obtain a birth certificate because the parent of illegal status does not possess these documents. Since their marriage is illegal, there is no need to provide such documents of both parents, just those of one. Therefore, the child of an illegal immigrant and a Chinese citizen will possess an ID card and household registration, as well as Chinese nationality.

However, this raises another question: can one parent who does not have Chinese nationality apply for it on the grounds that their child is a Chinese national? The legal basis is Article 7 of the *Nationality Law*, which stipulates that foreign nationals or stateless persons who are willing to abide by China's *Constitution* and laws and who are near relatives of Chinese nationals may be naturalized upon approval of their applications. It was mentioned above that foreign nationals or stateless persons are eligible for naturalization if they have a legal parental relationship (a parental relationship acknowledged by China's current laws) with their children who are Chinese nationals. If that is the case, then is the parental relationship between the parent without Chinese nationality with their child who has already become a Chinese national acknowledged by China's current law? According to Article 25 of China's *Marriage Law*, children born out of Wedlock shall enjoy the same rights as those born in Wedlock, and no one may harm or discriminate against them for such a reason. The natural father or mother who does not directly bring up a child born out of wedlock shall bear the child's living and educational expenses until the child can support themselves. This provision aims to protect the rights of children born out of wedlock and impose the natural father or mother of a child born out of wedlock the obligation of raising the child. Its legislative purpose is to acknowledge the parental

[43] Based on Article 4 of the *Nationality Law*, which stipulates that "any person born in China whose parents are both Chinese nationals shall have Chinese nationality.".

relationship between the child born out of wedlock and their natural father or mother. Even if a child is born out of wedlock, their relationship with their parents is equally protected by China's laws. Therefore, their parents without Chinese nationality can apply for it on these grounds.

Now, we have clarified the qualifications for naturalization. The next question is, can one parent without Chinese nationality provide requested supporting documents?[44] The answer is that, no, they cannot apply for naturalization if they are not able to provide these documents.

2.3 *Judicial Assistance*

Judicial assistance refers to the cooperation between countries in taking certain legal actions on behalf of the other side based on the international treaties they concluded or joined and the principle of reciprocity. China's judicial authorities must establish judicial assistance mechanisms with their counterparts in relevant countries to build international cooperation on illegal immigration governance to more effectively combat illegal immigration and related crimes.

On October 19, 1998, China and Vietnam signed the *Treaty between the People's Republic of China and Socialist Republic of Vietnam on Judicial Assistance in Civil and Criminal Matters*. The provisions regarding illegal immigration governance are those concerning judicial assistance in criminal matters. Chapter four of the *Treaty* specifies the scope of judicial assistance, such as the service of documents (Article 22), investigation and evidence gathering (Article 23), court appearance and protection of witnesses and expert witnesses (Article 24), transfer of misappropriated funds and goods (Article 25), notification of criminal convictions (Article 26) and refusal of judicial assistance in criminal matters (Article 27).

On January 25, 1999, China and Laos singed the *Treaty between the People's Republic of China and Laos People's Republic on Judicial Assistance in Civil and Criminal Matters*. In the *Treaty*, Article 27 stipulates the scope of judicial assistance in criminal matters between the two countries: the contracting parties shall, upon request, conduct service of litigation documents on behalf of the other side; collect evidence for investigation from witnesses, victims and expert witnesses; interrogate suspects and defendants; conduct identification, examination and other legal actions related to evidence gathering; arrange the attendance of witnesses or expert witnesses at trials; notify criminal convictions; and recognize the convictions regarding civil damages and litigation fees in criminal cases.

China has not concluded any agreements of judicial assistance with Myanmar or joined any international treaties in this field to which Myanmar is also a party.

[44] Supporting documents refer to: (1) a photocopy of the applicant's passport; (2) a photocopy of the applicant's permanent resident card; (3) documents to prove the applicant has acquired foreign citizenship at birth if one or both parents are Chinese nationals; and (4) other documents deemed by the authorities that are responsible for accepting the application to be relevant to the application for naturalization as a Chinese national.

Therefore, the two countries cannot seek judicial assistance according to any existing treaties. Moreover, any possible treaties of judicial assistance to be signed between the Chinese government and the governments of special regions of Myanmar may not be implemented in these regions. At present, the legal systems of these governments of special regions are either incomplete or nascent. Principal government officials have the final say in regard to serious cases and events and possess the power of final adjudication, despite the existence of judicial departments.[45] Therefore, the judicial departments in the Yunnan border areas will have to communicate with the governments of Myanmar's special regions to build cooperative mechanisms for illegal immigration management and control.

Nevertheless, there is a sensitive issue involved in this kind of judicial cooperation. Will the communication and cooperation between the judicial authorities of the Yunnan border areas and the governments of Myanmar's special regions constitute a violation of Myanmar's sovereignty? In other words, without the authorization of Myanmar's federal government and the legal basis of judicial assistance treaties between China and Myanmar, will such acts constitute interference in Myanmar's internal affairs?

In my personal opinion, such acts will not constitute interference in Myanmar's internal affairs for the following reasons. First, the governments of Myanmar's special regions cooperating with the judicial departments of the Yunnan border areas did not claim independence in the name of "states." Instead, in external exchanges, they continued to refer to themselves as the Government of Special Region 1 of Shan State or the Government of Special Region four of Northern Shan State. They believe that they are parts of the federal government from the perspective of international law. For example, the Government of Wa Special Region two explicitly stated that it belonged to the federal government during the 6th Border Counter-Narcotics Meeting with Pu'er Narcotics Control Committee. Second, the key to the interference in Myanmar's internal affairs is whether the cooperation between the governments of Myanmar's special regions and the judicial departments of the Yunnan border areas is approved by Myanmar's federal government. Since the federal government has never protested or raised the issue with the Chinese government, we can interpret this as its tacit acceptance of the legality of such acts. That is, the federal government does not believe that the country's internal affairs have been meddled with. Third, the relationship between the federal government and the governments of special regions has improved in recent years. With the exception of a small number of ethnic militia groups, 40 such groups have achieved reconciliation with the federal government. The relationship between the federal and local governments has become more clearly defined, and the former recognized the external exchanges of the latter. However, I anticipate that an agreement of judicial assistance will soon be signed between the Chinese government and Myanmar's federal government to combat illegal immigration and related crimes.

[45] "Yang Ronggang, Research on Local Judicial Assistance in the China-Myanmar Border Areas," source: http://www.gy.yn.gov.cn/Article/Print.asp.ArticleID=15,385. Accessed October 10, 2011.

In the case where Vietnam signed the *Treaty on Judicial Assistance in Civil and Criminal Matters* with China, the judicial authorities of the Yunnan border areas cooperated extensively with their Vietnamese counterparts.

For example, in June 2002, a delegation of the Yunnan Provincial Procuratorate visited upon invitation of the Procuratorate of Lao Cai Province in Vietnam, and both sides signed the *Meeting Minutes Between the Delegation of Yunnan Provincial Procuratorate of the People's Republic of China and Delegation of the Procuratorate of Lao Cai Province of the Socialist Republic of Vietnam*. In August 2003, a delegation of Yunnan Provincial Procuratorate paid another visit to the Procuratorate of Lao Cai Province and later made return visits on two occasions. Over all these years, the procuratorial authorities of Yunnan Province have achieved remarkable judicial cooperation with the procuratorial or judicial authorities of neighboring countries' border areas, successfully collected evidence across borders, and received strong support in overseas arrests.[46] Hekou County Procuratorate and Vietnam's Lao Cai Municipal Procuratorate, the departments authorized with liaison tasks by both countries, implemented the *Meeting Minutes* to enhance judicial assistance, which has protected the social and economic orders of border areas, and laid a foundation for the combat against illegal immigration and related crimes. In addition, the Hekou County Court held several judicial meetings with Vietnam's Lao Cai Municipal Court.[47]

On September 15, 2010, in Beijing, the Chinese and Vietnamese Ministries of Public Security signed the *Minutes of the 2nd China-Vietnam Public Security Ministerial Meeting on Cooperation against Crimes* and the *Agreement on Enhancing Cooperation in Preventing and Combating Human Trafficking between China and Vietnam*. On October 22, 2010, the Honghe Public Security Bureau held a working meeting with the Lao Cai Provincial Public Security Department in the city of Lao Cai, Vietnam. Both sides took stock of the public security tasks jointly taken in 2009 and made some suggestions, including the following: increasing cooperation in improving policing performance in border areas, cracking down cross-border criminal offenses, enhancing cooperation in exit and entry management and safeguarding social orders in border areas, improving policing cooperation mechanisms and strengthening policing management in border areas. In addition, both sides stated that they would build on effective policing cooperation in 2009 to continue the battle against criminal activities such as illegal border crossing, gambling abroad, trafficking of women and children, and transboundary drug abuse and drug trafficking.[48]

---

[46] For the documents of judicial cooperation between the procuratorial authorities of Yunnan Province and the procuratorial or judicial authorities of neighboring countries' border areas, see Wang Ruiqi and Zhu Chunli, "The Status and Suggestions Regarding Judicial Assistance in Criminal Matters of the Procuratorial Authorities of Yunnan Province," source: http://www.ynjcy.gov.cn/ynjc/722,264,790,239,543,296/20050921/915.html. Accessed October 9, 2011.

[47] See "The 7th Judicial Working Meeting Between Chinese and Vietnamese Judges in Port Areas," source: http://www.gy.yn.gov.cn/Article/Print.asp?ArticleID=12,034. Accessed October 10, 2011.

[48] See "The 2010 Working Meeting between Honghe Public Security Bureau and Lao Cai Provincial Public Security Department," source: http://www.hh.cn/news_1/xw01/201010/t20101025_329685.html. Accessed October 10, 2011.

The Hekou County Public Security Bureau also held several work meetings with the Lao Cai Municipal Public Security Bureau on enhancing border management and patrol and combatting illegal trafficking.[49]

References

I. Books

(2008). *Practical Chinese Dictionary*. Beijing: The Commercial Press.
Binggao, J. (2007). *General Discussion on Ethnic Theory*. China Minzu University Press.
Hathaway, J. C. (2005). *The rights of refugees under international law*. Cambridge University Press.
[United States] Henkin, Louis. (1997). *The Age of Rights*. Translated by Xin Chunying. Beijing: Knowledge Publishing House.
Jin, S. (2000). *International law*. Peking University Press, Higher Education Press.
Qiliang, W. (2010). *Toward the law deeply embedded in the social and cultural context*. China Legal Publishing House.
Wenxian, Z. (1999). *Jurisprudence*. Higher Education Press and Beijing University Press.
Yunnan Provincial Department of Finance. *Indo-Chinese Refugees in Yunnan*, 1977 (unpublished).
Zhiping, L. (1996). *The customary law in Qing dynasty: Society and state*. China University of Political Science and Law Press.

II. Articles and Dissertations

Fangtian, Li. (2009). *The research on international immigration and immigration policies*. Nankai University.
Hu Xingdong. (2011). Customs or the customary law: Forms of customs in the legal system. *Jurisprudence & Historical Science of Law* reprinted by the Book and Newspaper Information Center of Renmin University of China, no. 9.
Junhua, Xu. (2005). *The study on the problems of legal control of illegal immigration*. Wuhan University.
Liang Shuying. (2008). Principles of dealing with illegal entry refugees. *Law Science Magazine*, 6
Minghuan, Li. (2005). The study of international migration: Its scope, frameworks and significance. *Journal of Xiamen University*, 3.

[49] See "The Working Meeting between Hekou County Public Security Bureau and Lao Cai Municipal Public Security Bureau," source: http://www.ga.yn.gov.cn/sgat/743138219628953601/20091121/15183.html. Accessed October 10, 2011.

Chapter 6
Policy Response to Illegal Immigration in Yunnan Border Areas with a High Concentration of Ethnic Minorities

This chapter elaborates on the de jure status of illegal immigration governance in Yunnan border areas with a high concentration of ethnic minorities. Dejure status is proposed based on scientific and objective analysis due to various parties' dissatisfaction with the current situation. In addition, we must indicate concrete elements and specific approaches when depicting desired prospects.

1 Border Policies

The policies regarding illegal immigration in the Yunnan border areas with a high concentration of ethnic minorities are representative of China's related policies, or they could be regarded as the specific manifestation or implementation of such policies in these areas. Only when national policies are established can they be applied to specific areas of the country. The implementation of national policies must be adapted to local circumstances. Moreover, we must draw on the successful experience of and lessons learned by other countries when developing China's policies regarding illegal immigration.

1.1 What China Can Learn from Border Policy in France, the US and Russia

Generally, the common practices to handle illegal immigrants are either to repatriate or dispel them or to naturalize them. Various methods have been adopted by different countries or the same country at different times. It is instructive to review the policies of three specific countries, i.e., France, the US and Russia, for the development of China's policies regarding illegal immigration.

G. Luo, *The Issues of Illegal Immigration and its Solutions in the Minority-Border Regions in Yunnan Province, China*, https://doi.org/10.1007/978-981-19-1249-8_6

(1) **France**

EU member states currently face numerous obstacles for future development, such as unreasonable structures of the labor market, a shortage of high-tech talent, aging populations, longer life expectancy and decreasing birth rates. They must introduce many immigrants to fill the gaps and resolve these problems. Therefore, a rather bizarre phenomenon has occurred among European countries: they have opposed the influx of illegal immigrants, while at the same time also issuing work permits to them, thus leading to a vicious cycle of illegal immigration.[1]

Let us first take France as an example.[2] It was a traditional migrant-sending country before World War II. After the war, the plummeting domestic population and labor shortage severely affected its reconstruction and economic recovery. In response to this, the French government launched a recruitment plan for overseas immigrant workers. In particular, during the "Glorious Thirty" period (the 30 years of rapid economic growth from 1945 to 1974), faced with the prominent economic profits brought by immigrants, the government turned a blind eye to the increase in illegal immigrants beginning in the late 1950s, believing that combatting illegal immigration would hamper economic development. On the other hand, the government could not stand idly when facing such a problem; thus, it adopted a legalization policy toward illegal immigrants.[3] In 1968, 82% of illegal immigrant workers in France were legalized.[4] On July 3, 1974 (the final year of the Glorious Thirty period), the French government enacted a decree to "temporarily" suspend the inflow of overseas immigrant workers to the country.

In 2002, due to the 9.11 terrorist attacks, France began to enhance the scrutiny of foreigners who had entered its borders illegally, and law enforcement was permitted to hold illegal immigrants in detention for 30 days before sending them back to their home country. In addition, to ensure the effective implementation of the new immigration law enacted in 2002, French authorities took measures to dispel foreigners who were staying there illegally.[5]

In 2005, French riots wreaked havoc upon the whole country. It all began with an incident on October 27, in which two boys died from electrocution while hiding from police at Clichy-sous-Bois in the northern suburbs of Paris. Several hundred teenagers participated in protests, during which they burned vehicles and trash bins, smashed shops and government buildings, and clashed with police. Later, such protests spread to other cities in France. The riots broke out mainly in the poorest neighborhoods in the suburbs of Paris, and the perpetrators mainly consisted of Islamic immigrants

[1] Wen Feng, "The Research on European Union's Governance on Illegal Immigration" (PhD diss., Jinan University, 2010), 69.

[2] The materials regarding the illegal immigration governance in France, cited from Yuan (2010).

[3] Legalization, also referred to as amnesty, is the system by which the destination country's government grants illegal immigrants permanent residence permits and finally makes them nationals by policies or decrees. It is unscheduled and, in most cases, derives from the need for workers or due to other political reasons. Therefore, it is policy-based and significantly unstable (Xu, 2005).

[4] Yuan (2010).

[5] Ibid., 245.

from northern Africa, who had long been excluded from mainstream society for various reasons and had suffered from systematic discrimination.

I personally believe that the Paris riots reflected the errors that France had made in its immigration policies. First, immigrants (including illegal immigrants) were unable to integrate with the local community due to their heterogeneity. The immigrants in France mainly hailed from the French colonies in the Middle East and northern Africa and followed Islamism. Most of them had not received much education and performed manual labor. This is why they faced discrimination in their daily lives, employment and political rights[6] and why they had always held a grudge against being treated as "second class citizens." On the other hand, the French government had settled them in the suburbs of Paris, which led to their separation from mainstream society and the rapid spread of dissatisfaction among them.

France needed to absorb a great number of workers to replenish its inadequate workforce caused by the war, the declining birth rate and the aging population. This prompted the French government to introduce many immigrants or even to legalize illegal immigrants. On the other hand, slow economic development, changes in public attitude, heterogeneity of immigrants and social problems caused by them were the reasons behind the increasingly strict policies toward illegal immigrants, which was further exacerbated by the constant swing between restrictive and relaxed immigration policies.

In recent years, after reviewing and assessing the previous immigration policies, the French government adopted a selective immigration policy, which aimed to continue to introduce high-end professionals, crack down on undocumented immigrants and illegal workers, and pursue a proper immigration policy that was neither too restrictive nor relaxed. A pattern of "relaxed-restrictive-selective" immigration policies can be observed in France, but this pattern is unstable and may reverse.

In 2007, soon after taking office as President of France, Nicolas Sarkozy passed a new immigration law to intensify efforts to combat illegal immigration. First, it removed the automatic regularization of illegal immigrants who had illegally resided in France for over 10 years. Nationality would be granted based on performance, and unqualified immigrants would be expelled from the country. Second, foreigners applying for family reunification or immigration for marriage were required to meet the housing and income requirements for family reunion and pass language proficiency tests and tests of French values or attend adequate training. Third, foreigners applying for family reunification were required to undergo DNA tests if the authenticity of their identification documents was questionable. In addition, Nicolas Sarkozy launched multiple voluntary and mandatory repatriation schemes against illegal immigrants, namely, those who stayed in France illegally were subject to one year of imprisonment, a penalty of 370 euros and a three-year re-entry ban. After the new immigration law was enacted, the French government dispelled 33,000 illegal immigrants in 2011 and planned to expel 35,000 more in 2012. In 2011, a total of 182,595 resident permits were issued, a decrease of 3.6% from 2010, and the

[6] In 2002, the unemployment rate among immigrants in France was 22%, 2.4 times France's average unemployment rate (Song, 2007).

number of professional immigrants and family immigrants dropped by 26% and 14%, respectively. The number of naturalized immigrants approved by the French authorities decreased to 66,000 in 2011 from 94,500 in 2010, a decrease of 30%. In 2012, Francois Hollande was sworn in as the new president, and his immigration policies have yet to be observed. However, he suggested "intelligent immigrants" in his election campaign and advocated flexible assessment of illegal immigrants' application on a case-by-case basis.[7]

(2) **The US**

The US has received the largest number of immigrants of all global nations, as it has been a major and traditional immigrant-receiving country since its founding. According to the research of Ruan Zhengyu, immigration has played an indispensable role in promoting the US's economic development and protecting its economic safety.[8] Immigrants are net contributors to the US's tax revenues, i.e., social and medical insurance and have contributed lucrative economic benefits. Over 70% of immigrants are over 18 years old, which means that the costs of childcare and education of 17.5 million immigrants are borne by their home countries instead of US taxpayers. Illegal immigrants also play an important role in large American companies, particularly in the construction, catering and agricultural industries. Without them, many American companies will face labor shortages. In recent years, US labor unions have changed their attitudes against illegal immigrants and assisted them in becoming union members due to their increasing proportion in the American labor market.

If the economic contribution of immigrants (including illegal immigrants) is the only consideration, then the US immigration policy should be "wide-open." However, economic factors are not the only ones affecting immigration policies, and the evolving policies have been the result of various factors. Li Fangtian builds on the research of Michael LeMay and divides US immigration policies into four eras in different periods and contexts: (1) the free immigration era (before 1880); (2) the door ajar era (1880–1920); (3) the strictly restrictive era (1920–1965); and (4) the selective immigration era (1965–2009).[9] From the description of these four eras, we may see that the US has also adopted the "relaxed-restrictive-selective" model in its immigration policies. Economic factors have played a decisive role in these policies, and the heterogeneity of immigrants and social problems brought on by them were still the main reasons for the increasingly tightened immigration policies. Meanwhile, war, external policies, racism, major events and their implicit factors may also have affected immigration policies. For example, the US took a heavy blow to its national security during the 9.11 attacks in 2001, which made combatting terrorism and protecting national security the priority national strategy.

[7] Bi Zhenshan, "Illegal Immigration: A Cross to Bear," source: http://world.workercn.cn/c/2012/05/25/120525032851473336362_1.html. Accessed May 25, 2012.

[8] See the role of immigration on America's economic development stated by Ruan Zhengyu, cited from Zhengyu (2003).

[9] Regarding the analysis of the four eras of the US immigration policies, cited from Li (2009).

As the attacks were somewhat associated with immigration, the US government also transferred the functions of the former Immigration and Naturalization Service to two other entities, the Citizenship and Immigration Service and the Immigration and Customs Enforcement. The *Patriot Act* and the *Enhanced Border Security and Visa Entry Reform Act* were enacted in 2001 and 2002, respectively, to enhance the investigation of foreigners crossing US borders and safeguard national security. The US also adjusted its immigration policies and imposed strict restrictions on Muslim immigrants from the Middle East, particularly from Arabic countries.

There are two key points in President Barack Obama's measures against illegal immigration. First, illegal immigrants who have committed felonies will be deported under the "Secure Communities" program. This requires local police offices across the country to provide fingerprints to cross-check with exit and entry records in the Department of Homeland Security's database. When illegal immigrants are discovered, immigration officers must decide on the issuance of warrants, deportation or local police actions. In 2011, the US deported 396,000 illegal immigrants under this program, an increase of 89% from 2008. Among them, 55% were criminals who committed felonies such as murder, rape and sexual assault against children. Second, employers will be prosecuted, penalized or even punished by imprisonment for hiring illegal immigrants. Since Barack Obama took office, the US has investigated over 3,200 companies for suspected recruitment of illegal immigrants, 225 companies or individuals have been punished, and penalties totaling 50 million US dollars have been imposed. At the beginning of 2012, the US's largest window and door manufacturer was fined two million US dollars for employing illegal immigrants. The company also promised to hire a full-time compliance officer to supervise recruitment to ensure that no more illegal immigrants would be employed. However, Obama did not shut the door on the regularization of illegal immigrants. Instead, he actively promoted the *Dream Act*, which aims to grant naturalization for illegal immigrants who have arrived in the US before the age of 16 and have resided continuously in the US for at least five consecutive years since the date of their arrival without committing any crimes. People who meet the following requirements are eligible for the naturalization application: they have graduated from an American high school, obtained a GED, attended college or served in the army for two years, no more than 35 years, and demonstrate good moral character. However, as of yet, this *Act* has not been passed by the federal legislature.[10]

This transition from relaxed to selective immigration policies in the US coincided with the changes in French policies.

(3) Russia

After the dissolution of the Soviet Union in 1991, the Russian Soviet Federative Socialist Republic became the largest country in the world (17,075,500 km^2), and its name was changed to the Russian Federation (or Russia). However, the Russian population was only 141 million (as estimated by the Russian government in 2008),

[10] Bi Zhenshan, "Illegal Immigration: A Cross to Bear," source: http://world.workercn.cn/c/2012/05/25/120525032851473336362_1.html. Accessed May 25, 2012.

and it underwent negative population growth for 12 consecutive years from the 1990s. UN experts have predicted that the Russian population will decrease to 126 million by 2025 and 104 million by 2050. In addition, Russia still faces rapid population aging and severe labor shortages. The proportion of the aging population was nearly 19% in the 1980s and 17.3% in 2006. The Russian government must absorb immigrants to alleviate threats to population security.[11]

According to the World Bank, there are currently over 12 million immigrants in Russia, making it the second-largest destination for immigrants, next to the US.[12] However, the statistics of illegal immigrants are inconsistent. The Federal government stated that there were no more than 1.3–1.5 million illegal immigrants in Russia in 2000–2001; according to Federal Frontier Defense authorities, the number was three million; the data provided by the Ministry of Internal affairs showed 1.5 million, while the Federal Immigration Service stated there were six to ten million illegal immigrants.[13]

Russia's immigration policies have also evolved, although the Russian government took power only 20 years ago.[14] (1) In the early 1990s, immigration policies focused on increasing refugee problems. The Russian government adopted the *Refugee Law* and the *Law on Forced Migrants*. It designated 13 districts in the coastal and frontier areas as places to settle immigrants temporarily, which reflected its urgent need to absorb overseas immigrants. (2) From the mid-1990s to the beginning of the twenty-first century, the government focused on controlling immigrant workers and combatting illegal immigration in response to the second immigration wave. (3) The enforcement of laws and regulations, such as the *Federal Law on Migration Registration of Foreign Nationals and Stateless Persons in the Russian Federation* of January 2007, exemplifies the increasingly mature and controllable management of immigrants in Russia. We can see three stages of immigration policies in Russia: immigration flows in the early 1990s due to a policy vacuum, strict control from the mid-1990s to the beginning of the twenty-first century, and selective adjustment after 2007. Russia shares the same changes in immigration policies with France and the US, i.e., relaxed-restrictive-selective policies.

Russian President Dmitry Medvedev called for combating illegal immigration and ordered the Migration Service to pay attention to the residence of foreign nationals in Russia. He held that "most Russian nationals are concerned about this issue. Unfortunately, it has led to deteriorated situations and conflicts based on ethnic problems, which should not be ignored." In addition, he emphasized that the expulsion of foreign nationals should be conducted based on the laws of Russia.[15]

---

[11] Xiaoyun (2010).

[12] Ibid., 67.

[13] Ibid., 67.

[14] Ibid., 101–102.

[15] See "*Russian President: The Expulsion of Tajik Illegal Immigrants Is Not a Campaign but a Coincidence,*" source: http://rusnews.cn/eguoxinwen/eluosi_duiwai/20111114/43211516.html. Accessed February, 22, 2012.

The research performed by Qiang Xiaoyun indicates that the opponents of mass migratory flows advocate tough and restrictive immigration policies due to their concerns over the threats of immigrants to economic, social, identity and homeland security, while supporters hold that Russia should attract immigrants to protect the country's population and economic security. Both sides consider protecting national interests and ensuring national security as the basis of their arguments, despite the differences in their views regarding immigration.[16]

Of course, economic development is part of the considerations when formulating Russia's unique immigration policies. However, a more important matter is resolving its urgent population pressure. In addition, Russia prioritizes the introduction of overseas ethnic Russians and immigrants from former Soviet Union countries. This is of particular significance: a lesser degree of heterogeneity between immigrants and locals, common languages, religious beliefs and living habits can help to better facilitate integration with the local society and reduce the negative impact of illegal immigrants.

1.2 China's Border Policies: Establishment and Basic Principles

We must consider two factors when establishing China's policies of illegal immigration governance. First, China's particular conditions and the evolution of immigration policies of other countries. Second, the purposes of China's policies, i.e., ultimate objectives of related policies.

(1) The Establishment of China's Border Policies

Migratory flows may attract high-end professionals and legal immigrant workers, along with various kinds of illegal immigrants who may pose considerable threats to national security. We must face this trend and prepare for the future when formulating relevant policies. Prior experience is one of the prerequisite considerations. Therefore, examining the countries that underwent immigration flows and analyzing their evolving policies will be instructive for the development of China's future policies.

Despite the differences in national conditions and the factors affecting their immigration policies, France, the US and Russia have adopted the same model, i.e., relaxed-restrictive-selective policies. To meet the urgent need of immigrant workers during rapid economic development, their governments have implemented policies to encourage the inflow of immigrants, promoted the introduction of immigrant workers for further economic development, or even regularized illegal immigrants on the grounds of policy or legal vacuum. However, when matters are pushed to the extreme, pushback tends to occur. The massive inflow of immigrants also led to a series of social problems and exacerbated the negative impacts on the receiving countries' political, economic and social orders. These negative impacts challenged

[16] Xiaoyun (2010).

the governance capabilities of these countries and affected the relationship between receiving countries and other countries, especially receiving countries, to whom these negative impacts also posed security threats. Therefore, these governments had to adjust their immigration policies to limit the inflow of immigrants, enhance border management, and combat illegal immigration. As a result, immigration flows ebbed, and the number of immigrants reduced. However, at the same time, their economies continued to grow, and there was still a need for immigrants. Moreover, strict limitations on legal immigrants may attract illegal immigrants, which renders immigration policies a dilemma. Consequently, "compromising" immigration policies were launched, which inaugurated a new era of selective immigration. On the one hand, these countries welcomed the inflow of immigrants but were selective about their number, quality and origins. That is, they controlled the number of immigrants to ensure their quality and preferred homogeneous or less heterogeneous immigrants. On the other hand, they amended the laws and regulations or developed new ones to strengthen entry and exit management and increase efforts to combat illegal immigrants. In other words, the so-called selective policies were welcoming, yet differentiated immigration policies were formulated based on national interests.

I believe that in the future, there will be massive migratory flows into China. We have determined the evolution of immigration policies in other countries, which will aid us in making use of late-mover advantages to prevent us from repeating the same mistakes.

First, we must formulate far-sighted policies.

Since we anticipate inevitable migratory flows into China, we must take action to prevent or delay these flows and attempt to eliminate their negative impacts. There are various factors regarding the inflow of immigrants. We cannot alter the positive factors involved, such as China's rapid economic development, stable political situation, harmonious social environment and national strategies of further opening China to the world. The trend of aging populations and decreasing growth rates is also unstoppable. It is restricted by China's laws and regulations, such as the *Constitution* and the *Population and Family Planning law* for Chinese citizens to have more children to increase the supply of the labor force. China must take advantage of the current policies and their flexible provisions and implement guidelines and policies conducive to introducing high-end professionals and legal immigrant workers. Meanwhile, China must adopt flexible and pragmatic foreign policies to coordinate with other countries, especially neighboring ones, and create a harmonious international environment and communication platform for the introduction of high-end professionals and legal immigrant workers.

For the Yunnan border areas with a high concentration of ethnic minorities, we must pay attention to the following three aspects to formulate far-sighted policies. First, make full use of the national guidelines and policies, such as developing China's vast western region, developing border areas and improving the lives of locals, and constructing Yunnan as a bridgehead in the opening to southwestern China, to promote the rapid and comprehensive economic and social development in these areas. This will provide a space for fostering local talent and workers and more opportunities to attract talent and workers from elsewhere. Second, we must make full use of the regional national autonomy enshrined in the *Constitution* and the *Law on Regional Ethnic Autonomy*. We must set out and implement personnel and employment policies adapted to the local conditions in autonomous regions and institutionalize these policies to create a thriving work environment for talent to stay. Third, we must make full use of Yunnan's geological advantages of sharing borders with three countries and facing more countries to the southwest. We must make closer connections with counterpart departments or local governments with countries to the southwest and develop approaches to introduce high-end professionals and workers under the state's permit.

Second, we must formulate science-based policies.

The countries described above have all followed the pattern of relaxed-restrictive-selective immigration policies. This demonstrates their flexibility in developing policies, but they have also paid a price for it. We should learn from their lessons, avoid unnecessary policy changes, and directly select the policies that have proven effective with minimal costs. Such policies are the most cost-effective ones based on science. Specifically, China must not repeat the same pattern of relaxed-restrictive-selective immigration policies. We have sufficient wisdom and capability to formulate and implement selective policies. We should, on the one hand, control the number and quality of immigrants and select homogeneous or less heterogeneous immigrants; on the other hand, we must strengthen entry and exit management and increase efforts to combat illegal immigrants by amending relevant laws and regulations or enacting new ones.

In the face of the increasingly challenging illegal immigration in the Yunnan border areas, we must not repeat the pattern of relaxed-restrictive-selective immigration policies but instead choose the selective model of immigration control by respecting the objective law of illegal immigration governance, thus minimizing governance costs and unnecessary efforts.

Third, we must formulate flexible policies.

Formulating and implementing selective policies does not signify that China's illegal immigration governance is a single-step process. It is an option based on other countries' experience, China's national conditions, the objective law of illegal immigration governance, and China's political advantages. However, selective policies are not a panacea that remains unchanged or fits all situations. They require continuous tests and improvement and may be replaced by new and better policies. In other words, the policies themselves are in constant change and may encounter emerging problems in implementation. We must adjust these policies in different circumstances to ensure their flexibility.

How flexible these policies should be will depend on practice to determine. In addition, we must also consider the following two aspects. First, the coordination between policies and laws and regulations. Theoretically speaking, the CPC's and the state's guidelines and policies are completely consistent with China's current laws and regulations regarding the basis, interests and fundamental purposes. However, the conflict between flexible policies and lagging and stable legislation leads to contradicting provisions between the two. The only solutions would be to adjust the policies, launch new policies to adapt to the laws, adjust the laws or enact new laws to adapt to the policies through coordination. In addition, different circumstances of China's various areas must be taken into consideration in policy implementation. We must make adjustments in implementing governance policies in the border areas based on the local conditions, without running counter to the overall national policy, to demonstrate the flexibility of policies and better resolve the existing practical problems.

(2) The Purposes of China's Policies

We must consider the ultimate goals and core demands in policy development. When formulating China's illegal immigration governance policies, we must determine the purposes of these policies, that is, to have a clear understanding of their ultimate goals without contradicting the *Constitution* and relevant laws. I believe that these policies have the following three purposes.

i. Ensure Policy Consistency and Safeguard China's Image

Looking into the governance process of the countries discussed above, we may find that their policies were constrained by different needs in different phases of economic and social development. When countries were in urgent need of overseas immigrants due to rapid economic and social development, they kept their doors wide open to illegal immigrants in migratory flows or even regularized their status. However, when the economy was disrupted or stagnant, illegal immigrants took its brunt, and legal immigrants also faced strict restrictions. This pragmatic approach undermined legal immigrants' identification with the receiving country and tempted illegal immigrants to wait for regularization. In other words, pragmatic policies will become an alternative pull factor of illegal immigration.

At the same time, pragmatic policies also undermined policy continuity and directly impacted the receiving country. Only policies featuring consistent and clear purposes can bring long-lasting social and economic benefits. China is building itself into a responsible major country. As soft power has become a critical element of the competition among countries, the continuity of a country's policies is a significant factor in improving its soft power.

Therefore, introducing high-end professionals and legal workers in a selective and appropriate manner and combating illegal immigration must become the CPC's and the state's consistent immigration policies, as well as the ultimate goal and core demand of China's governance policies.

When handling illegal immigration in the Yunnan border areas, we must consider the overall policies and their ultimate goals and the continuity of policies. However, maintaining continuity does not signify that these policies are unchangeable. Rather, it means that their fundamental principles or ultimate goals are unchangeable. We must consider combating illegal immigration as the guiding principle, and we shall not allow impunity for illegal immigration and related crimes on the grounds of "specific conditions in the border areas."

ii. Insist on Value Orientation and Protect National Security

The purposes of formulating and implementing the policies of illegal immigration governance are to regulate immigration order, combat illegal immigration, and satisfy the need for overseas immigrants for economic development. At the same time, this also involves combating illegal immigration and related crimes and protecting national security.

Under distorted value orientation, France, the US and Russia have loosened up control over illegal immigration to meet the demand of economic development. After realizing the threats of illegal immigration to their national security, they quickly halted these policies but had already paid the price. China must make use of its late-mover advantages to put national security at the core of its relevant policies and make the right choice between accelerating economic development and protecting national security.

In the Yunnan border areas with a high concentration of ethnic minorities, the impact of illegal immigration may not be evident at present. However, we cannot postpone the combat against illegal immigration and related crimes until the situation worsens. We must nip them in the bud and put protecting national security at the core of our policies.

As indicated previously, the illegal immigration problem that China will have to face is a hidden crisis. There is a Chinese saying that goes, "misfortune often stems from trivial mistakes, and one's wisdom and courage are often wasted by their obsession." Many countries have headed toward decline and destruction in history due to the accumulated and extended effects of unnoticeable crises. We must make top-level and long-term designs for state governance and the reform and opening-up. In addition, we must prepare ourselves for future risks, build risk awareness, and have the wisdom and means to identify and prevent hidden crises.[17]

iii. Insist on the Legality of Policies and Protect the Dignity of the Legal System

As indicated previously, the CPC's policies are consistent with China's national policies. At the same time, the CPC's policies and China's laws are highly consistent in terms of class nature, economic foundation, guidelines, fundamental principles and social objectives. There are no conflicts of fundamental interest between the two. In fact, policy legality and policy legitimation have seldom been explored. In his book *Introduction to the Study of Public Policy*, published in 1977, Charles O. Jones argues that there are two levels of policy legitimation: the legitimacy of the political system and the legitimation of policies, and the two processes are interdependent and indispensable. Therefore, instead of legitimation, we must focus on the policy legitimacy of the ruling party, i.e., how does the ruling party consciously translate the public interests into its policies?[18]

What are the elements of policy legitimacy? One scholar holds that there are three elements: (1) the legitimacy of the subject of policies; (2) the formulation and

[17] Editorial Department of People's Tribune: *Frontiers: Research on Unnoticeable Crises*, source: http://www.rmlt.com.cn/qikan/2012-05-10/. Accessed May 22, 2012.

[18] Yang (2010).

implementation of policies are science-based, legitimate and democratic; and (3) the legitimacy of the policies themselves.[19] Regarding the policies of illegal immigration governance covered in this book, the first two requirements are attainable, and the key is the third requirement, i.e., the legitimacy of the policies themselves. The scholar holds that public policies are the governance tool of the government or its political output. In this sense, the government should be a devoted defender of the public interests, and its policies should reflect the fundamental interests of the vast majority of the people and serve their interests. Otherwise, the policies are contradictory to the fundamental purposes of the government and the laws and have no legitimacy.[20] I believe that his understanding of policy legitimacy is based on the nature of policies. In terms of the wording of policies, they should at least not conflict with China's current laws and regulations.

Specifically, when formulating policies related to illegal immigration, we must compare them with the current laws and regulations and refrain from setting out contradictory policies. Meanwhile, we must check if these policies run counter to the laws and regulations and then alter the policies or amend the laws and regulations to ensure the legality of the polices and protect the dignity of the legal system.

2 The Rule of Law

Now that we have examined the policies of illegal immigration governance, let us review the current laws and regulations. They are the basis of illegal immigration governance and a significant part of the governance process, yet they are also fragmented and contradictory. Apart from legislation, another crucial part of the implementation of laws is law enforcement. This is a critical step to put laws and regulations into practice and a way to verify their scientific basis and applicability and achieve the fundamental purpose of the legislation, i.e., illegal immigration governance.

2.1 Legislation

We have previously stated that China's laws regarding illegal immigration are international law and domestic law. The latter includes China's *Constitution*, laws, administrative rules, local rules, autonomous rules, administrative regulations and the laws of Special Administrative Regions. There are no provisions regarding illegal immigration in the current domestic legal system, and the legal basis of handling such cases is the provisions of the exit and entry of Chinese nationals and the entry, residence and exit of foreigners. However, the problems of mixed forms of law, lagging rules, and inconsistent provisions and penalties still occur in practice. Should we

[19] Ibid.

[20] Ibid.

establish an immigration law or maintain the fragmented status of legislation? To answer this question, we must consider our national conditions and learn from the legislative experience of other countries.

France, a county with a civil law legal system, enacted a specific law on immigration in 1945. In July 1993, the then Interior Minister Charles Pasqua proposed a *New Immigration Law* to the Parliament and emphasized that France "no longer wants to be a country of immigration."[21] In September 2010, the National Assembly began to consider an amendment to the *Immigration Law* (the sixth amendment since 2002), which suggested depriving the French nationality of some immigrant criminals and expelling foreigners to overstay temporary visas and threaten public order. The purpose of the amendment was to promote selective immigration policies.[22] The new *Immigration and Integration Law* enacted in the summer of 2007 aimed to encourage high-skilled immigration, restrict family immigration and fight illegal immigration more effectively. Through new amendments, France adopted a harmonized legislature framework and adapted its immigration law to ever-changing circumstances.

As a typical common law country, the US adopts a massive legal system regarding immigration comprised of various laws influenced by immigration policies and cases of different periods. Some critical US laws regarding illegal immigration governance include the following[23]: (1) the *Chinese Exclusion Act of 1882*, which indicated the beginning of restrictive and selective immigration policies; (2) the *Immigration and Naturalization Act of 1965*, a milestone in the history of the US immigration law and the start of comprehensive reform of the US immigration policies; (3) the *Immigration Reform and Control Act of 1986*, which granted legal status to undocumented immigrant workers residing in the US (most beneficiaries were undocumented Mexican immigrants in the agricultural industry); (4) the *Illegal Immigration Reform and Immigrant Responsibility Act of 1996*, that showed intense hostility toward immigrants; (5) the *Patriot Act* enacted on October 26, 2001 and the *Enhanced Border Security and Visa Entry Reform Act* enacted on May 14, 2002, which aimed to strengthen the investigation of foreigners crossing the US borders to enhance the national security after the 9.11 attacks; and (6) the *Maritime Transportation Security Act* of 2002 signed by President George W. Bush, which aimed to carry out port security plans, improve crew identification systems, and prevent terrorists from launching attacks on the US via maritime transportation systems.

Russia is a traditional European country whose legislation is influenced by common law. It adopts a separate approach to legislation regarding immigration (including illegal immigration) governance.[24] From 1991 to 2003, the Russian government approved 37 federal laws, 10 presidential decrees, 62 federal rules, 26 departmental rules and nine international agreements regarding immigration,

---

[21] Feng (2010).

[22] See "France Reviews the Proposal of the New Immigration Law Today," source: http://bjyouth.ynet.com/article.jsp?oid=69534857. Accessed September 26, 2011.

[23] The materials regarding the US laws on illegal immigration governance, cited from Xu (2005).

[24] The Materials regarding the Russian laws of immigration, cited from Qiang (2010).

including the *Law on Refugees of 1993* and the *Law on Forcibly Displaced Persons of 1993*; the *Federal Law of the Russian Federation on the Procedure for Exit from the Russian Federation and Entry Into the Russian Federation of 1996* (amended in January 2003); and the *Federal Law on Legal Status of Foreign Citizens in the Russian Federation of 2002*. In addition, the *Federal Law on Migration Registration of Foreign Nationals and Stateless Persons in the Russian Federation* and the newly amended *Federal Law on Legal Status of Foreign Citizens in the Russian Federation* came into effect in 2007.

China mainly implements a civil law legal system, and it should adopt the French legislative model to establish a unified immigration law. However, since the founding of the PRC, and particularly since the reform and opening-up, China has been sending many migrants to other countries. China has conducted research mainly on controlling the emigration from Fujian and other provinces but has not paid sufficient attention to inbound migration. Moreover, the relevant laws and regulations are mainly related to the exit and entry of Chinese citizens and the entry, residence and exit of foreigners. The terms of immigrants and illegal immigrants cannot be found in these laws and regulations. In fact, during my investigation, I observed that substantive departments were not very familiar with these terms. More importantly, due to the small number of illegal immigrants in China, governmental departments tend to not pay due attention to the risks involved, especially the threats of illegal immigration to national security.

I believe that China is not equipped to establish a uniform law on immigration in terms of its legislative basis. Considering that legislation should be moderately advanced, competent departments must prepare for a uniform immigration law, including current situation investigation and the collection and analysis of overseas legal documents. At the same time, legislative departments must accomplish the following:

First, resolve the practical problems in the current laws and regulations regarding illegal immigration governance, such as mixed forms of law, outdated rules, and inconsistent provisions and penalties. The recommended responses are: 1. The departments that formulated the lagging laws and regulations shall be responsible for amending them or setting out new ones; 2. For inconsistent penalties, competent authorities must summon the departments that enacted these rules to set standardized penalties; 3. The mixed forms of law refer to the various complicated provisions in the laws, local rules, local governmental regulations, additional rules, implementation rules and regulations, despite a sound legal system of border management. I believe that the key is to combine the laws of the same level. For example, the former *Law on the Control of the Exit and Entry of Citizens and the Law on Administration of the Entry and Exit of Foreigners* were combined into the *Exit-Entry Administration Law*. We must integrate the *Yunnan Province Administrative Rules for Entry-Exit of External Border Residents in the Chinese-Myanmar Border Areas*, *Yunnan Province Provisional Administrative Rules for Entry-Exit of Chinese Citizens in the China-Myanmar Border Areas*, and *Yunnan Province Administrative Rules for Entry-Exit in the China-Vietnam and China-Myanmar Border Areas* into the *Yunnan Province Administration Rules for Personnel and Materials Entry-Exit in the China-Vietnam,*

China-Laos and China-Myanmar Border Areas as soon as possible. In doing so, we will be able to combine different rules on the same level into one set of uniform rules, which is a simple and practical way to deal with the mixed forms of law.

Second, we must formulate uniform yet more comprehensive local or autonomous rules regarding the management of cross-border immigration and illegal immigration in the Yunnan border areas. Considering that China lacks a uniform immigration law, the relevant laws and regulations are based on the rules of the exit and entry of Chinese nationals and the entry, residence and exit of foreigners, and the competent authorities and the public are not familiar with the terms of "immigration" and "illegal immigration."

Therefore, according to Articles 100 and 116 of the *Constitution* and the requirements in Articles 63 and 66 of the *Legislation Law*, I suggest first developing trial rules in Yunnan Province or Honghe Hani & Yi Autonomous Prefecture, such as the *Administrative Rules on Cross-border Migration of Yunnan Province* and the *Administrative Rules on Cross-border Migration of Honghe Hani & Yi Autonomous Prefecture*. Such rules must include the management of exit and entry in border areas and a series of relevant issues regarding the residence, nationality and naturalization of cross-border immigrants. We must also specify the difference between regular *sanfei* and illegal immigrants and formulate corresponding penalties in such rules.

2.2 Law Enforcement

As previously noted, the discussions with relevant departments revealed that, aside from inadequate staffing and limited budget, other law enforcement problems include multiple border management departments (China's primary departments of illegal immigration control) with overlapping responsibilities. In addition, the inconsistent understanding of border management, unreasonable exercise of power, and unclear division of mandates among public security, armed police, foreign affairs, customs, inspection and quarantine and civil affairs authorities have rendered it difficult to pursue collective efforts. I believe that this distinctly Chinese style of comanagement by multiple departments can be found in the management of illegal immigration and other issues, which in turn leads to low effectiveness and efficiency. In addition to common understanding, clear division of responsibilities and distribution of tasks, we also need an effective solution. The systems and experiences of other countries can aid us in better solving this problem.

In France, the Immigration Department oversaw the management of overseas immigrants. After Nicolas Sarkozy became President, he enacted a series of stricter immigration policies in 2007 and set up a new Ministry of Immigration, Integration, National Identity and Codevelopment. Following this, the government decided to adjust the number of family immigration and economic immigration applications and combat illegal immigration more effectively.

In the US, there are four departments that oversee immigration management (i.e., the US Department of State, US Department of Homeland Security, US Department of Labor and US Department of Health and Human Services), with a clear division of responsibilities.[25] The Department of State implements the *Immigration Law* through the US embassies and consulates across the world. The most important task of embassies and consulates is to issue visas. According to regulations, foreigners who wish to enter the US, including immigrants and nonimmigrants alike, must first obtain valid visas from overseas US embassies and consulates. The enforcement of immigration law was previously entrusted to the Minister of Justice, whose mandates do not include matters related to immigration law authorized to other departments (including the Department of State and Department of Labor). The Minister of Justice typically authorizes the Immigration and Naturalization Service (INS) and the Executive Office for Immigration Review to handle the issues related to immigration. On January 15, 2003, the US Department of Homeland Security was established. Since this time, the INS was no longer part of the Ministry of Justice, and its functions were combined with two units of the Department of Homeland Security, i.e., the Bureau of Citizenship and Immigration Service and the Directorate of Border and Transportation Security. The US Department of Labor is responsible for assessing and verifying whether immigrant workers (applicants for permanent residence) will be taking jobs away from American workers when they obtain permanent employment. The Department of Health and Human Services is required to inspect the medical examinations of international medical graduates prior to their entry and determine if schools are eligible to receive international students, then provide related information to the Minister of Labor.

The Russian executive body responsible for immigration matters is the Federal Immigration Service under the Interior Ministry. According to the *Regulations on the Federal Immigration Service* released on July 16, 2004, the Federal Immigration Service exercises the functions of control, supervision and rendering state services in the sphere of immigration and coordination with other departments in immigration management. The Federal Service for Labor and Employment under the Ministry of Health and Social Development of Russia is also involved in immigration management.[26]

There are two common aspects in the immigration management authorities in these three countries: 1. a separate immigration management body regardless of which department it belongs to and 2. a clear division of labor, although different departments are involved.

According to Article 4 of the *Exit-Entry Administration Law*, "The Ministry of Public Security and the Ministry of Foreign Affairs shall, within the scope of their respective responsibilities, be responsible for administering exit-entry affairs. Embassies and consulates of the People's Republic of China and other institutions stationed abroad entrusted by the Ministry of Foreign Affairs (hereinafter referred to as "the visa-issuing authorities abroad") shall be responsible for the issuance of entry visas to foreigners. Exit-entry border inspection authorities shall be responsible for carrying out exit-entry border inspections. Public security organs under

[25] Regarding the division of labor among the US law enforcement departments, see Xu (2005).
[26] Xiaoyun (2010).

local people's governments at or above the county level and their exit-entry administrations shall be responsible for the administration of the stay and residence of foreigners. The Ministry of Public Security and the Ministry of Foreign Affairs may, within the scope of their respective responsibilities, entrust exit-entry administrations of public security organs or foreign affairs departments under local people's governments at or above the county level to accept foreigners' applications for entry, stay and residence in China. In the administration of exit-entry affairs, the Ministry of Public Security and the Ministry of Foreign Affairs shall strengthen communication and cooperation, cooperate closely with relevant departments under the State Council, and exercise functions and powers and bear liabilities within the scope of their respective responsibilities in accordance with the law." We can see that China does not have any specific authorities that administer immigration affairs. We can learn from the countries described above and establish a Department or Administration of Immigration directly under the State Council and corresponding entities at provincial, municipal and autonomous regional levels. These entities would be responsible for immigration management and coordination with related organizations. However, before such entities are established, the only solution is to enhance the management of foreigners' exit, entry and residence.

3 Overcoming Difficulties

Illegal immigration governance in the Yunnan border areas with a high concentration of ethnic minorities involves many issues at the macro level. The fundamental problems or difficulties are as follows: First, how can strict restrictions be placed on illegal border crossing to block the entry of illegal immigrants? Second, how can the legal status of illegal immigrants and their children be coped with, and if regularization is possible? The difficulties in border control in these areas are caused by many factors. The question is, can we learn from the experience of other countries and adopt a new model of border control to address illegal border crossing more effectively? In addition, for illegal immigrants who are unlikely to be repatriated after years of residence in China, is it possible to regularize their status by following the practices of other countries? To address the issue of illegal immigration, it is important to prevent new illegal immigrants, while regularizing the status of illegal immigrants and their children is equally important.

3.1 Border Management

Border management systems vary among states. It is a sovereign state's internal affair to adopt its border management system and legitimize it based on its national conditions. At the same time, this often involves relations with neighboring countries. The two sides may coordinate border management by concluding bilateral agreements with each other. If one sovereign state joins an international organization or an international treaty, then the provisions regarding border management in the organization's charter or the treaty shall be the basis of border management.

(1) EU: Strict External Control and Relaxed Internal Control

The EU is an influential regional integration organization that is both a political and economic entity. In December 1991, the Maastricht Summit of the European Community approved the *European Union Treaty* (the *Maastricht Treaty*), which came into force on November 1, 1993, marking the birth of the EU. At present, the EU has 27 member states with a combined population of 500 million. One of its objectives is to promote balanced economic and social development among member states by building a borderless space, enhancing coordinated economic and social development and building an economic and currency union using a common currency. EU countries carry out relaxed border management among themselves but strict border control toward other countries. This kind of strict external control and relaxed internal control is realized through two agreements.

1. *Schengen Agreement*

In June 1985, Germany, France, the Netherlands, Belgium and Luxembourg signed the *Agreement on the Gradual Abolition of Checks at Common Borders* (the *Schengen Agreement*) in Luxembourg's border town Schengen. It includes the following policies: (1) no border checks between signatory states; (2) foreigners, when authorized to enter Schengen areas, are allowed to travel freely across the signatory states; and (3) the establishment of police cooperation and a legal assistance mechanism, the Schengen Information System, and a shared archive of offenders. Later, several newcomers joined the *Schengen Agreement*, and at present, a total of 25 member states have signed it. With the exceptions of Norway, Iceland and Switzerland, the other Schengen countries are all EU member states. In contrast, two EU members, the UK and Ireland, have yet to sign it. The purposes of the *Schengen Agreement* are to abolish mutual checks at the common borders, coordinate border control toward other areas, and create a "borderless" Europe.

2. *Convention on the Crossing of External Frontiers*[27]

The purpose of the *Convention on the Crossing of External Frontiers* (the *Convention on Frontiers*) is to control the crossing by nationals of a third state at the external frontiers of EU member states, especially illegal crossings. It defines external frontiers as a member state's land frontier that is not adjacent to a frontier of another member state, maritime frontiers, and airports and ports outside of the common frontiers. Nationals of a member state or a third state who embark in a member state from a third party must present valid travel documents and are subject to checks.[28]

---

[27] The *Convention on the Crossing of External Frontiers* (the *Convention on Frontiers*) was signed by the European Community member states in June 1991. It was intended to come into force on December 31, 1994, yet remained on the table due to a dispute between Spain and the UK over the status of Gibraltar. However, the other provisions of the Convention were agreed upon by all parties (Xu, 2005).

[28] Feng (2010).

External frontiers are governed by member states (including frontier checkpoints, land frontiers, coastlines, airports and ports). According to the *Convention on Frontiers*, any person who is not a national member state may be authorized to enter the territories of the member states for a short stay provided that they (1) present a valid passport; (2) present a valid travel document; (3) do not represent a threat to public policy or national security; (4) present an employment verification letter; and (5) have sufficient means of subsistence for the stay and to return to his country of origin.[29]

(2) US: Strict Prevention and Control

The US's control over its land frontiers has been challenged by the influx of illegal immigrants into the country from lands. Let us take the US-Mexico border as an example. The border protection zone built by the US Border Patrol (USBP) covers only approximately 128 km, compared with approximately 3,200 km in total of the US-Mexico border. The overstretched border patrol agents have long been toiling along the frontiers, but their operations ended up like a cat-and-mouse game. The long border and the USBP's manpower shortage are the main reasons for this ineffective border control.[30] In 2005, after two days of heated debate, the US House of Representatives voted to adopt a strict immigration bill that included increasing the number of Border Patrol agents, using drones for border patrol, and building approximately 1,120 km of fence along the US-Mexico border. In 2006, people in major East and West coast cities attended the protests and rallies against the new immigration law and the building of walls along the US-Mexico border. However, the House of Representatives eventually passed a bill to permit the building of 594.5 km of wall and 804.6 km of fence along the border to prevent illegal immigrants from entering the US across the border without barriers.[31]

Meanwhile, the US government increased the funds for relevant authorities, increased the staff number of the CIS and customs offices, and assigned the National Guard for assistance to enhance border control.

(3) The Chinese Model: US or EU Model?

During the investigation, the officials in Hekou County agreed on the difficulties in managing the China-Vietnam border and attributed the issues of illegal immigration governance to poor border control. They concluded that if the current situation remained unchanged, then other issues related to illegal immigration governance could not be completely resolved.

The officials in Hekou County disagreed with my recommendation of adopting the US model to take strict prevention and control measures along the border, such as building wire fences to prevent illegal border crossing, for the following reasons. 1. The southern part of Hekou County shares a border of 193 km (120 km land boundaries and 73 km water boundaries) with Vietnam's Lao Cai city, Muong Khuong

[29] Xu (2007).

[30] Hao (2002).

[31] Li (2009).

County and Bat Xat County. It will require tremendous human and physical resources to construct wire fences. In addition, it is inconvenient to do so, as the water boundaries are usually rivers (natural boundaries or geological boundaries by law) and the boundary line is the midline of the river. 2. Numerous staff members will be needed to guard 193 km of borderlines if wire fences are built. 3. It will hinder the passing of border residents, create tensions along the border, and break the close bond between the Chinese and Vietnamese people. 4. This may undermine the friendly relations between China and Vietnam.

I believe that the first and second reasons, i.e., the problems of human, physical, financial and technical resources, can easily be solved. The wire fences can be built on China's side. Moreover, Vietnam has already built a dam on Vietnam's side of the boundary river. I believe that the fourth reason does not apply because the dam built on Vietnam's side has not affected relations between China and Vietnam. The third reason is worth pondering over. Freely crossing borders is a long-established habit of border residents. Furthermore, border residents mainly consist of minorities who are accustomed to striding across the border. After negotiations, China and Vietnam issued exit and entry permits for border residents and allowed free passing via ports. However, due to the limited number of these ports and poor transportation, most border residents prefer to use unauthorized crossing points, which must be controlled to ban illegal border crossing.

If we take a closer look, we may find that the same border management problems also exist in border areas in Yunnan other than Hekou County. In theory, it is plausible to construct wire fences to strictly prevent illegal movement across the border, but in practice, it is not feasible, at least at present.

Let us take Hekou County as an example. Is it possible to sign a multilateral agreement, similar to the *Schengen Agreement*, among China, Vietnam, Laos and Myanmar? Or to sign such an agreement among China and ASEAN countries on the basis of the China-ASEAN free trade area, to abolish the checkpoints along the border between China and ASEAN countries, coordinate border control outside these countries, and create a "borderless" China-ASEAN free trade area?

I believe that this proposition is even more unattainable. The *Schengen Agreement* was concluded based on the high level of political and economic integration among EU member states. In addition, these countries do not differ greatly in terms of history, culture, national system, religious beliefs, values and customs; this is also the main reason for the effective implementation of the agreement. However, there are substantial differences in these aspects between China and ASEAN countries and among themselves. Moreover, China and most ASEAN countries are still developing countries, but their levels of economic development vary. For example, the GDP and purchasing power of Vietnam, Laos, Myanmar and Cambodia, which recently joined the ASEAN, are much lower than those of early members such as Singapore and Brunei. The "China threat theory" lingers on under the manipulative propaganda of the US and other countries, and China and some ASEAN countries dispute over the South China Sea islands and maritime rights. The basis of high political and economic integration is lacking, and it is impossible for this to be created in a short period of time. This is why the chance of signing an international treaty similar to the *Schengen Agreement* with those countries is slim.

Neither the US nor EU model applies to border management in the Yunnan border areas. The current approach is problematic and ineffective, and this leads to difficulties in border control. Therefore, we must find a solution to solve border management problems in these areas.

In my personal opinion, the key is to renew our conceptions.

First, we must reflect on our attitude toward the current border management approach. We have realized that the current management approach is problematic, but we have not realized the severe consequences of the difficulties in border control. Therefore, there is insufficient pressure to solve these problems. This attitude stems from the perception that persistent illegal border crossing has not led to severe consequences, and there is no need to examine or resolve these problems. It is challenging to call on the government or civil society to focus on what they deem not severe. Second, massive migratory flows into China have yet to occur. The threat of immigrants (especially illegal immigrants) to the stability and security of border areas with a high concentration of ethnic minorities is not evident. This is why people do not have an adequate understanding of the relations between illegal border crossing and illegal immigration and underestimate the negative effect of illegal immigration. We must be aware that protecting the safety of border crossings in border areas is safeguarding national security. While massive migratory flows into China have yet to occur, as the old saying goes, "preparedness ensures success, and unpreparedness spells failure." A precautionary approach is the optimal attitude of problem solving.

I believe that we can take pilot measures of border management in Hekou County, i.e., strict management and control along the border to prevent illegal border crossing. At the same time, considering the specific conditions of these areas, we must be flexible in implementing relevant laws and regulations.

(4) Moderate Flexibility in Implementing the Law

There are two aspects of moderate flexibility in implementing the law: it must be carried out within the framework of China's laws and regulations, and the implementation must be moderately flexible and take actual effects into consideration.

Flexibility within the framework of China's laws and regulations signifies that there must be a legal basis. As indicated previously, according to Article 100 of the *Constitution* and Article 63 of the *Legislation Law*, Yunnan Province has established adaptive rules regarding the penalties against illegal border crossing (see the previous table). In addition, according to Article 116 of the *Constitution*, Article 66 of the *Legislation Law* and Article 19 of the *Law on Regional Ethnic Autonomy*, autonomous regions in the border area shall have the power to enact regulations on the exercise of autonomy and separate regulations in light of the political, economic and cultural characteristics of the reality of autonomous regions in the border area. They shall also implement relevant policies and measures with certain alterations. Article 90 of the *Exit-Entry Administration Law* stipulates that "upon approval by the State Council, provinces and autonomous regions bordering on neighboring countries may, in accordance with the boundary administration agreements signed by China with relevant countries, formulate local regulations or local government rules to regulate the association of residents in border areas of the two countries." Together, these form the legal basis of flexibility in implementing the law by local governments.

We must understand that the purpose of flexibility is to better resolve the relevant problems, and the metric by which to measure this is the effectiveness of problem solving. If the altered rules or measures are ineffective in controlling illegal border crossing, this means that the alterations have failed. As previously discussed, the amount of penalty and duration of detention for illegal border crossing differ from one another. Any border resident who illegally crosses the national border shall be given a warning and fined a penalty of different amounts, ranging from 10 yuan to 50 to 100 yuan. There is a considerable discrepancy between local punishment and punishment written in national legislation. Furthermore, punishment is inadequate to prevent any future occurrence of the same behavior.

Therefore, the effectiveness of problem solving is a way to assess whether the alterations are successful or appropriate. If the answer is no, then we must amend or improve the local regulations as soon as possible. This is in fact an issue of how to exercise local legislative powers reasonably. We must amend the "three rules" formulated by the Yunnan Provincial Government in a timely manner to impose stronger punishment. After all, flexibility does not mean "ignoring offences" or "reducing punishment." Instead, tougher punishment is another alternative permitted by law. In the Yunnan border areas with a high concentration of ethnic minorities, people are accustomed to lenient punishment for breaking national legislation without assessing the implications of such acts. In some cases, this may run counter to the fundamental purposes of legislation.

We can build a specific management model for Yunnan border areas with a high concentration of ethnic minorities. For example, I have built a "Hekou border management model" as follows:

First, the US practice of strict prevention and control should be adopted along the border, and anyone entering or exiting the border must comply with the laws and regulations. We do not necessarily need to construct wire fences, but we should be aware of strict border control.

Second, subordinate ports or patrol stations should be established at settlement areas with a high concentration of border residents who frequently cross the border, in addition to the four existing ports in Hekou County, to facilitate the crossing of border residents holding exit and entry permits. Nonborder residents must cross the border through the existing ports and shall not pass subordinate ports or petrol stations.

Third, border control tasks should be assigned at subordinate ports or petrol stations to the authorities responsible for port management. We can build upon the practice of traffic police assistants and hire local people to participate in border control after training to build a border management model featuring cooperation between police and local residents.

Of course, the Hekou border management model is currently a theoretical concept, and many problems will occur during its implementation. However, without theoretical innovation, no new practices will be carried out.

I am pleased to note that the Lincang Border Defense Force has done an outstanding job in controlling illegal border crossing in the Yunnan border areas. From January to July 2011 alone, they arrested 890 people from entering and exiting the border illegally, seized 167 kg of drugs, and effectively contained such illegal activities[32] in the following ways. First, they built three defense lines of blockade at ports, public security investigation within the jurisdiction, and examination and control at checkpoints. Second, they performed unscheduled field investigations at places where people who often illegally enter and exit the border stay and hide, such as business units, transportation stations, construction sites and recreational venues. They also registered and examined temporary residents from other places, set up barriers at main transportation routes, and checked the personnel and vehicles entering the border. Third, they built an information monitoring network along the border and a digital communications system by installing surveillance cameras at border ports and routes to monitor routes 24/7 and left no room for illegal border crossing.[33]

The practices of the Lincang Border Defense Force have strongly underpinned the theory of the Hekou border management model. Their experience in building an information monitoring network along the border and installing surveillance cameras at border ports and routes has been proven economically and technically feasible. In addition, it has made 24/7 border monitoring possible, which is instructive for practicing strict border management and control and for implementing the rule of border crossing by law.

3.2 *Legal Status*

From the perspective of international law, the legal status of foreigners refers to the rights and obligations of foreigners in the country of residence, including foreigners shall abide by the laws of the country of residence and the regulations of their entry, residence and exit and shall enjoy their due rights.[34] People who reside within the territory of China and do not have Chinese nationality are not necessarily foreigners. They cannot enjoy the rights granted to foreigners by China unless they present proof of their foreign nationality or stateless status. They must also abide by China's laws and regulations regarding their entry, residence and exit.

As stated earlier, illegal immigrants who have long resided in China typically cannot prove their foreign nationality or stateless status. They are unlikely to obtain

---

[32] Regarding the experience of Lincang Border Defense Force in controlling illegal border crossing, see "*Lincang Border Defense Force Arrests 890 People for Illegal Border Crossing and Captures 167 kg of Drugs in Six Months,*" source: http://www.legaldaily.com.cn/zfb/content/2011-08/16/content_2869581.htm?node=22,950. Accessed October 20, 2011.

[33] See "*Lincang Border Defense Force Arrests 890 People for Illegal Border Crossing and Captures 167 kg of Drugs in Six Months,*" source: http://www.legaldaily.com.cn/zfb/content/2011-08/16/content_2869581.htm?node=22950. Accessed October 20, 2011.

[34] Jin (2000).

Chinese nationality or be repatriated. They are not foreigners, nor stateless people, let alone Chinese. However, we cannot simply ignore them, as they have been living in China. The problem is how to identify their legal status, and is it possible to regularize their status?

Regularization (also referred to as amnesty) is a process in which irregular foreign immigrants are granted legal status by the country of residence. The typical practice is to grant irregular immigrants legal status so that they are no longer deemed unacceptable.[35] In other words, it is a way to make them legal immigrants through specific procedures, accept their naturalization, or grant them residence permits. Although regularization differs in methods and provisions among countries, it is often influenced by immigration policies. It depends on the immigration policies of different periods to decide whether to regularize their status or the scale, scope and methods of regularization.

In 1981, the Socialist Party of France came to power. It restricted the inflow of immigrants but offered amnesty to illegal immigrants who had lived in France for a long time. In 1998, the Party took power again and enacted the *Chevènement Law*, which allowed undocumented immigrants who met the following requirements to apply for regularization: they were legal spouses of French nationals; they were parents of children who were born in France; they could present the proof of their residence in France for over 10 years; or they could present proof of their connection with France (spoke fluent French, had jobs and paid taxes). The number of illegal immigrants was not reduced after three large-scale regularization campaigns, and President Nicolas Sarkozy began to take strict actions in response. In 2012, the newly elected President Francois Hollande stated that the regularization of illegal immigrants must be controlled.

Italy has long been a transit country for illegal immigrants from northern Africa to the EU because of its geological location. Every year, Italy's border police must investigate numerous smuggling cases. In the meantime, many people have successfully entered the Italian border and arrived in other EU countries, and the ensuing social and humanitarian problems have caused great trouble for EU member states. Among the EU members, Italy has granted the greatest number of amnesties, and it has done one large batch every few years. In 1990, 1996 and 1997, Italy regularized 716,000 illegal immigrants from Maghrib, Balkan and other Asian regions. In 2003, 630,000 illegal immigrants were regularized by amnesty in Italy, setting a record of the largest number of regularized immigrants within the shortest time under the simplest procedures. The Italian government issued 520,000 residence permits in 2007 and another 170,000 permits to non-EU workers in 2008, among which 95% were illegal immigrant workers in Italy who were then able to obtain legal residence.[36] Despite several amnesties to illegal immigrants, Italy is aware of the danger of illegal immigration, and Italian Prime Minister Silvio Berlusconi began to enact severe measures against illegal immigration.

---

[35] Graziano Battistella, Irregular Migration, *World Migration Report 2008*, 225. Cited from Feng (2010).

[36] Feng (2010).

The US once kept its door wide open to immigrants, which led to massive inflows of illegal immigrants into the country. According to the latest report of the Pew Research Center, as of March 2010, there were nearly 11.2 million illegal immigrants in the US, which was approximately the same as the previous year. The US media reported that there were approximately 11.5 million illegal immigrants at the time (May 25, 2012).[37] Mexico is the largest country of origin of illegal immigrants in the US. As of March 2010, there were 6.5 million illegal immigrants from Mexico, accounting for 58% of the total number.[38] In 2006, the US president George W. Bush proposed the *Guest Worker Program*, which aimed to grant undocumented immigrants and workers from abroad three-year work permits, and these permits could be extended for another three years. The authorities would decide on these people's naturalization according to their performance and would regularize seven to eight million illegal immigrants among a total of 12 million. The program was objected by many congress members and the public, and it was not approved. Later, President Barack Obama illustrated the US government's immigration policies. First, illegal immigrants shall be liable for breaking US laws. No large-scale amnesty would be granted to illegal immigrants in the future, and the 11 million illegal immigrants would be responsible for their illegal actions according to law. Second, illegal immigrants would be provided with naturalization procedures. It is impossible for the US government to expel all illegal immigrants, considering its economic development and repatriation costs. In the future, illegal immigrants would be asked to register their information, pay the fines of illegal border crossing and outstanding taxes, learn English, and become legal US citizens by legal means.[39]

Illegal immigrants constitute a high percentage of the immigrants in Russia. It is estimated by the Russian Immigration Service that there are over five million illegal immigrants in the country who pose multiple threats to its social stability in terms of the following aspects:

Financial losses caused by tax evasion. Illegal immigrants are outside of the regular employment and taxation systems due to their status, thus seriously affecting the national economy. The Director of the Federal Migration Service Konstantin Romodanovsky once told the media that the Russian economy suffered a loss of eight billion UD dollars due to tax evasion every year. (2) Deteriorated national security. Some illegal immigrants ignored the law and committed criminal activities. Many felonies, such as arms, drugs and psychotropic substances trade, were committed by illegal immigrants. (3) Fewer jobs for local workers and an increase in unemployment rates. Illegal immigrants have to take away low-end jobs from local workers for survival, leading to an oversupply of cheap laborers, a decrease in wages, and an increase in unemployment rates. (4) Nationalist sentiment among some Russian

---

[37] Bi Zhenshan, "Illegal Immigration: A Cross to Bear," source: http://world.workercn.cn/c/2012/05/25/120525032851473336362_1.html. Accessed May 25, 2012.

[38] Du Jing, "11.2 Million Illegal Immigrants in the US," source: http://news.xinhuanet.com/world/2011-02/03/c_121049078.htm. Accessed September 28, 2011.

[39] "*Barack Obama Makes His First Formal Speech on the Reform of Immigration Policies,*" source: http://www.cnr.cn/china/gdgg/201007/t20100702_506675566.html. Accessed September 28, 2011.

people. In recent years, some extremist nationalist organizations have become active in some major cities in Russia, the most notorious of which are the Skinheads, whose members mainly consist of youths. These organizations have attacked foreigners and ethnic minorities by terrorist means and created a growing trend of extremist criminal cases. According to the investigation of an authoritative agency, the Levada Center, over half of the Russian population believed that the inflow of for immigrants should be restricted, and 34% of the respondents believed that poverty in Russia was caused by non-Russian ethnic minorities. Only 20% of the respondents held positive views regarding immigrant workers from neighboring countries.[40]

The Russian government took severe measures against illegal immigration in response to the negative impact of the influx of illegal immigrants. At the same time, due to its rapidly aging population and labor shortages, in recent years, it has implemented a series of immigration laws and regulations to alleviate the ensuing social problems through institution building and government guidance. It has also formulated preferential measures to prioritize the introduction of ethnic Russians from abroad, including streamlining entry registration and naturalization procedures, ensuring immigrants' legitimate rights, providing employment support and exempting several years of business tax, and guiding the movement of immigrants to less populated areas such as the Far East and Siberia.[41] According to the Russian media, the country is developing a bill of immigration amnesty, which is expected to legalize five million illegal immigrants in Russia. Russia's 21st Century Migration Foundation has begun to formulate a bill regarding immigration amnesty to assist with the government's work on immigration strategies. It is suggested in the bill that illegal immigrants who have not committed any crime shall be able to report to the authorities and obtain legal status when their work permits expiration. This will be the largest-scale amnesty among the 25 amnesties for illegal immigrants in the past. The Foundation stated that the draft bill would be submitted to the government in six months.[42]

In conclusion, I believe that the French government's responses went from one extreme to another. The illegal immigrants in France experienced drastic changes from massive regularization to a complete lack of large-scale regularization of undocumented immigrants. Although widely known for its frequent amnesties, the Italian government awakened to the truth and decided to clamp down on illegal immigration under social pressure. The US took reasonable and pragmatic measures to demonstrate its demeanor as a large immigrant-receiving country. The Russian government carried out stern measures against illegal immigration but at the same time began to formulate a bill regarding immigration amnesty, thus reflecting the dilemma faced

---

[40] Cao Yan and Wei La, "Migrants in Russia: Intensifying the Combat against illegal immigrants," source: www.xinhuanet.com, cited from http://edu.ce.cn/html/2012/ymymzx_0523/15643.html. Accessed May 26, 2012.

[41] Cao Yan and Wei La, "Migrants in Russia: Intensifying the Combat against illegal immigrants," source: www.xinhuanet.com, cited from http://edu.ce.cn/html/2012/ymymzx_0523/15643.html. Accessed May 26, 2012.

[42] "*Russia Establishes the Migration Amnesty Law,*" source: Shenzhen Special Zone Daily, cited from http://edu.ce.cn/html/2012/ymymzx_0507/13967.html. Accessed May 26, 2012.

by a young government. China, which is bound to embrace massive migratory flows, must have a long-term perspective and make preparations for handling illegal immigrants who have long resided in the country. Meanwhile, we must also develop our own countermeasures in light of the experience of other countries and our national circumstances.

First, we must distinguish regular *sanfei* from illegal immigrants, establish identification standards, and take respective management measures. In terms of the current laws and regulations and the *Exit-Entry Administration Law of the People's Republic of China* to be enacted soon, there will be no legal barriers in identifying and managing regular *sanfei*. However, considering the lack of a legal basis for identifying illegal immigrants, we must conduct a thorough investigation within the territory of China to distinguish regular *sanfei* from illegal immigrants. We must explore the responses to resolving the legal status of illegal immigrants with Chinese characteristics based on China's own conditions by learning from other countries, taking relevant international treaties as a reference, and defining the legal concept of illegal immigrants.

Second, it is not necessary to resolve the legal status of illegal immigrants by regularization. When viewing the management experience of the countries mentioned above, we may observe that regularization is merely an option out of necessity in particular periods. If we can strictly control the inflow of illegal immigrants and absorb laborers by legal means of immigration, then there will be no need for regularization, as it is a remedy that comes with a price. More importantly, regularization is a double-edged sword that grants illegal immigrants legal status and offsets the negative impact of illegal immigration to a certain extent but leads to a more significant effect, i.e., encouraging illegal immigration.

Based on China's current circumstances, it is a poor choice to deal with the legal status of illegal immigrants by regularization. We should resort to repatriation as much as possible, permit temporary stays and give humanitarian treatment to those who cannot be transferred or repatriated.

The Hekou management model of illegal immigrants that I have conceived includes the following steps:

First, apply the model to strictly control illegal entry and exit and prevent the inflow of regular *sanfei* and illegal immigrants. On this basis, perform a thorough investigation of the illegal immigrants residing in Hekou County and record the information of their country of origin, duration of residence, marital status and children, and their willingness to return.

Second, for those who wish to return, relevant departments shall communicate with the counterpart departments of the country of origin (Vietnam or other countries) to inspect their identities and negotiate for their return. If they are accepted by their home country, then we can provide allowances and send them back through ports. For those who do not wish to return, relevant departments shall also communicate with the counterpart departments of the country of origin (Vietnam or other countries) to check their identities and send them back based on the repatriation agreement concluded by the two countries (bilateral repatriation), provided that the other country accepts their repatriation.

Third, for those who do not wish to return home, or even if they do yet their home country cannot confirm their identities and thus do not accept their return or repatriation, we may reregister their information and treat them as specially illegal immigrants.

Fourth, we may learn from the practice of setting up a refugee office in the Civil Affairs Bureau of Hekou County and establish an office in charge of the affairs of illegal immigrants as follows. 1. Increase awareness among illegal immigrants regarding China's laws, regulations and policies and encourage their return to their home country. 2. Coordinate communication between China's departments and their counterparts of the country of origin for cooperative repatriation. 3. Provide humanitarian assistance for illegal immigrants who cannot be transferred or repatriated in forms such as hardship relief and educational assistance for their children.

Fifth, issuing temporary residence permits for specially illegal immigrants who have resided in China for years and have abided by China's laws and regulations. However, they shall not be able to obtain ID cards or household registration booklets, apply for Chinese nationality (except those who married Chinese citizens and are naturalized by law), or enjoy corresponding political rights.

There are three principles to be followed when establishing a model to identify the legal status of illegal immigrants:

First, China should place strict restrictions on illegal immigrants, especially their regularization requirements and procedures. If specially illegal immigrants who have resided in China for years and abided by China's laws and regulations are issued ID cards and household registration booklets, then their legal status will be equivalent to that of refugees. Illegal immigrants and refugees, although closely related, are not the same, and their differences shall be reflected. Second, enhance international cooperation and build mechanisms for information sharing and bilateral repatriation with immigrant-sending countries on an equal footing to jointly resolve the repatriation of illegal immigrants. We must not adopt unilateral repatriation in practice, as it lacks legal basis, fails to abide by the agreement between two countries and is not conducive to maintaining friendly relations among states. Third, humanitarian treatment should be provided to specially illegal immigrants to ensure their basic subsistence.

References

Feng, W. (2010). *The research on European Union's Governance on illegal immigration*. Jinan University.

Hao, Q. (2002). *An ethnic study of Americas Hispanics: A case study of Cuban and Mexican immigrants*. China Social Science Press.

Jin, S. (2000). *International law*. Peking University Press, Higher Education Press.

Li, F. (2009). *The research on international immigration and immigration policies*. PhD diss., Nankai University.

Song, Q. (2007). *European immigration research: European immigration process and European immigration problems in the 20th century*. Jinan: Shandong University Press.

Xiaoyun, Q. (2010). *Impact factors of immigration on the current Sino-Russia relations: An analysis from the perspective of nontraditional security*. Current Affairs Press.
Xu, J. (2005). *The study on the problems of legal control of illegal immigration*. Ph.D. diss., Wuhan University.
Xu, J. (2007). *The study on the problems of legal control of illegal immigration*. Wuhan: Huazhong University of Science and Technology Press.
Yang, C. (2010). Public participation and the ruling party's policy legality. *New Heights*, no. 1.
Yuan, T. (2010). *Immigrants and national security: The research on the derivation of threats and their conditions*. World Affairs Press.
Zhengyu, R. (2003). *Cross-border Immigration and National security: A study on Nontraditional Security*. Jinan University.

Chapter 7
Conclusion: Building China's Illegal Immigration Governance System

When referring to illegal migrants, many people automatically think about the tens of thousands of Chinese people who have traveled across the oceans by smuggling to make a living in foreign countries. China is a traditional migrant-sending country, and previous studies have primarily focused on how to prevent its people from smuggling and how to protect their rights to live and dignity in other countries. However, circumstances have changed, and China has witnessed an insidious immigration flow. Despite their small number and trivial influence, immigrants have begun to exert impacts on our country. While taking delight in the country's rapid economic and social development, the Chinese people may feel more delightful at the arrival of immigrants without knowing the spread of their negative impacts.

The terms immigrants and illegal immigrants are not found in China's current laws and regulations. The substantive departments have made great efforts in expelling *sanfei*, i.e., foreigners of illegal entry, illegal residence and illegal employment. However, comanagement of this issue by multiple departments is still adopted, which leads to fragmentation and lack of synergy. In fact, illegal immigrants are part of *Sanfei*, the only difference being that illegal immigrants have resided in China for longer. China has now been fully integrated with the world, and we should look into the problems in China from a global perspective.

Although lagging behind other places, the Yunnan border areas with a high concentration of ethnic minorities share long borders with Vietnam, Laos and Myanmar, without natural barriers, due to their unique geological location. Despite the existence of state boundaries, border residents have been used to crossing the border freely for generations. Many of them, although from different countries, are either related or have the same ethnic origins. This is why they have built close bonds through marriage and daily interactions such as market fairs and cross-border grazing. Due to the convenience of border crossing, illegal immigrants who were repatriated before could return to China easily, which has caused difficulties in border control. Consequently, the number of illegal immigrants continues to increase, and their negative impacts become more prominent as a result of illegal marriage, extended residence, and repatriation challenges. Such unseen crises often stem from people's

G. Luo, *The Issues of Illegal Immigration and its Solutions in the Minority-Border Regions in Yunnan Province, China*, https://doi.org/10.1007/978-981-19-1249-8_7

reluctance to look into facts. Many people tend to neglect warning signals and ignore their hunches to overlook reality and deny hidden crises for subjective reasons. They typically use groundless facts to prove that such crises do not exist, which will only lead to unseen outbreaks of crises and enormous damage.[1]

To avoid such damage, we must formulate a solution to resolve these crises. This book takes Hekou County as an example for analysis, yet the following suggestions are widely applicable.

First, enhance entry and exit management and block the inflow of illegal immigrants. The prerequisite and fundamental guarantee of eradicating illegal immigration are to build a strict and sound mechanism of entry and exit management, regardless of the specific conditions of illegal immigrants, i.e., illegal entry and illegal residence, or legal entry and illegal residence. Ineffective control over the inflow of illegal immigrants will lower the costs and risks of illegal immigration and undermine the effectiveness of managing illegal immigrants who have resided in China. Therefore, for both the Hekou border management model proposed in this book and the Lincang model that has previously been proven effective, the ultimate goal is to strictly control the unauthorized crossing points taken by illegal immigrants.

Second, international cooperation should be enhanced for the repatriation of illegal immigrants. Repatriating illegal immigrants is the fundamental principle of illegal immigration governance. However, the precondition is the conclusion of bilateral repatriation agreements between the sending and receiving countries or compliance with multilateral repatriation conventions. In addition, relevant parties must effectively and strictly implement these agreements and conventions. This relates to the image of a country as always fulfilling its commitments and to the coordination of relations among countries. Therefore, it is a crucial step to enhance international cooperation in illegal immigration governance.

Third, strengthen investigation and research and identify the legal status of illegal immigrants. Instead of ignoring immigrants who cannot be repatriated, we must identify their legal status and secure their subsistence. I am opposed to any regularization measures toward illegal immigrants. Although in specific historical contexts, such measures were adopted by some countries and therefore played positive roles, eventually they have been abandoned by most countries. The Hekou model of illegal immigration governance proposed in this book does not call for the regularization of illegal immigrants; instead, it merely suggests providing basic subsistence guarantees and granting temporary residence rights based on humanitarian grounds.

Fourth, institution building should be intensified, and awareness of governance should be built by law. There are many methods and concepts regarding the governance of illegal immigrants. By referring to governance by law, this book advocates addressing the issues of governing bodies, the basis of governance and difficulties in governance, and more importantly, promoting the rule of law and addressing the relations between laws and policies and between the rule of law and [economic] development to integrate illegal immigration governance into the rule of law.

[1] Peng Gang, "Rebuilding the Thinking of Crises: Unnoticeable Crises," source: http://www.rmlt.com.cn/qikan/2012-05-10/. Accessed May 22, 2012.

At the same time, we must not neglect to learn from others' errors.

France, the US, Russia, Italy and other countries have taken the lead in implementing immigration policies. They once enjoyed the benefits of immigration but eventually paid a heavy price for the ineffective governance of illegal immigrants. Upon reflecting on their failures, they amended immigration policies, enacted new bills and established new mechanisms to moderately control legal immigrants and seriously combat illegal immigrants. Massive migratory flows have yet to arrive in China, but we must make preparations based on our late-mover advantages to build governance mechanisms.

The concept of a "mechanism," which originally referred to the structure and operating principle of a machine, is now widely used in natural and social phenomena. According to its current definition, a mechanism can also refer to the internal structure and operating principle and plays a fundamental role in any system. In the best-case scenario, an effective mechanism can make a social system almost self-adaptive. In the face of uncertain external changes, it can automatically respond to and adjust the previous strategies and measures to realize optimized goals. To better understand a mechanism, we must focus on two points. First, the component parts are the precondition of a mechanism because they bring out the coordination among the different parts. Second, the coordination among the different parts is a particular operating method. Therefore, a mechanism is an operating method that connects the various parts and coordinates their operation.[2]

To build a mechanism of illegal immigration governance, we must clarify three components. First, governing bodies (vertical and horizontal structures of governing bodies). Vertical bodies include international organizations, states and local governments, while horizontal bodies include military, public security and judicial authorities. Second, the basis of governance was statutory law (China's *Constitution*, laws, administrative rules, local rules, autonomous rules, administrative regulations and the laws of Special Administrative Regions) and unwritten law (policies and customs). Third, governing methods in four aspects. One, establish a uniform immigration law. Considering that it is premature to establish such a law, we must resolve existing problems in the current laws and regulations and give full play to their roles. Two, establish a department or administration responsible for immigration affairs and the coordination of relevant departments. Three, enhance the publicity of relevant laws, regulations and policies regarding illegal immigration. Fourth, build the Hekou border management model and Hekou illegal immigration governance model to deal with two difficult tasks, i.e., controlling illegal entry and exit and identifying the legal status of illegal immigrants (see Fig. 1).

In addition, we must understand that the mechanism is an operating method of coordinating three components. With the governance mechanism, we shall realize the coordination among governing bodies and the basis of governance and the positive interaction and coherence between governing bodies and the basis of governance. Once the mechanism is established, it can be applied to the governance of illegal immigration in Hekou County, other border areas with a high concentration of ethnic

[2] Source: http://baike.baidu.com/view/34249.htm. Accessed September 18, 2011.

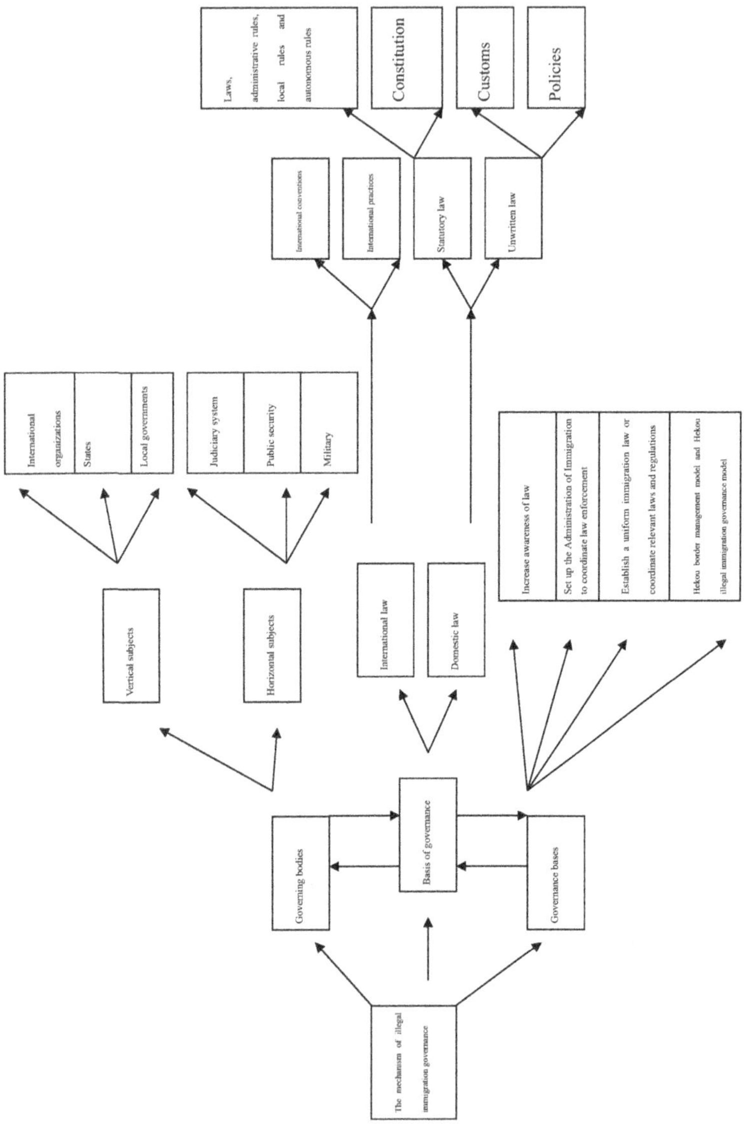

Fig. 1 Mechanism of Illegal Immigration Governance

minorities in Yunnan, and the country as a whole. Furthermore, it will make illegal immigration governance a self-adaptive system that rapidly responds to uncertain external changes and adjusts the previous governance strategies and measures for the best results. Governing methods are the operating methods used by governing bodies on the basis of governance. Although implemented by governing bodies, they shall not deviate from the basis of governance. Finally, the basis of governance is used to regulate governance activities, constrain governing bodies, and assess governance results.

Therefore, establishing a mechanism of illegal immigration governance is the starting point and the ultimate goal of this book. I hope my studies have achieved the expected goals.

Afterword

I originally met my Advisor, Professor Ren Xinmin, by chance, and his words during that delightful first conversation gave me the courage to "go back to school." His brief comments keep me alert when I am complacent, and his laughter cheers me up when I feel down. He is a knowledgeable and eloquent scholar who inspires me to enjoy academic research. Serious yet humorous, he is both a teacher and a friend who guides my exploration of the world outside of books.

My gratitude to him is beyond words, and I will keep it in my heart forever.

I would also like to express my gratitude to several other professors, including Wang Wenguang, He Ming, Zhou Ping, Na Lin, Chen Guoxin, Dong Yunchuan, Zhang Jucheng, Lu Gang and Li Ruoqing, for helping build my respect for and perseverance in academic study.

I would like to thank the officials of the People's Procuratorate of Yunnan Province, Department of State Security of Yunnan Province, Entry and Exit Administration Bureau of Department of Public Security of Yunnan Province, Political and Legal Affairs Commission of Pu'er City, People's Procuratorate of Lincang City, People's Procuratorate of Honghe Prefecture, CPC Committee and Government of Hekou County and other relevant departments for instructing me on how to understand the gap between theory and reality.

Thank you to all the department heads and my teachers and friends at the School of Marxism Studies, School of Ethology and Sociology, Law School and Graduate School of Yunnan University.

Thank you to my friends at the Editorial Department of Law Press China.

Thank you to my friends in Yunnan and Guizhou. You are the driving force in my way forward.

Finally, I owe my gratitude to my parents, my wife and my daughter. You are my motivation for everything I strive for.

G. Luo, *The Issues of Illegal Immigration and its Solutions in the Minority-Border Regions in Yunnan Province, China*, https://doi.org/10.1007/978-981-19-1249-8

This book is adapted from my PhD dissertation. Finally, to the Dean of School of Ethology and Sociology, Professor He Ming, Dean of Law School, Professor Chen Yundong, Deputy Dean of Law School, Professor Wang Qiliang and Mr. Gao Shan, editor at the Law Press China, I would like to express my deep gratitude for your strong support in publishing this book!

July 1, 2012 Luo Gang

Bibliography

I. Books

[France] Ada, Jacques. (2000). *Economic globalization*. Translated by He Jing and Zhou Xiaoxin. Beijing: Central Compilation & Translation Press.
[U.K.] Albrow, Martin. (2001). *The global age: State and society beyond modernity*. Translated by Feng Ling and Gao Xiangze. Beijing: The Commercial Press.
[United States] Baldwin, David A. (2001). *Neorealism and neoliberalism*. Translated by Xiao Huanrong. Hangzhou: Zhejiang People's Publishing House.
Brochmann, G. (1999). *Mechanisms of immigration Control*. Berg Press.
Castles, Stephen, & Miller Mark, J. (1993). *The age of migration: International population movements in the modern word*. Houndmills: Macmillan Press.
Hammar, T. (1985). *European immigration policy: A comparative study*. Cambridge University Press.
Hongbo, L. (2006). *Immigration and globalization*. China Social Science Press.
[United States] Hunt, Michael H. (1998). *Ideology and U.S. foreign policy*. Translated by Chu Lüyuan. Beijing: World Affairs Press.
[United States] Huntington, Samuel. (1999). *The clash of civilizations and the remaking of world order*. Translated by Zhou Qi, Zhang Liping et al. Beijing: Xinhua Publishing House.
[Germany] Kohler-Koch, Beate, Thomas Conzelmann et al. (2004). *European Integration and EU Governance*. Translated by Gu Junli et al. Beijing: China Social Sciences Press.
[United States] Koehn, Peter H. (2004). *Expanding roles of Chinese Americans in U.S.-China relations: Transnational networks and trans-pacific interactions*. Translated by Yin Xiaohuang, Yu Ningping et al. Beijing: Xinhua Publishing House.
[United States] Kwong, Peter. (2001). *Forbidden workers: Illegal Chinese immigrants and American labor*. Translated by Wang Bin et al. Beijing: World Affairs Press.
Maoxin, L. (2000). *The research on the US immigration policies*. Northeast Normal University Press.
[United States] Myers, Norman. (2001). *Ultimate security: The environmental basis of political security*. Translated by Wang Zhengping et al. Shanghai: Shanghai Translation Publishing House.
[United States] Nye, Joseph S. (2003). *Governance in a globalizing world*. Translated by Wang Yong et al. Beijing: World Affairs Press.
[United States] Rosenau, James N. (2001). *Governance Without Government*. Translated by Zhang Shengjun, Liu Xiaolin et al. Nanchang: Jiangxi People's Publishing House.
Ruihua, C. (2009). *On research methods of jurisprudence*. Peking University Press.

G. Luo, *The Issues of Illegal Immigration and its Solutions in the Minority-Border Regions in Yunnan Province, China*, https://doi.org/10.1007/978-981-19-1249-8

Sassen, S. (1988). *The mobility of labor and capital: A study in international investment and labor flow*. Cambridge University Press.
Wei, D. (2004). *A comparative study on migrant smuggling*. Law Press China.
Xiaotian, F. (2001). *Social research methods*. China Renmin University Press.
Yugang, C. (2002). *A comparative study on the theory of national and supranational European integration*. Shanghai People's Publishing House.
Zhenglai, D. (2006). *Whither Chinese law: Construct an ideal picture of the Era of Chinese law outline*. The Commercial Press.

II. Articles and Dissertations

Chen Gong. (2005). Security and population security: Development and discussion of its concept. *Market and Population Analysis*, 2.
Fang Tie. (2007, September). The distribution, origins and characteristics of cross-border ethnic groups in Yunnan province. *Journal of Guangxi University for Nationalities (Philosophy and Social Science Edition)*, 5.
Hu Shiyun. (2005). The research on contemporary illegal immigration and management measures: A case study of illegal immigration in Eastern Coastal Areas. MA diss., East China Normal University.
Lin Shengzhong, & Qu Xiuqin. (2004). The role of population security in the harmonious development between human and nature. *Population and Family Planning*, 2.
Li Buyun, & Zhao Xun. (2005). What are good laws? *Chinese Journal of Law*, 6.
Li Qi. (2009). The research on controlling illegal migration in China and Russia through legal means. MA diss., Xinjiang University.
Papadelnetriou, Delnetrios G. (2006, March). *Europe and its immigrants in the 21st century: A new deal or a continuing dialog of the deal?* MPI and the Luso-Americin Foundation.
Qiheng, S. (2006). *The formation and governance of illegal migration in Fujian*. Fujian Normal University.
Qiu Liben. (2005). The research on international immigration: History and current situation of international immigration and China's countermeasures. *Overseas Chinese Histories Studies*, 1.
Xiaojing, C. (2005). *The study on ethnic self-identification in the pattern of pluralistic unity of the Chinese nation: Theoretical exploration and empirical analysis of the needs of Bai people in Han communities*. Yunnan University.
Xiaoying, C. (2004). *The study on Vietnamese refugees and boat people in Hong Kong*. East China Normal University.
Xu Junhua. (2007). Thoughts on illegal immigration from the perspective of international law. *Law Review*, 1.
Zhou Ping. (2004). Rethinking on nation countries. *Political Science*, 9.
Zhou Ping. (2010). Transformation and reconstruction of China's frontier governance. *Journal of Yunnan Normal University (Philosophy and Social Sciences)*, 2.

The manufacturer's authorised representative in the EU is Springer Nature Customer Service Centre GmbH, Europaplatz 3, 69115 Heidelberg, Germany. If you have any concerns regarding our products, please contact ProductSafety@springernature.com

Printed and bound by CPI Group (UK) Ltd, Croydon, CR0 4YY
01/10/2026
02226300-0011